Guide to
Stress Reduction

L. John Mason, Ph.D.

CELESTIAL ARTS
Berkeley ▪ Toronto

*To my mother and my father,
and all those who wish to take
responsibility for their own health.*

Celestial Arts
P.O. Box 7123
Berkeley, California 94707
www.tenspeed.com

Distributed in Canada by Ten Speed Press Canada, in the United Kingdom and Europe by Airlift Books, in New Zealand by Southern Publishers Group, in Australia by Simon & Schuster Australia, in South Africa by Real Books, and in Singapore, Malaysia, Hong Kong, and Thailand by Berkeley Books.

Cover and interior design by Toni Tajima
Cover photograph by Doug Plummer

PERMISSIONS:
Holmes and Rahe Social Readjustment Rating Scale from *Journal of Psychosomatic Research,*
    Vol. 11, pp. 213–18. Copyright 1967. Pergamon Press, Ltd. Reprinted with permission.
Secondary Gains from *Getting Well Again* by O. Carl Simonton, M.D., Stephanie Matthews-
    Simonton and James Creighton. Copyright 1978. Published in hardcover by J. P. Tarcher, Inc.,
    Los Angeles. Used by permission of Bantam Books, Inc.

Library of Congress Cataloging-in-Publication Data

Mason, L. John, 1950–
    Guide to stress reduction / L. John Mason.
        p. cm.
    Includes bibliographical references (p.   ) and index.
    ISBN 1-58761-091-4 (pbk.)
    1. Stress (Psychology) 2. Relaxation.   I. Title.
    BF575.S75 M35 2001
    155.9′042—dc21

                                        2001028233

Original edition published by Peace Press, 1980.
Celestial Arts edition First Printing, 1985.

Printed in Canada

1 2 3 4 5 6 7 — 05 04 03 02 01

Contents

WITHDRAWN

Acknowledgments

A SPECIAL THANKS to all the people at Celestial Arts and Ten Speed Press for their support and encouragement. Especially the late David Hinds, for bringing my first book to Celestial Arts and his appeal for me to write the second book, *Stress Passages: Surviving Life's Transitions Gracefully*. I hope that this edition will bring them the profits they deserve.

My family has been gracious and loving through my long professional process. I want to acknowledge and thank my wife, Barbara Ehlers-Mason, R.N., for her love and patience. My mother, Evelyn Mason, who has always been my strongest supporter and has shown me a way to live and flourish with a gusto for life into her tenth decade. And thanks to my two sons, who motivate me to be the best person and parent that I can be. I hope that they succeed in their dreams and follow pathways of service that make them proud.

To my clients, who have been my focus since 1977. They have shared with me their challenges and their successes. I have learned more from these experiences than I can ever acknowledge. Every connection with these individuals or groups has taught me and opened me to greater possible acts of service with the spirit of giving that we all require to thrive. Many of these people I have come to care for as friends and will maintain my connections with them as long as I can be conscious of my memories.

Finally, I want to thank my special friends who have supported and influenced me through the years. Too many to name all of these great folks, I will list but a few. Hobart "Red" Thomas, Stachu

Geurtsen, Stephen Snyder, Stephen Topple, Ken and Kathy Gibson, Jim and Jennifer Hulac, Gary and Cheryl Salinger, Lou Callait, Morry and Dawn Edwards, Adam Crane, P. E. Langer, Hank Sherman, Keith and Sheree Pellemeier, Jerry Cornacchio, Celia Mason, Dan and Kathleen Roberts, Andrea Salvemini, Len DiGiovanni, Tim Warren, and many others.

Introduction

YOU HAVE THE RIGHT to relax, to feel good, to be happy. You do not
have to accept headaches, insomnia, backaches, indigestion, and
other discomforts as irreversible facts of life. These physical complaints may be the way your body responds to stress, even if you
don't realize you are experiencing it. *The stress of modern life is real—
there is no denying it. But the way you respond is up to you.* You can
react to stress in a positive way and counteract the damage stress
may be doing to your health. This book will teach you how to
reduce excess tension with stress-reduction techniques.

Your stress response is the product of conditioned habits
adopted early in life for coping with difficult and painful situations.
It is possible to drop these seemingly protective and habitual
responses which have become unquestionably harmful to your
health and well-being. If stress is viewed as an insoluble problem,
you are easily reduced to fretting and self-pity; this just increases
your tension and produces a vicious cycle from which there seems to
be no escape. If stress is interpreted as a challenge, the mind and
body respond with renewed vigor and creativity.

We have never been taught how to relax, how to take care of
ourselves in a positive, nurturing way (not just going on a vacation
or out for an expensive dinner). Twenty minutes of deep relaxation
a day will aid your mental growth, improve your physical health and
emotional stability, and possibly even increase your spiritual awareness. You will use your energy more efficiently and have more time
for your family, friends, and yourself. You will be on a more even

keel, not on the roller coaster of life with its traumatic ups and downs. This does not lessen the great joys of life but allows you to progress more evenly with less backsliding and distress.

How do you feel stress? As a pain in your back that's with you from your first cup of coffee in the morning to your last cigarette at night? As a migraine headache that propels you to the medicine cabinet? Your negative response to stress is individual, uniquely your own. So will be the more positive way of coping with stress and its negative effect on your health.

The first step in reducing stress is identifying your own unique stress response. Become more aware of the events that trigger it. What causes you the most distress? A mailbox full of unpaid bills; rush hour traffic twice a day? Your boss in his office reading the memo you just wrote? After you have recognized the situations that cause you the most discomfort, listen to your body's signals and locate where you feel stress. *We have desensitized ourselves to our bodies' messages until they literally reach out and shake us.* Do you treat symptoms as warning signals or barriers to be conquered? Do you consider your body a reliable friend or disabling foe? When your stress level is too high, do you stop and consider how to lower it? We must step back inside our bodies to change this pattern of neglect, to treat these signals and messages as helpful guides and tools. Illness or pain may be trying to tell you something—but it's up to you to pick up the signals and decode the message.

Prolonged, unrelieved stress has been proven to cause organic disease. Your daily tension headache may be the prelude to more serious dysfunction and even to the eventual breakdown of your immunological system. Practicing stress reduction on a regular basis can help you cope with pain, prevent disease, and improve the quality of your life.

As a stress-reduction therapist, both in private practice and as a teacher of classes and seminars, I have seen the rewards of this work on individual lives. It is gratifying to see a person with a twenty-five-year history of debilitating migraine headaches respond quickly and within a few weeks report 100 percent prevention of these headaches. To see a person racked by chronic pain for five years due to an industrial accident find freedom from the most severe, crippling complaint and begin reaching out in life to begin a new positive existence. To work one-to-one with people emotionally disabled by their own fears and insecurities and to watch them take control of their lives and break through the barriers which have held them from living truly peaceful, positive lives. To help vibrant, productive people who have been struck down by stress-related disorders such as high blood pressure, heart problems, arthritis, and ulcers to become aware of negative habits and restructure their lives to be productive without the cost of their health or happiness. For these reasons, seen over and over, I felt the need to reach out to more people than I could touch in my own practice, to help them reduce their pain and crippling complaints. I could not find a book which provided an overview of the relaxation techniques, in a form accessible to the layperson, so I undertook the writing of *Guide to Stress Reduction*.

No other book discusses such a wide variety of approaches; no other book teaches the layperson how to benefit from home practice of these methods and exercises. My suggestions for managing various physical diseases and disabilities are all based on actual experience and practice. The case studies will give you an idea of how these techniques have helped others with problems similar to your own. Step-by-step instructions will make it easy for you to combat the effects of unnecessary and inappropriate stress on your body and mind.

This book will not solve all your problems, nor can it eliminate all the stress from your life. The exercises will teach you to become more attuned to your body and subtle levels of building tension. *When the effects of stress start to take hold in your body, you will be able to release that excess tension before it gets out of hand.* You will be able to choose not to get upset—to relax instead. After a while you may find that previously upsetting experiences will fall away from you, like water shed off a duck's back. In a profound state of deep relaxation, you may discover new depths in yourself, reexperience and reclaim lost feelings.

If you want to start doing something good for yourself and grow older in health and happiness, practice stress reduction.

By becoming more aware of how your body responds to life's pressures, you can take personal responsibility for enhancing your quality of life. People often make excuses like they "do not have time," and then complain about their aches, pains, and terminal (often preventable) conditions. Starting now, get back in control of your life.

Built into each one of us, through our genetic coding, is a very primitive response mechanism that has been used for personal survival for millions of years. This coding is similar to what early mammals needed 70 million years ago to prevent becoming someone else's lunch. This prepares us, just as it did our ancient ancestors, to fight or run away to save our lives when we are threatened.

Stress/change management techniques are relevant not only for the quality of our lives, but also for survival in this stress-filled world. The primitive fight or flight response that is born into every one of us is a potential danger that we must learn about and learn to control, or we will suffer from inefficiency and perhaps serious life-threatening conditions. The system built to protect us can also kill us!

As an example, the first editions of this book came out in the early 1980s. Has the world changed since then? Look at some of the basic technological changes that have "enhanced" our lives since then. Communication at every level has been altered significantly. We now routinely use fax machines, cellular phones, pagers, home computers with e-mail capabilities and access to the Internet, and voice mail. Televisions have forty to five hundred channels, satellite access, instantaneous news from around the world, and even VCRs to record extra programs we are not free to watch when they are first broadcast (but know we will find time to watch at some later date).

Even if you do not own a cellular phone, pager, fax machine, or home computer with e-mail/Internet capability, are you stressed out by the knowledge that you may be falling behind in the Information Age? Are you worried your children will be growing up in an even more information-pressured world? Have you ever been on the freeway and worried that another driver may be distracted by the cellular call he is receiving while driving in the lane next to yours?

What does your primitive survival response do with the insults from the advanced technologies that hammer us more each day? Do you work more now than you did ten years ago? Do you now work at night or on weekends just to catch up with your week? Do you feel insecure because the work world is changing so fast that your department or your company may be obsolete within the next few months? Seventy million years of evolution have not kept up with the past one hundred years of technological change and so we feel "overwhelmed." If we are not aware and vigilant about our self-care, our bodies will respond by grabbing our attention with some physical or emotional symptom.

Because we do not have much control over evolutionary processes, we need to develop our coping skills to minimize, if not eliminate, potentially dangerous responses to surviving in this fast-paced world.

As young adults, we are generally more resilient, flexible, and can even "muscle through" the problems and obstacles we face. But as we age, we lose some of our strength and flexibility, and even some of the resilience we were formerly able to depend on. This is often when symptoms of societal stress begin to rob us of efficiency and quality of life.

The fight or flight response does not serve us in the modern world. We can no longer run away or physically beat people up if they cause us stress. Our bodies are forced to sit still at meetings with the boss. We eat dinner while watching wars, violence, and crime on the television news, just to save some time while staying informed. We commute to work surrounded by angry, hostile, and stressed-out wage earners.

You may believe that you have no control over your work schedule, your boss, your children, your relationship partner, the economy, your family, your neighborhood, or the government. But you do have control over the way you respond to these outside forces. You can develop awareness and the skills to get back in control of the way you respond and the energies that you spend to survive in the modern world.

If you do not do this for yourself, then learn how to do this as an example for your children and the people around you. They, too, are growing and living in an ever more rapidly paced world.

Stress is nothing new. It has been in the news for more than twenty years and in our lives much longer. While most everyone experiences extreme stress at some point in their lives, few of us cope with it well. And now, life has gotten much more stressful in just the past few decades.

To review, let's begin with the 1960s. The 1960s gave us an economic explosion, an unpopular Asian war, a change in social attitudes, and an increased pace due to the advances of technology. Then, the 1970s continued with great economic and social changes. But even greater changes—and additional stressors—have come with the explosion of the Information Age.

In the past few years our society has been confronted by inflation, recession/depression, reduction of job and economic security (decertification of labor unions, high unemployment, changes in the status of social security), growing data about the negative environment in which we live (toxic waste problems, air and drinking water pollution), and increased political awareness of the harsh realities of the nuclear age. As we live each day, we are surrounded by the increased speed and needs of technology. The news media communicates a startling barrage of facts, information, issues, and points of view—faster and more widespread than ever before.

Each of these factors alone can result in stress and the need to change. Our society must cope with ongoing change, and whether the change is good or bad, we are still forced to adjust to something very new on a regular basis. That adjustment leads to stress that can create serious symptoms and illness, drug/alcohol abuse, suicide attempts, accidents on and off the job, and disruption in personal and social relationships, marriage, and parenting.

The era of computers brings both joy and terror to many people. The technology is greeted with mixed feelings for many reasons. The fear of something new and unknown is the initial reaction of many. Not until you sit down and explore the possibilities do the major terrors and frustration of the computer age truly strike. Although I think of technology as a friend, just the scope and power of the basic microcomputers make me uneasy. For everything that I learn and begin to master, ten new avenues appear for me to explore. Computer literacy is now a necessity and the new field is unparalleled in history for speed and dimension of growth. This is stressful and intimidating.

To make matters worse, sitting at a computer for long periods is an entirely new territory of stress to explore. Eye strain, back problems, lighting, computer frustration, and many more stressors are plaguing the computer adventurers as they chart the dimensions of this space-age world. The computer is a time-saver and great asset to human beings, but the transition into this new world may foster many symptoms of stress.

In my private practice, I see many individuals who manifest the symptom of anxiety related to particular issues of the day, such as the fear of nuclear disintegration.

And anxiety itself—as a symptom—also seems to be on the rise among very capable people who in the past may have coped exceptionally well with even severe work-related stresses. Some of these people come to feel out of control with the internal terror of anxiety which is stress-related. Very often they seek professional medical advice fearing heart problems because of their anxiety responses of chest pain and shortness of breath. Many try to escape through alcohol or prescribed or illegal drugs. This only increases the depression/anxiety symptoms and, in a vicious cycle, creates heightened feelings of loss of control.

Insomnia is another common referral for my private practice, and this can often be traced to the stress experienced today which was once tolerable and dealt with more appropriately. Small amounts of residual stress from a normal day can be just as irritating as static noise. This leads to distraction from the relaxation necessary for sleep. The stress management techniques described in this book can offer relief from these daily stressors.

But there have been many positive developments in the field of stress management in the last few years. Among these, the control of high blood pressure without the need for medication or costly treatment is now possible. The theory of wellness and preventive health care has grown from holistic attitudes into cost-effective methods utilized by major corporations. Also, techniques for control of chronic pain now offer positive alternatives to surgery and medication. But perhaps the most exciting and potentially most positive development is the birth of a new discipline called psychoneuroimmunology. This long name describes the new field of study about the connections between mind/emotion and the body's immune system.

Stress is not always bad. Nearly everyone finds a certain level of stress both stimulating and necessary for motivation. Some important research on job stress and burnout suggests that jobs with too little stress may be potentially as hazardous to our health as jobs with too much stress.

Only you know where to draw that line. When you fully understand your own particular needs, then, with the help from the following pages, you can create a program for stress management that will be best suited for you.

Chapter 1
Understanding Stress and Relaxation

Your First Step

S TRESS IS INHERENT in every healthy form of life; it is the force exerted by any one thing against another. Stress is, always has been, and always will be a part of being alive. People cannot maintain an erect posture without the tension of opposing muscles that balance each other and keep the skeletal system erect. Eating puts some stress on the digestive system; active exercise puts stress on the cardiovascular system. Your immunological system is constantly killing off bacteria in your body. Subtle balances shift, and tension between one force and another is inherent in being alive. With normal stress, the overall physiological equilibrium is maintained. *We are not concerned with such essential stress or tension, but with undesirable, excess tension that threatens the body's well-being.* Everyone suffers the effects of this excess stress; what is important, is how you learn to cope with it.

Let's look at the historical source of the stress response. The body responds most extremely to the most extreme stress: a threat to the survival of the organism. If placed in a life-threatening situation, an organism automatically responds with the fight or flight response, identified by Dr. Walter Cannon in the 1930s. The stress response is an instinctual reaction under a life-threatening situation; all animals respond automatically when the danger is real.

Imagine that you are coming home late from work one evening. It is already dark. As you go to unlock your door, you realize that it is open. Your heart begins to pound, and sweat starts to drip down your forehead. Someone has been in your apartment. Who could it have been? As your mind races through the possibilities, your breathing quickens; your hands are clammy on the doorknob as you push open the door. You flick on the lights. The lamps are knocked over, your grandmother's porcelain figurines are not in their place— the living room is a disaster. You have been robbed! The robber may still be in your apartment. Your knees are weak, and there's a knot in your stomach as you grab a bookend to defend yourself. Or should you run?

FIGHT OR FLIGHT

In the case of such an extreme threat, a variety of physiological changes occur with dramatic suddenness to allow you to survive, either by fighting off the threat or by fleeing from it. What typically happens?

- The heartbeat increases to pump blood throughout the necessary tissues with greater speed, carrying oxygen and nutrients to cells and clearing waste products more quickly.

- As the heart rate increases, the blood pressure rises.

- Breathing becomes rapid and shallow.

- Adrenaline and other hormones are released into the blood.

- The liver releases stored sugar into the blood to meet the increased energy needs of survival.

- The pupils dilate to let in more light; all the senses are heightened.

- Muscles tense for movement, either for flight or protective actions, particularly the skeletal muscles for the thighs, hips, back, shoulders, arms, jaw, and face.

- Blood flow is greatly constricted to the digestive organs.

- Blood flow increases to the brain and major muscles.

- Blood flow is constricted to the extremities, and the hands and feet become cold. This protects you from bleeding to death quickly if the hands or feet are injured in fight or flight, and allows blood to be diverted to more important areas of the body.

- The body perspires to cool itself, since increased metabolism generates more heat.

The major stress response occurs if you are in a life-threatening situation or experiencing an exciting, highly stimulating activity, such as racing a car or riding on a roller coaster. After the danger has passed, you stop, assess your survival, and then breathe a "sigh of relief"; your body must return to equilibrium after this taxing experience. (You may go to the other extreme and collapse in shock.) The surge of energy subsides and your metabolism slows down. Some people are actually addicted to this adrenaline rush and need to do dangerous things to get their "kicks." Others addicted to the rush will eat a lot of sugar quickly, which raises the blood sugar level. During the fight or flight response, the body releases stored sugar into the blood. When ingestion of large quantities of sugar raises the blood sugar level, the body responds as if under threat and triggers the fight or flight response. Eating a hot fudge sundae may elicit the same response as a roller-coaster ride.

The fight or flight response is appropriate if you are confronted by a robber in your home or by some other threat to your life. But often this response, or some of the characteristics of it, is triggered inappropriately by a situation which is stressful but not life threatening. You may be suffering a chronic stress response worrying over unpaid bills. The ultimate result of not paying your bills may be death: if you go bankrupt, your creditors might come and shoot you; if you fail to pay your utility bill, the heat may be turned off and you might freeze to death. These possibilities are neither immediate nor likely, but your body cannot distinguish between the hypothetical threat you imagine and an immediate, genuine one. Consciousness has developed to the extent that stress responses can be triggered by emotions, ideas, memories, and expectations. Abstract thought produced in the sophisticated, higher centers of the brain (cerebral cortex) can trigger the autonomic survival reflexes located in the lower centers.

Your chronic stress response may include some of the characteristics of the fight or flight response, not necessarily the entire physiological configuration. You may not even feel threatened. The tension headache is a good example of a chronic response to stress. Just as in the fight or flight configuration, muscles tense to prepare for action. In the case of tension headache, muscles in the forehead, face, eyes, jaw, neck, and shoulders are held rigidly, although no real physical threat exists. After a prolonged siege of such rigidity, the constricted muscles go into spasm (extreme contraction). This is the result of prolonged, unrelieved tension. *If we just stop and relax, resting our muscles briefly during the day, realizing that we do not need to brace ourselves physically against a nonphysical threat, our tension headaches and other stress complaints may be totally prevented.*

Hans Selye, an endocrinologist and the world's leading researcher into the effects of stress upon the body, states his theory in *The Stress of Life.* When the brain perceives stress, either consciously or unconsciously, the message is transmitted to the hypothalamus. This switching station carries signals in and out of the brain. The hypothalamus sends impulses to the pituitary gland, the master endocrine gland. The pituitary releases hormones such as adrenaline. A life-or-death situation may trigger this response, but the brain may respond in a similar way to persistent lower levels of stress. *If a stress response is chronic, the constant presence of stress hormones begins to wear down the body's immunological system; whatever part of the body is weakest will show signs of dysfunction first.* Selye calls the body's total effort to cope with stress, and its process of adapting, the general adaptation syndrome (GAS). As the immunological system is weakened, the body becomes more susceptible to infections and diseases, even cancer. For example, in the case of cancer, the body would normally eliminate a mutant cell; but if the system is dysfunctional, the cell may take hold and develop into a tumor. Hormone balance may also be upset, so that the body overcompensates when it swings back from the stress response, turning against its own healthy tissue.

So, stress is related, even though seemingly indirectly, to many, maybe even most, diseases. Over the years, continually triggering the stress response for inappropriate situations causes wear and tear on the body. We may not be conscious of the stress until we are confronted with pain. Stress-reduction techniques will not only prevent or alleviate a tension headache, or other stress-related complaints, but also act to prevent future disease.

Do you suffer from any of the stress-related complaints on the following questionnaire? As much as 90 percent of all disease can be traced directly or indirectly to stress, and if you suffer from any of these ailments, stress reduction may help you. For your own awareness, number any conditions you may experience according to the following ratings. If you require medication for any of the symptoms, place a star next to the number.

- 1   Hardly noticeable
- 2   Mildly disturbing
- 3   Irritating—continually at the back of your mind
- 4   More intense—but still able to function
- 5   Incapacitating—requires cessation of all functioning

Complete this worksheet before you begin to use stress-reduction techniques. Redo after one month into your stress-reduction program and again after six months.

STRESS-RELATED COMPLAINTS

CONDITIONS	NOW	AFTER 1 MONTH	AFTER 6 MONTHS
Tension Headache			
Muscle Cramps, Spasms			
Back Pain			
Neck and Shoulder Pain			
Jaw Tension (Bruxism)			
Chronic Pain			
Migraine Headache			
Raynaud's Syndrome			
Cold Hands and Feet			
High Blood Pressure			
Skin Problems			
Allergies			
Asthma			
Arthritis			
Stomach Pain			
Digestive Disorders			
Abdominal Disorders			
Constipation			
Diarrhea			
Frequent Colds			
Infectious Diseases			
Cancer			
Metabolic Dysfunction (Hypoglycemia, Hypothyroidism, etc.)			
Stroke			
Irregular Heart Rate			

CONDITIONS	NOW	AFTER 1 MONTH	AFTER 6 MONTHS
Insomnia			
Fatigue			
Breathing Irregularities			
Profuse Perspiration			
Overeating			
Alcohol or Drug Abuse			
Sexual Dysfunction			
Anxiety			
Depression			
Emotional Instability			
Fears and Phobias			
Learning Disabilities			
Living in Past or Future			
Forgetfulness			
Clumsiness			

Certain disorders such as ulcers, allergies, asthma, high blood pressure, colitis, and insomnia are directly related to stress. You may be aware that such conditions are considered psychosomatic, meaning that mental or emotional states contribute to or cause the illness. Other conditions generally considered to be organic in cause by the orthodox medical standard are indirectly related to stress. However, the prevailing medical model is not invalid when it defines the disease process. Medicine can treat the symptoms, but treating the symptoms does not get to the root of the problem. The doctor may aid you, support you, and convince you of future health, but your body performs the magic of healing and so repairs itself. Medical intervention can help you create the atmosphere for better health—the knitting or mending of tissue is solely the body's ability. *You are ultimately responsible for healing yourself.*

SECONDARY GAINS

Your illness may be fulfilling some psychological needs, and you may not really want to get well. These needs may be unconscious, and though you think you don't want to be sick, you may be fighting yourself. Unconscious motivations for illness are called secondary gains. Carl and Stephanie Simonton worked with patients suffering from cancer and other serious illnesses and found that certain psychological needs are often met through illness. In *Getting Well Again,* they identified the following as the five most common unconscious motivations for sickness:

- Permission to be excused from a troublesome problem or situation

- Attention, care, and nurturing

- Opportunity to deal with a problem or gain a new perspective on your own terms

- Incentive for personal growth or for modifying undesirable habits

- Not having to meet your own or others' high expectations

Most of us can take this list and, if we are honest and aware, find needs that are being met through illness. If we can develop an awareness of our own psychological and emotional requirements, we may not have to become sick to fulfill them. We can learn how to receive support in more positive ways and lead healthier, happier lives. Even if secondary gains don't play a large role in your illness, the way you choose to respond to stress may be intrinsically unhealthy.

THE NEW SCIENCE OF PSYCHONEUROIMMUNOLOGY

Psychoneuroimmunology is quite a mouthful! Since 1991 researchers have begun to make major breakthroughs in understanding the connections between the mind/emotions and changes in health (physiology).

PNI—an acronym for "psychoneuroimmunology"—is the new science that may eventually lead to the prevention and/or treatment of certain traumatic ailments such as rheumatoid arthritis, other autoimmune diseases, and various cancers. We are finding that the mind can be used in very positive ways to enhance the functioning of the body's defense mechanism—the immune system.

Stress suppresses the function of the immune system. If stress is chronic and unrelenting, as is often the case because stress is experienced daily and is below the level of normal consciousness, then certain glands of the body which normally help to produce an active defensive protection against disease shut down. Over time this weakens the body's ability to fight off infection or a severe disease such as cancer.

The process seems to affect the hypothalamus of the lower brain, which is very sensitive to emotion and stress, and then the hypothalamus sends direct and indirect messages to the adrenals and the thymus glands. These glands then alter their production of hormones to deal with the stress. The thymus gland seems to shrink under stress, and this means that its normal function—which is to help produce certain killer white blood cells called T cells from the immune system—is discouraged, and an important component of the defense mechanism is disarmed. Without this part of the hunt-and-destroy system, the immune response does not seek out and eliminate the invaders to the body, so tumors may begin to develop.

PNI is working to explain this very complex series of connections between the mind and the body. Once this is more fully understood, the treatment for many diseases will be altered to include the use of relaxation techniques and specially created visualizations. The visualizations will be powerful, positive suggestions enhancing the natural healing process so that the body can do the best job of removing the illness.

Relaxation and visualization are already used to aid present therapies, but PNI will provide more information and thus help gain greater support from the medical community.

Perhaps a time will come when prevention will be both booster shots of vaccines and "booster shots" to the psyche to bolster the natural immune processes. Do not be surprised if laughter and joy therapy become the strongest medicines of our future.

THE SOCIAL READJUSTMENT RATING SCALE

Life changes, beneficial or detrimental, can be stress producing. Holmes and Rahe researched stress and statistically developed the patterns of certain typical life events and the proportionate degree of stress they elicited. The ratings are relative to the number and degree of health changes (disease) that occurred in the group of 7,000 people surveyed. Life changes are rated according to their stressfulness and the degree of readjustment required. Add up your score, based on the events that you have experienced over the past twelve to eighteen months. If the total is over 150, you have been under a lot of stress, requiring a high degree of adaptation.

The significance of such life changes may depend on your own lifestyle. Taking out a mortgage over $10,000 may not be particularly stressful if you invest regularly in real estate; moving may be considerably more stress producing if you only move once every twenty years than if you move all the time. Even positive events add to your stress level because you must adapt to a new situation. If you get married, all of your habit patterns (eating, sleeping, lifestyle) change. Your body has to adapt to these changes, and even though they are positive, this still adds stress.

EVENT	VALUE	YOUR SCORE
Death of a Spouse	100	
Divorce	73	
Marital Separation or End of Relationship	65	

EVENT	VALUE	YOUR SCORE
Jail Term	63	
Death of Close Family Member	63	
Personal Injury, Illness, Abortion, or Miscarriage	53	
Marriage	50	
Fired from Work	47	
Marital or Relationship Reconciliation	45	
Retirement	45	
Change in Family Member's Health	44	
Pregnancy	40	
Sexual Problems	39	
Addition of New Family Member	39	
Business Readjustment	39	
Change in Financial Status	38	
Death of Close Friend	37	
Change to Different Line of Work	36	
Change in Number of Marital Arguments	35	
Mortgage or Loan over $10,000	31*	
Foreclosure of Mortgage or Loan	30	
Change in Work Responsibilities	29	
Son or Daughter Leaving Home	29	
Trouble with In-Laws	29	
Outstanding Personal Achievement	28	
Spouse Begins or Stops Work	26	
Starting or Finishing School	26	
Change in Living Conditions	25	
Revision of Personal Habits	24	
Trouble with Boss	23	

EVENT	VALUE	YOUR SCORE
Change in Work Hours or Conditions	20	
Change in Residence	20	
Change in Schools	20	
Change in Recreation	19	
Change in Church Activities	19	
Change in Social Activities	18	
Mortgage or Loan under $10,000	17*	
Change in Sleeping Habits	16	
Change in Number of Family Gatherings	15	
Change in Eating Habits	15	
Vacation	13*	
Christmas Season	12*	
Minor Violation of the Law	11	
TOTAL		_____

(*) Our economy has of course gone through major changes since this list was developed in the early 1960s. For example, in California, the mortgage break point would now be over $200,000 instead of $10,000. Some of these life events may thus elicit a different degree of stress now than was indicated above.

If you have experienced stress under any of these situations, do you recognize the connection between the event, the symptoms of stress, and their effect on your general health? Offset the negative effects of the stress you have suffered, and are still suffering, by beginning a stress-reduction program.

THE RELAXATION RESPONSE

Stress reduction reverses the adverse effects of stress. *The goal of all stress-reduction techniques is to evoke the relaxation response.* Dr. Herbert Benson, noted cardiologist and stress researcher, coined this term for the state physiologically opposite to the fight or flight response. You can elicit the feeling of deep relaxation and calm associated with the physiological state of relaxation. Your breathing becomes deep and slow. Your heart rate decreases, and the blood flow to the extremities increases. Muscles relax and return to their normal resting state. Hormonal equilibrium is established, and the overall metabolism is slowed.

If you can elicit one characteristic of the relaxation response, then you can break into the chain of physiological changes that occur when you relax. Deep breathing will probably slow your heart rate and generalize to an overall state of relaxation. Increased blood flow to the extremities, achieved through autogenics, will aid in muscular relaxation. Muscular relaxation, achieved through progressive relaxation, will contribute to increased blood flow to the extremities. Focusing the mind in meditation can slow the heart rate, and if you have hypertension, will help decrease your blood pressure. The various exercise techniques focus on different physiological responses, but they all elicit the relaxation response.

YOUR STRESS-REDUCTION PROGRAM

The chapters and exercises within each chapter are arranged in a logical progression. I recommend that you move through the book from beginning to end. However, if one technique doesn't appeal to you, feel free to move on and try another. The breathing exercises are crucial to all the other techniques that follow. (Deep breathing alone can significantly reduce your stress level.) *Try the breathing exercises before going on to any of the other approaches.*

Set aside a regular time and place for stress reduction. You should practice at least twenty minutes a day, twice a day if you have the time and feel the need. Find a quiet location where you will not be disturbed; take the phone off the hook and ask your family not to interrupt you. Your health and well-being are worth these minor inconveniences. By taking this time for yourself, you will be better able to give time and energy to the people and projects in your life.

Make a decision not to worry about anything during your relaxation period. This time should be nonnegotiable. No matter how hectic your life or how distracted you feel, allow these twenty minutes of time for relaxation. Try to practice on an empty stomach, and avoid practicing immediately after eating. If you are under a doctor's care or taking any medication, discuss your relaxation program with your doctor. Medication levels must be checked periodically, since the relaxation exercises are potentially powerful body-regulation techniques, and medication needs may radically change. Do not use the exercises as a substitute for medical care and advice. I do not work with anyone without a medical referral and always insist on a follow-up examination by the referring physician. *If you have a medical problem, please see a doctor.*

The questions that follow the exercises can help you probe more deeply into your own process of relaxation. *Answers are individual, and the answers provided are meant to provoke awareness, not curtail further discussion.* Do not be concerned if you think you are not "really relaxed," and don't compare your rate of progress with anyone else's.

When you first begin to practice relaxation techniques, you may encounter some resistance in yourself. You may find yourself fighting relaxation and holding on to your state of tension. You may not want to let go. Letting go is the hardest part for most people. Examine why you want to hold on to the tension. Do you believe that relaxation is a weakened state and that, as an adult, you must be on top of things, feeling the full burden of your responsibilities all the time? Do you believe that to be relaxed is to be vulnerable and that holding on to tension is staying in control? Relaxation actually teaches greater control, because you become more aware of your true feelings. When the noise of the stress response is stilled, you become in touch with feelings long repressed.

Are you afraid to feel all those emotions that the constant state of tension has masked? *When you relax, feelings will come up and emotions stored in your body will surface.* We have been programmed to deny and repress our feelings. These blocked and stored emotions can develop into stomach pain, high blood pressure, muscle tension, depression, or anxiety. Through stress reduction, stored and blocked emotions will be released so that you will be able to live more in the present and waste less energy on old feelings and old wounds. You will gain the ability to consider life and long-term change in your life in a serene state of mind, rather than in a state of anxiety.

Include a "wake up" at the end of your stress-reduction period or at the end of your tape. Don't jar yourself out of relaxation; come out of the state slowly and easily, gently carrying the feelings of deep relaxation and calmness with you. Tell yourself to begin awakening slowly, carrying the joy of relaxation into a fully alert state. You might want to use a 1-to-5 count, counting forward while suggesting to yourself that you will be more alert with each succeeding number. When you count 5, tell yourself to become fully alert, take a deep breath and stretch. Repeat the suggestion: "I am refreshed and fully alert." You might want to repeat this several times if your relaxation has been very deep. Become fully alert before returning to your ordinary activities.

TAPING THE EXERCISES

Many people find it easier to learn the relaxation exercises when guided by a tape. Some of the exercises are lengthy, and the visualizations, which are complex, especially lend themselves to being taped. Using a tape allows you to focus all your awareness on relaxing, rather than trying to learn the exercise and memorize its details. Straining to remember the exact wording of an exercise, or the exact sequence, will not make it easy for you to relax. You should not become too dependent on a tape, since your goal is to be able to induce relaxation at any time, anywhere, and under almost any condition. If you start with a tape, attempt to wean yourself from it after a while.

Sometimes a tape may be essential. *Keep a "first-aid" tape on hand for anxiety attacks, traumatic events, and the "worst days of your life."* The 10-to-1 Passive Progressive Relaxation makes an excellent first-aid tape and can be modified to meet your needs. You may find a visualization that works particularly well for you and might want to tape it. The type of exercise you use for this purpose is unimportant; the important thing is that it works for you.

You can record tapes yourself or have a friend record them for you. If you are making your own tapes, begin by repeating the exercises into the tape recorder, and then playing them back. You will first need to get over any self-consciousness you might feel about hearing your own voice on tape. Read the exercises in a slow, calm monotone at about one-quarter your normal rate of speaking. Pause frequently as this allows time for the suggestions to manifest and for the listener to sink more deeply into relaxation. Do not rush. Take it slow and easy. The exercises are designed to be peaceful, calm, repetitive, and somewhat monotonous. Speak with little inflection and avoid displaying any excitement or emotion. *Attempt to identify with the experience you are trying to induce.* If you suggest heaviness of the arms, for example, in the autogenics phrases, attempt to experience the same sense of heaviness in your own arms while reading the exercise onto a tape. I am usually deeply affected by an exercise while reading it. When you use a tape for the autogenics exercises, you may find it more effective to speak the phrases along with the tape.

When reading the "wake up" at the end of an exercise, raise your voice from a monotone, add inflection and emotion, and speed up your rate of speaking. Your tone of voice and volume should induce alertness and indicate that the relaxation period is over. Repeat the ending phrases several times, and if necessary, add a counting exercise.

In using a tape, just allow yourself to flow with it, letting it lead you into a state of deep relaxation. It is surprising how the initial self-consciousness melts away and how comfortable people become, allowing their own voices to lead them to relaxation. You may find the sound of yourself relaxing the best cue for future relaxation.

If you would like some professionally prepared guided relaxation exercises, I have taken exercises from this book and developed these as tools for my clients. You can find information about these stress management exercises and ordering information at the Stress Education Center's website, www.dstress.com. (Look for the page dedicated to audiotapes.)

MUSIC TO PRACTICE BY

Music, in conjunction with relaxation techniques, can lead you to a new experience—an experience so profound that you will always be able to remember what relaxation feels like. Certain types of music are better than others for this purpose, and since taste in music is so individual, you may have to experiment to find the music that perfectly suits your temperament and vibrations.

The most important element in any music for relaxation is the calming effect; music that builds to a crescendo or is highly emotional, such as Beethoven or Mozart, would be unsuitable. Fairly monotonous music is more conducive to relaxation than progressive, random music, such as John Cage, or loud rock and roll. Any music that creates emotions independent of the state of relaxation is undesirable, and most vocal music falls into this category.

I encourage people to begin with Steven Halpern's music, composed specifically to induce a relaxed, calm feeling. I particularly enjoy *Spectrum Suite* and *Zodiac Suite* from the *Anti-Frantic Alternative Series*. The first is piano and flute; the second is violin, flute, wind chimes, and piano. To obtain Steven's music, you can contact him directly at Inner Peace Music, PO Box 2644, San Anselmo, CA 94979; (800) 909-0707; www.innerpeacemusic.com.

My second choice is *Music for Zen Meditation* (MGM-Verve Records). This music gives a nice flow to your unconscious mind as it resonates with the rhythmically calming tones. Japanese koto and flute music is also very appropriate. The koto is a seven-to-thirteen-stringed instrument, similar to the zither. Many of the flutes used in this type of Japanese music are the original folk instruments made of wood and bamboo; the music has a soft, gentle sound that seems to flow from the instruments like wind through the trees. There is also a series of environmental sounds—

birds singing, waves washing on the seashore, rain falling—that are extremely peaceful. Though some people prefer classical music for a calming background, I feel that music specifically composed for a relaxing, calming effect will help you reach a deeper state of relaxation.

Music can cover up background noise. It can also be used as a meditation in itself—when you focus only on the notes and sounds, rid your mind of anything else, feel the vibrations throughout your body, and let the music fill you completely.

Chapter 2
First, Breathe . . .

W HEN YOU WERE BORN, you took a deep, full breath. Learning to breathe deeply again is the first step in learning to relax, and the deep, diaphragmatic breath is the core of the relaxation exercises discussed in this book. It is also used in the treatment of asthma, in the practice of yoga and meditation, and as a method of relaxation in childbirth.

Place one hand just below the rib cage (above the stomach). Take a deep breath, and as you inhale, notice the movement of your hand. Does it move in or out? Does it move at all? If you breathed properly, your hand moved outward. Be aware of how deeply you breathe.

We have been taught to hold our stomachs in and our chests out. Unfortunately, this posture inhibits healthful breathing. In proper breathing, the diaphragm (the muscle that separates the lung cavity from the abdominal cavity) moves slightly down to create a vacuum in the lung cavity. As a result of the downward movement, the abdomen is forced forward.

Imagine that your lungs are divided into three parts. The deep, full breath begins with the diaphragm moving downward and the lowest part of the lungs filling with air; the middle part fills; then the chest expands; and finally the upper part of the lungs fills with air. The shoulders may move slightly upward. Take another deep breath and try to imagine this progression. Is this the way you usually breathe?

Take another deep breath. Do you inhale through your nose or through your mouth? How do you exhale? Do you exhale fully and completely? In breathing for relaxation, remember to breathe in through your nose and fill your lungs completely. Breathe again, inhaling through your nose. Visualize your lungs filling slowly with air; feel the movement of your abdomen. Then, exhale through your mouth and feel the warm air leave your body. You may find it uncomfortable to breathe exclusively through your nose. *Don't be confined by a rigid pattern—do what feels right.* But begin to breathe the deep, slow, healing breath instead of the rapid-shallow-shoulder-chest breath.

Inhale and hold your breath for ten seconds, feeling the tension in your throat and chest. Exhale through your mouth with a slight sigh; feel the "sigh of relief" release the tension. Sighing may not feel comfortable at first—give it a fair chance, as this may be a way for you to instantaneously release tension. The quietest or calmest time of the breath is between the exhalation and the inhalation. If you can feel the stillness at that moment directly after exhaling, at the end of the sigh, then you are learning how to relax. Inhale again; exhale with a slight sigh. As you exhale fully and completely, feel all the tension leaving your body, melting away. *Be aware of the quiet time of the breath.* Whenever you find yourself in a stressful situation, remember this feeling, and try to re-create that moment of peace and calm.

Why the deep, full breath? Breathing properly is healthful; it increases the amount of oxygen in the blood and strengthens weak abdominal and intestinal muscles. When you are tense or upset, your breathing becomes shallow and irregular, and your heart rate tends to accelerate. When you are relaxed, your breathing deepens and your heart rate decelerates. Breathing is the easiest physiological system to control. If you can breathe the deep, slow breath inherent in relaxation, then you can trigger the rest of the characteristics of the relaxation response. Once you become aware of your breathing patterns and know how to use breathing to reduce tension, you may gradually notice how you hold tension throughout your body.

The proper breath is the basis for a variety of breathing exercises. It can be learned quickly and may be easily integrated into your busy day. Don't wait for a stressful event to practice deep breathing. When people become tense, they often forget to breathe and develop a pattern of locking up the chest muscles and the diaphragm. Take a deep, slow breath and you may be surprised to discover how quickly your tension melts away.

Take at least forty deep breaths every day. *(This is a very important technique to try. Please work with this for two weeks to give it a fair chance to benefit you.)* To remind yourself to practice deep breathing, associate it with something commonly done during the day. If you are in a busy office, and the telephone seems to ring incessantly, don't grab the phone on the first ring. Let it ring an extra time and take a deep breath. Exhale fully and completely. Remember the quiet time of the breath and pick up the phone—relaxed and free of nervous tension.

All the time you spend driving from place to place can make you tense and edgy, and if you find yourself in a traffic jam, you may be grinding your teeth by the time you arrive home. If you drive a great deal, try taking a deep breath and relaxing at each stop signal, or use billboards and highway turnoff signs as reminders. Every time you inch forward in rush hour traffic, instead of frantically beeping your horn at every stop, take a deep, full breath and exhale fully and completely. As you breathe, check your shoulders and your forehead to see if they are tense. You really don't need to drive with your shoulders or your forehead.

A dramatic but not unusual story was told to me by a man who had attended one of my stress-reduction lectures. He had a very high-pressure job and was going through a difficult custody fight for his son. The added pressure of the legal battle made it almost impossible for him to function well at work. He was having difficulty meeting deadlines and relationships with his co-workers were rapidly deteriorating. After signing up for the entire five-week course, he attended the introductory lecture. I didn't see him at the second and third lectures and began to wonder what had happened to him; the course had been closed and he had been very insistent that I allow him to enroll. When he didn't show up for the fourth lecture, I decided to call him at work. He told me the following story:

I had recommended that clock-watchers put a piece of tape on the office clock; every time they turned to check the time they would be reminded to take a deep, full breath. After the first lecture he realized that he was constantly looking at his watch while working. He placed a piece of tape (in his case it was bright blue) on his watch and took a deep breath when he checked the time. Exhaling fully and completely, at first very difficult for him, became easier with each day. Even though he couldn't attend the second lecture because of work responsibilities, he continued to practice deep breathing. On the ninth day of practice he actually counted the times he took a deep breath and was amazed to discover that he had taken fifty-three deep breaths in just one workday. On the tenth day of practice he was approached by an office secretary who commented on the change in his personality; she wanted to know what drug he was taking because it had obviously helped him so much. She didn't believe that deep breathing had effected such a radical change, but when he showed her the tape on his watch she finally believed him. Breathing cues, combined with proper deep breathing, had worked for him; he apologized for not returning to class, but he felt that deep breathing exercises were enough to keep him relaxed and free from tension.

The simple deep breathing exercise may not be enough for you—but if you learn how to take a deep, full breath and exhale fully and completely, you will have mastered the first technique for relaxation. If none of the breathing cues is appropriate for your lifestyle, find a recurring event in your daily schedule to use as a trigger for deep breathing and relaxation.

BREATHING EXERCISES

Practice these initial exercises to control tension. They may or may not be enough. Try each one three times a day for a week; you will probably find that one or two feel most comfortable for you. Pick a quiet spot for your practice session. If this is impossible and you are in a noisy place, just try to concentrate on the exercise and shut out the distractions. Always get into a comfortable position before attempting any exercise.

1-to-8 Count

Take a deep, slow breath and close your eyes. Exhale fully and completely, making sure to get the last bit of air out of your lungs. Breathe in again. As you inhale, try to see the number *1* in your mind; at the same time focus on the inhalation. Hold your breath for three seconds. Exhale, and as you breathe out the air fully and completely, mentally say "two" and visualize the number *2* in your mind. Breathe in again and mentally say "three," focusing on the number *3* and the inhalation. Hold your breath for three seconds. Exhale fully and completely, while mentally visualizing and saying *4*. Inhale, counting *5*; exhale, counting *6*. Remember to visualize the number and focus on the inhalation. Inhale, counting *7*, and exhale, counting *8*. Repeat the entire sequence from *1* to *8*. Slowly open your eyes.

Do you feel calmer?

Did you have any difficulty visualizing the numbers?

Were you able to focus on the inhalation?

Did you finish the exercise?

If you had any trouble focusing on the inhalation or visualizing the numbers, try to clear your mind of any distractions and try again. You might have been trying too hard if you didn't finish the exercise. Remember, trying too hard will only make you tenser. This exercise is not a race. Learn to be patient with yourself and the exercise; breathe slowly and pause between breaths. Do not try to force relaxation—this will only make it harder for you to relax, and you may find this very frustrating. *Instead, find a way to give in to relaxation.*

1-to-4 Count

Take a deep, full breath. Exhale fully and completely. Inhale again, and mentally count from *1* to *4*. Hold your breath, and again count from *1* to *4*. Slowly count from *1* to *8* while exhaling fully and completely. Repeat the sequence four times.

While exhaling, did you run out of breath before reaching number 8?

If you did, try again. On the second try, take a deeper breath and exhale more slowly. Be aware of full inhalation and full exhalation. If you had your eyes open and found it difficult to mentally count, close your eyes on the second try. This is a very powerful exercise if done correctly.

5-to-1 Count

Say the number *5* to yourself, and as you focus on the number, take a deep, full, slow breath. Exhale fully and completely, making sure to get the last bit of air out of your lungs. Mentally count *4* and inhale. As you begin the exhalation, tell yourself: **"I am more relaxed now than I was at number 5."** Be sure not to rush the thought. Inhale, mentally counting *3*. Tell yourself: **"I am more relaxed now than I was at number 4,"** as you exhale fully and completely. Count number *2* and then number *1,* mentally repeating the phrase: **"I am more relaxed now than I was at number 2."** Allow yourself to feel the deepening relaxation. As you approach number *1,* you should feel calmer and more relaxed.

Three-Part Breathing

Take a deep, diaphragmatic breath. Imagine that your lungs are divided into three parts. Visualize the lowest part of your lungs filling with air. Use only your diaphragm; your chest should remain relatively still. Imagine the middle part of your lungs filling, and as you visualize the expansion, allow your rib cage to move slightly forward. Visualize the upper part filling with air and your lungs becoming completely full. Your shoulders will rise slightly and move backwards. Exhale fully and completely. As you empty your upper lungs, drop your shoulders slightly. Visualize the air leaving the middle portion of your lungs, and feel your rib cage contract. Pull in your abdomen to force out the last bit of air from the bottom of your lungs. Repeat the exercise four times.

Did you have any trouble visualizing your lungs expanding and contracting?

Were you able to complete the inhaling visualization before you started to exhale?

If you had trouble visualizing, take a moment to put your thoughts out of mind. You can get back to them later when you are calm and relaxed. The visualization may seem more complex to you than it actually is; if you found yourself exhaling while still visualizing the inhalation, try and inhale more slowly. Be sure to exhale completely and push all of the carbon dioxide out of your lungs. This allows more room for life-giving oxygen to fill your lungs when you inhale.

Alternate-Nostril Breathing

Once you are comfortable with Three-Part Breathing, try this more difficult exercise. Place your right forefingers over your right nostril, pressing lightly to close off the nostril. Take a deep, full breath, inhaling with your left nostril. Visualize your lungs filling fully and expanding completely. Remove your finger from the right nostril and lightly close off the left nostril. Exhale slowly through the now open right nostril. Be certain to exhale fully and completely. Inhale through the right nostril. Close off the right nostril, and exhale fully and completely through the left nostril. Repeat slowly and rhythmically for ten more breaths.

Did you find it difficult to breathe through your nose?

Did you find one nostril easier to breath through than the other?

If you repeat this exercise at different times during the day, you will find that sometimes it is easier to breathe through the right nostril and sometimes the left. This happens because your primary breathing nostril changes about every four hours. This exercise will make you more aware of the changes in your breathing patterns.

Alternate-Nostril Breathing Variation

When you have mastered Three-Part and Alternate-Nostril Breathing, attempt this more advanced version of Alternate-Nostril Breathing. Pinch off one nostril with your mind, rather than with your finger. Visualize the air entering and leaving through the chosen nostril. Do not allow air to enter or leave the "closed" nostril. Then reverse, and try the other nostril. This exercise requires concentration and may prove difficult initially, but keep trying. It is very effective in developing self-regulation and relaxation.

If, after practicing breathing exercises for a week or two, you are still experiencing some of the symptoms of your stress response, do not despair. Even though you are breathing properly and calmly, you may still be holding tension in some part of your body, especially if you have been holding tension there for years. Don't just use proper breathing during a stress-producing situation—practice deep breathing throughout your day. Try to recall that peaceful feeling, that quiet space, after the exhalation and just before the inhalation.

Evoke this feeling whenever you feel caged in by tension. The battle for stress reduction is 50 percent awareness of your own stress response and 50 percent letting go. The other stress-reduction techniques discussed in this book will help you zero in on your own particular stress response. But, whatever exercise you are doing, remember to first, breathe....

Chapter 3
Autogenics

Your Body Listens

SOMETIMES YOU FEEL that you are a victim of your body, with its physiological processes beyond your control. When you feel well, you probably don't have this sense of helplessness. But when you are tense or anxious, you may suddenly feel out of control. Your hands and feet are icy; you jump at the slightest sound; trying to maintain an even keel consumes all your energy. You wish that you could tell yourself to calm down—and have your body listen. Though you may not be able to eradicate the stress-provoking incidents, with autogenic training you will be able to exert some control over your physiological processes and not feel so helpless. You will learn to recognize the signs and symptoms of tension and be able to reduce their effect on your life. *You do not have to be a victim of your own stress response.*

Once you have mastered deep breathing, autogenics can be the next step in your relaxation program. This method is easily learned and success usually increases with practice; the more you practice the exercises, the sooner you will effect a change in your tension level. You can use autogenics whenever you start to feel tense: for a few minutes at your desk, on the bus or in the subway, before going to sleep at night, or at any time you set aside during the day.

In autogenic training you attempt to induce specific physical sensations that are associated with relaxation. By inducing any of the characteristics of the relaxation response, such as warmth and heaviness, you can break into the chain of physiological changes that occur when you are relaxed. Imagine that these changes are a row of dominoes, carefully stood on end and regularly spaced so that slightly pushing one domino causes all the others to topple over, one after the other. The warmth that you strive for is your perception of increased blood flow throughout the body, especially to the extremities (unlike the stress response, which constricts blood flow to these areas). The heaviness is your perception of the skeletal muscles relaxing (unlike the tensing of the stress response). If you can teach yourself to elicit warmth and heaviness at your command, then the other physiological changes that occur when you relax will follow, as in the domino analogy.

Johannes H. Schultz developed the autogenic method from his experiments with hypnosis. Schultz observed that hypnotized subjects, who had been commanded to relax and were in a state of deep relaxation, experienced two powerful and pleasurable sensations—warmth throughout the body and a feeling of heaviness in the limbs. Schultz developed the autogenic program for people wishing to achieve profound relaxation through self-suggestion, without the help of a hypnotist. Simple, yet effective, word phrases suggest relaxation to the unconscious mind, which then manifests the desired responses in the body.

Some people who practice the autogenic method have learned how to exercise considerable control over their automatic functions and can induce a variety of physical sensations as well as block out the feelings of pain. *Your body can listen, but you must abandon the will, rather than exercise it.* If you try to consciously control your body, you will fail. Passive concentration is the key— you focus on your body while in a state of deep relaxation. The effort necessary for mastering the autogenic technique is not in trying to do it; letting go and giving in to relaxation is the hardest part. Trying too hard will always create more excess tension and make it more difficult for you to learn to relax.

Autogenics produces a state of relaxation that is physiologically identical to that induced by meditation and other Eastern techniques.

Unlike Eastern methods, autogenics focuses on physical sensations rather than abstract mental states; the Westerner may be able to understand and achieve deep relaxation more readily by utilizing methods deeply seated in Western culture. Autogenics gives you something concrete to do and experience. *The feedback is fairly immediate—you know if it is working.*

In some people autogenics can work quickly. A registered nurse, who had experienced true migraine headaches for over twenty years, came to me for help. Her headaches occurred three or four times a week, usually while she was working. Aware of the problem of drug addiction in chronic pain sufferers, she did not want to take pain pills; yet she worried that due to her intense discomfort she might make a mistake that would endanger someone's life. If she had a migraine and was dispensing medication, she often found herself checking and rechecking to make sure that the dosages and recipients were correct. She was a highly motivated person and very much wanted relief from her headache problem.

At the initial session I taught her the basic autogenic training phrases, and directed her to practice the exercises by herself at home at least twice a day. When she walked into my office for the second session, she had a big grin on her face. I was surprised because I had not seen her smile during the entire first session, and asked her what had brought about such a radical change in her behavior. She had not had a migraine all week and felt that she finally had control over her headaches and her life. She was absolutely elated.

Twice a day, and when possible, three times a day, the nurse had practiced autogenic training. It worked the very first day. We discussed her rapid progress and what seemed to be, at this time, her cure. She returned for three more sessions, and to her relief, there had been no recurrence of her migraines. The exercises had also taken on a new meaning for her; she found them so relaxing and rejuvenating that she continued practicing and discovered that they were also positively affecting her spiritual growth.

Of course not all people respond so dramatically, but I have found autogenics particularly effective with migraine sufferers; the success rate is about 85 percent. It has also been highly successful in treating high blood pressure, abdominal pain, anxiety, and nervousness.

In Basic Autogenic Training, some phrases imply heaviness, others warmth, others overall relaxation. Suggestions of heaviness are designed to relax skeletal muscles, and when they work, the arms and legs should feel very heavy, as they do when you are deeply relaxed. For those of you who hold tension in the muscles, releasing this tension may dramatically generalize to an overall relaxation. Phrases of warmth suggest increased blood flow allowed by the relaxation of the smooth muscles surrounding the arteries of the vascular system. If you constrict these arteries unconsciously and respond to tension with cold hands and feet, then these phrases will be especially helpful.

AUTOGENIC POSITIONS

Begin the exercises in the sitting or lying position with your eyes closed. Before assuming a position, make yourself as comfortable as possible: loosen your clothing, remove any jewelry or glasses, take off your shoes. These are the basic positions for many of the relaxation exercises included in this book, and I will often refer you to these positions. Learn them now, as correct posturing will facilitate deep relaxation.

Sitting Position

Sit near the front edge of a straight-back chair. Find the spot and position most comfortable for you. Your knees should be bent so that the angle between the calf and thigh is slightly more than 90 degrees. Sit up, as if a string were pulling you straight up through the crown of your head. Let your arms hang down freely at your sides. Now, crumple straight down with your neck bent forward. When you crumple, do it straight down, not forward or backward. Gently pick up your arms and lay them on top of your legs, about an inch above the knees. Spread your fingers. If you feel yourself pulling backward, move your hands slightly forward; if you are pulled forward, move your hands slightly back. There may be a pulling in your neck or shoulders, but as you become accustomed to this position, you will gradually stretch out and become comfortable. This sitting position creates the least amount of muscular tension.

Lying Position

Lie flat on a bed or on the floor. You may support your neck and knees by placing a pillow under them. Some people even prefer to place pillows under each arm. Spread your legs slightly and move your arms away from your torso, keeping your palms down and your elbows out. Separate your fingers so that they are not touching each other. If you are cold, cover yourself with a light blanket. Personally, I prefer the lying position, but if you find yourself inappropriately drifting into sleep, use the sitting position to remain awake.

AUTOGENIC EXERCISES

I recommend exercising in the afternoon, before dinner, or in the morning before breakfast. It is always best to practice before meals rather than after eating. When you first attempt autogenics, try to reduce all outside distractions. Once you have become adept, you may be able to practice in an ordinary setting without preparation. Autogenics can be practiced for a few minutes at work; instead of grabbing a cup of coffee between phone calls, take ten minutes, request that someone take messages, and relax. Before attempting to practice in your office, you should have practiced at home and be familiar with the progression. There is no right way to experience these exercises; everyone's experience is unique. *Remember not to try too hard—it will only make it more difficult for you to relax.* Passive concentration is the key. Let any extraneous thoughts flow through you and out of you.

These phrases are easily read into a tape recorder; if you wish to use this method, see the section on using tapes in the first chapter.

This can be a vastly effective method of learning how to use autogenic training, though often people stop using tapes after they are familiar with the progression. The Autogenics and Deepening Visualization, which follows the Basic Autogenic Training, is most effective if read onto a tape or if someone reads it to you.

Basic Autogenic Training

Get into a comfortable position, either sitting or lying, and close your eyes. Take a deep breath, and exhale fully and completely. Remember to breathe properly throughout the exercise. Let the day's experiences and thoughts pass through you and out of you. Do not hold onto your thoughts; allow them to go. Watch them flow by as if on a movie screen or like billboards passed on the highway.

Repeat this mood phrase to yourself three times: **"I am at peace with myself and fully relaxed."** Remember to breathe properly, and on the exhalation, breathe away any tension.

Concentrate on feeling heaviness in your arms and legs. Right-handed people begin with the right arm; left-handed people with the left. Right-handed people begin: **"My right arm is heavy. My right arm is heavy. My right arm is heavy."** Left-handed people begin: **"My left arm is heavy. My left arm is heavy. My left arm is heavy."** Pause between each phrase—this is not a race. Take your time, and let any worries or thoughts that may enter your consciousness flow through you and out of you. Feel the heaviness in your arm. Proceed to the opposite arm and repeat the phrase to yourself three times: **"My left arm is heavy,"** or **"My right arm is heavy."** Feel the heaviness in your arm.

Then proceed to the legs, saying to yourself: **"My right leg is heavy. My right leg is heavy. My right leg is heavy."** Feel the heaviness in your leg. Remember to breathe naturally, and take your time, pausing between each phrase. Then the other leg: **"My left leg is heavy. My left leg is heavy. My left leg is heavy."** Feel the heaviness in your legs.

Then say to yourself: **"My neck and shoulders are heavy. My neck and shoulders are heavy. My neck and shoulders are heavy."** Feel the heaviness in your neck and shoulders. Take a deep, calm breath, and exhale fully and completely.

Concentrate on feeling warmth as you relax the smooth muscles in the walls of the arteries. Right-handed people begin: **"My right arm is warm. My right arm is warm. My right arm is warm."** Left-handed people begin: **"My left arm is warm. My left arm is warm. My left arm is warm."** Feel the warmth in your arms; be aware of the pulse and the flow of blood through your entire body. Go on to the other arm.

Then let go of the tension in your legs, saying to yourself: **"My right leg is warm. My right leg is warm. My right leg is warm."** Feel the warmth in your right leg. Continue with the other leg and repeat the phrase to yourself three times. Feel the heaviness in your legs. Remember to breathe slowly and naturally, and let any thoughts flow out of you.

Move on to your neck and shoulders and say to yourself: **"My neck and shoulders are warm. My neck and shoulders are warm. My neck and shoulders are warm."** Feel the warmth in your neck and shoulders, and feel the warm blood flowing through your body. Just allow yourself to remain relaxed, don't try to force the feeling, and be aware of any sensation of blood flow or temperature change. Remember to breathe naturally and calmly.

Slow and calm your heart by saying to yourself: **"My heartbeat is calm and regular. My heartbeat is calm and regular. My heartbeat is calm and regular."** Some people may experience discomfort when they turn their attention to their own heartbeat. If you feel nauseated or light-headed, or notice any other disturbing sensation, change the phrase to: **"I feel calm. I feel calm. I feel calm."**

To slow your breathing, say to yourself: **"My breathing is calm and regular. My breathing is calm and regular. My breathing is calm and regular."** Feel the air completely filling your lungs when you inhale, and on the exhalation feel the warm air leaving your lungs. Pause between each phrase, and say the phrases to yourself slowly and calmly.

Concentrate on warmth in your abdomen, saying to yourself: **"My abdomen is warm and calm. My abdomen is warm and calm. My abdomen is warm and calm."** If you have serious abdominal problems, bleeding ulcers, or diabetes, or are in the last trimester of pregnancy, change the phrase to: **"I am calm and relaxed. I am calm and relaxed. I am calm and relaxed."**

Move on to your forehead, repeating to yourself: **"My forehead is cool and calm. My forehead is cool and calm. My forehead is cool and calm."** Feel the excess blood flowing out of your head. Remember to breathe the calm, full breath; allow any extraneous thoughts to flow through you and out of you.

When you have completed the last phrase, rest for a moment. To bring yourself back to a normal state of alertness, repeat the phrase to yourself: **"I am refreshed and completely alert. I am refreshed and completely alert. I am refreshed and completely alert."** Take a deep, full breath, flex your arms and legs, and stretch. You may wish to repeat the last phrase several more times. Slowly open your eyes.

Were you able to feel heaviness?

Was the technique more successful for one part of your body than another?

Did you experience any sensation other than heaviness?

Were you able to feel warmth?

Any sensation of blood flow?

Did you find the exercise pleasant or disturbing?

Did you feel any resistance to letting go?

If you were unable to feel heaviness in your limbs you may be trying too hard. Remember not to hold on to your thoughts—let them flow through you and out of you. You may have found it easier to feel warmth or heaviness in your arms or abdomen; this is not unusual and the rest will come with practice. Feeling warmth, especially in the legs and feet, may take some time. It took me almost two months of daily practice to feel warmth in my legs, so don't be discouraged if you are having difficulty with this part of the exercise. The feeling of increased blood flow will also be easier to recognize after more practice. The phrase used for the forehead suggests cooling and calming to relax the muscles of the head and face. A warming suggestion would increase blood flow to the brain and scalp, possibly causing a headache for migraine sufferers. Remember that this is the first time you've done the exercise—be patient. If you were able to let go and flow with the phrases, then you are on your way to being a relaxed person.

Practice the entire sequence at least once a day, twice or more if you want to learn more quickly. After you have followed the routine for several weeks, you may find that you can decrease the number of phrase repetitions because your body will be reprogramming itself and responding more readily to the suggestions. Also, after a few weeks reread the questions, and see if your responses are different. You may even wish to keep a journal; but don't use the journal to push yourself too much. This may just make you tenser and make it more difficult for you to let go. Try these techniques for at least a month; it takes that long to learn the phrases and to become comfortable with the exercise. You may wish to add a visualization to your exercise after two to three more weeks. If the combined autogenics and visualization doesn't work after ten to fourteen weeks, you might consider trying a different relaxation exercise.

Autogenics and Deepening Visualization

The author's taped version of this exercise is available at www.dstress.com. Look for Tape #102.

Get yourself into a comfortable position, either sitting or lying, and close your eyes. Take a deep, slow breath, and pause for a moment after you inhale. Exhale fully and completely. Allow yourself to continue to breathe slowly and naturally. Repeat the autogenic phrases to yourself slowly, and allow yourself to feel the heaviness and the warmth.

The first phrase is: **"I am at peace with myself and fully relaxed. I am at peace with myself and fully relaxed. I am at peace with myself and fully relaxed."** Breathe naturally and slowly, remembering to exhale completely. Try feeling the heaviness in your arms, as you say to yourself: **"My right arm is heavy. My right arm is heavy. My right arm is heavy."** Allow yourself to let go of the muscles in your arms as you say to yourself: **"My left arm is heavy. My left arm is heavy. My left arm is heavy."**

Continue to breathe slowly and naturally, and say to yourself: **"My right leg is heavy. My right leg is heavy. My right leg is heavy."** Let go of the tension in your legs as you say to yourself: **"My left leg is heavy. My left leg is heavy. My left leg is heavy."** Now say: **"My neck and shoulders are heavy. My neck and shoulders are heavy. My neck and shoulders are heavy."** Let your shoulders drop; allow the muscles to relax fully and completely.

As you continue to breathe slowly and naturally, say to yourself: **"My right arm is warm. My right arm is warm. My right arm is warm."** Feel the blood flow through your arm and into your hand, and say to yourself: **"My left arm is warm. My left arm is warm. My left arm is warm."** Allow yourself to let go even more, and say to yourself: **"My right leg is warm. My right leg is warm. My right leg is warm."** Feel the blood flow through your leg and into your foot, as you say to yourself: **"My left leg is warm. My left leg is warm. My right leg is warm."** Now say to yourself **"My neck and shoulders are warm. My neck and shoulders are warm. My neck and shoulders are warm."**

Continue to breathe naturally and completely, while saying to yourself: **"My heartbeat is calm and regular. My heartbeat is calm and regular. My heartbeat is calm and regular."** Feel your strong, even heartbeat. Say to yourself: **"My breathing is calm and regular. My breathing is calm and regular. My breathing is calm and regular."** Feel your deep, full breaths and your complete, slow exhalations.

Continue on, saying to yourself: **"My abdominal region is warm and calm. My abdominal region is warm and calm. My abdominal region is warm and calm."** Then turn your attention to your forehead, and say to yourself: **"My forehead is cool and smooth. My forehead is cool and smooth. My forehead is cool and smooth."**

Breathe slowly and naturally, allowing yourself to breathe away tension with each and every exhalation. Imagine that any thought or experience running through your mind appears to you as a bubble, and just let the bubble float up and out of your consciousness. Just as if you were watching a glass of carbonated water, see the bubbles rise to the surface and burst. Let your thoughts or experiences rise up and out of your consciousness. Don't hold on to any of them—just watch them as they drift by. And just like in the glass of carbonated water, the bubbles gradually decrease in frequency, slowing and finally stopping, leaving the water clear and calm. As you continue to breathe slowly and calmly, your mind gradually becomes calm and clear as you let go of distractions and drift deeper into relaxation and peaceful calmness.

Imagine that you are at the top of a slow-moving escalator, and as you step on, you find yourself gradually riding down, deeper and deeper into relaxation. As you slowly ride down, you can feel yourself becoming more and more relaxed, deeper and deeper into relaxation. Gradually you can feel your muscles becoming heavier and more relaxed, as you allow yourself to drift deeper into a dreamlike state of calmness and relaxation. As you near the bottom of this slow-moving escalator, you can see yourself surrounded by your favorite outdoor landscape. It is a calm and beautiful day, and as you step off the escalator, look around at this peaceful, calm scene.

Drift slowly over to the most comfortable spot, and allow yourself to lie down, just sinking into the warm earth. Gradually any excess tension melts away and is replaced by calmness and deep relaxation. Feel the warmth of the sunlight as it gently shines down and warms your hands and arms. Imagine that the sun and warm breezes warm your legs and feet.

Let the warmth of the sun spread to every cell of your body, melting the tension and allowing you to become more calm and relaxed. As the sunlight and warmth flow freely and easily through your body, simply let go of tension and allow yourself to drift deeper into a peaceful, calm state. See yourself completely relaxed, feel the increasing heaviness of your arms and legs as you melt into the earth. Feel the deep state of calmness and relaxation and register it in your mind, so that you can remember it in a fully waking state. Let yourself drift in this state of calmness for just a few moments.

Every time you practice this exercise you will get better and better at it, being able to relax more deeply and more completely. Every time you practice, the will to control tension increases, and you can relax more quickly. The effects of the calmness and relaxation will carry over with you throughout your day. You will feel calm and relaxed and be aware of tension or excess energy whenever it manifests itself.

Now, gently bring yourself up and out of deep relaxation to a more alert state, gradually letting yourself become more aware of your surroundings, remaining calm and relaxed. Say to your-self: **"I am refreshed and alert. I am refreshed and alert. I am refreshed and alert."** Take a deep, full breath and stretch, let-ting the feelings of calmness and relaxation carry over with you into a fully alert state. You may wish to take another deep breath and stretch, and then gradually open your eyes.

Did you find this exercise more difficult than the basic exercise?

Did you have any trouble visualizing the bubbles?

Was it easier to feel warmth or heaviness?

Did you want to come out of the deep relaxation state?

Visualization can be extremely difficult for some people, so if this form of autogenics was more difficult for you than the basic exercise, don't feel that you have failed miserably. Once again, letting go and clearing your mind of distractions will make this exercise easier. If you had more difficult visualizing the bubbles in the carbonated water than visualizing yourself outside, you were probably more receptive by the time you reached the second stage of the visualiza-tion. Visualization is a skill that improves with practice. Warmth and heaviness, for some people, are easier to feel when the sugges-tions are accompanied by a visualization. If you found this to be true, then try to make it a practice to always accompany your auto-genic sessions with a visualization. Not wanting to come out of a state of deep relaxation is normal, especially if you have trouble relaxing most of the time. Just remember that once you have achieved this state, you can recall that peaceful, calm feeling throughout the rest of your day.

Chapter 4
Progressive Relaxation

From Head to Toe

IN AUTOGENICS WORDS ARE USED to trigger relaxation, focusing on the concrete sensations of warmth and heaviness. In active progressive relaxation specific muscles are contracted and released. Both autogenic and progressive relaxation techniques teach you how to focus on bodily sensations and how relaxation feels. Just as the act of inducing warmth and heaviness generalizes to an overall relaxation response, relaxing localized muscle tension generalizes to an overall relaxation response.

If you feel cut off from your body and find it hard to manifest warmth or heaviness through the autogenics technique, progressive relaxation may be a good method for you. If your tension expresses itself as a backache, muscle spasm, tight jaw, stiff shoulders, or a tension headache—all forms of skeletal muscle tension—this may be the method that works best for you.

Progressive relaxation teaches you to be more aware of daily tension. Imagine that it is 2:45 on a Friday afternoon. You are waiting in a long line at the bank hoping to cash your paycheck and thinking about all the taxes deducted from your weekly salary. Your neck is stiff, and your shoulders are hunched up around your ears. Because you have practiced progressive relaxation, you are aware of the tension and know how to release it. This tension, in the past, has often developed into a full-fledged backache; now you know how to prevent this tension from manifesting itself later as pain. You zero in on the tension and feel it in your neck and shoulders. After tightening the muscles even further, you take a deep, full breath. As you exhale, you release the muscle tension and feel it leaving your body with the warm breath. Two more full, deep breaths, accompanied by a tension-releasing exhalation, and you are a new person, free of tension and neck pain.

Edmund Jacobsen said, "An anxious mind cannot exist within a relaxed body." Fifty years ago he developed a series of over two hundred exercises designed to relax the muscles by teaching muscle awareness and relaxation through tensing individual muscles. These exercises progress through the musculature—thus the term "progressive relaxation." Jacobsen used the exercises to treat a wide variety of physical complaints, and his research forms the foundation for our understanding of the mind/body awareness processes, and the use of relaxation in healing.

Two kinds of progressive relaxation have been developed from Jacobsen's original exercises: active progressive and passive progressive. In the active mode you tense your muscles and then relax them; passive progressive takes the process one step further and teaches you how to relax your muscles without first tightening them. *I personally find passive progressive relaxation more effective than the active form.* Active progressive can aggravate tension for some people. If you wish, you may go on to the passive form.

ACTIVE PROGRESSIVE

Muscle tensing, followed by a conscious effort to relax the muscles, allows you to recognize clearly the difference between tension and relaxation. Once you feel your muscles tensed and then relaxed, it may be easier for you to induce relaxation. *These exercises are extremely beneficial for people who find it easier to concentrate while physically active.* I have not included Jacobsen's original exercise as it is too lengthy for most people, and it is not generally used for this reason. The first exercise follows his basic structure and incorporates the major muscles. The second, abbreviated version should only be practiced after you have used the first form.

These exercises work well on tape, and if you wish to tape them, follow the instructions in the first chapter. Many people are able to remember the sequence after practicing only three or four times and find tapes unnecessary. The sequence may be done quickly, but a slow initial session is most beneficial; you can speed up after you learn the basics of muscular relaxation.

Active Progressive Relaxation

Begin by sitting in a comfortable chair in a quiet room, or use the sitting or lying autogenic positions. Close your eyes gently and take a deep, diaphragmatic breath. Exhale fully and completely, letting the tension melt from your body. Pay attention to your slow breathing and let go of the day's tensions and uncomfortable experiences. Relax as much as possible. Remember not to strain to relax as this only creates excess tension.

■ ARMS AND HANDS

Make a fist with your right hand, and concentrate on the tension as you gradually tighten your fist. Hold your fist tight for a few moments and notice the tension. After a few seconds release your fist and relax your hand. Take a deep, full breath, feel the relaxation, and let the tension flow from you as you exhale. Take a few moments to relax even further. Be aware of all the sensations in your hand and lower arm. Tense your right hand again, and repeat the process.

Do not forget to breathe naturally and let go completely when relaxing. Study the difference between tensed and completely relaxed muscles; become aware of the subtle degrees of tension. Repeat the exercise a third time and focus on any tension you may be holding in your fingers. Feel the tension in each finger, and feel the relaxation. Feel the warmth as the blood flows freely into your hand and each finger. Recognize increased circulation. Breathe deeply and fully, allowing the tension to flow from you.

Make a fist with your left hand. Remember to tense completely and relax fully. Notice any difference in the sensations between the left hand and the right. After clenching your left hand for the third time, take a moment and relax completely. Feel the relaxation in both hands and your lower arms. Now move up your arms to your biceps.

Contract your right bicep as tightly as possible. Concentrate on the tension for a few moments. After a few seconds release your bicep, and relax your entire upper arm. Take a deep, full breath, feel the relaxation, and allow the tension to flow from your body as you exhale fully and completely. Do the exercise two more times, while remembering to breathe naturally. When you have tensed and relaxed your bicep three times, focus on the relaxation in your right arm as it rests limply by your side.

Turn your attention to your left arm. Tense your bicep, and then release it, just as you did with your right arm. Do the exercise three times, remembering to exhale completely after each full breath and to release all the tension. Feel the relaxation in both arms.

Refocus your attention on your right hand and wrist. Spread your fingers apart and bend your hand towards you at the wrist as far back as you can. Feel the tension between your fingers, in your palm, in your wrist, and in your lower arm. Hold this position for a few moments, then relax, letting your hand go limp and releasing any tension in your hand and arm. Breathe away any remaining tightness and relax fully. Do the exercise two more times, remembering to breathe naturally. Feel the deep relaxation in your right arm and hand. Become aware of the increased blood circulation and notice how heavy your right arm and hand have become.

Practice the same exercise with your left arm and hand. Be aware of the difference between tension and letting go into relaxation. Remember to do the hand-spreading, wrist-bending movement three times. Be conscious of the different degrees of relaxation and how total relaxation feels.

Return awareness to your right arm. Stretch the arm out straight at a right angle to your body, pointing your fingers out straight so that you feel tension and a pulling in your arm. Tighten your triceps and your whole arm and hand as much as possible. Remember to breathe naturally. Hold your arm in this taut position for a few moments, and then relax your arm completely and let it hang limp and relaxed at your side. Breathe fully and feel the relaxation. Straighten your right arm again; examine the tension and then relax. Repeat one more time and then take a few moments to relax completely, being aware of your right arm and hand. Repeat the entire sequence with your left arm and hand.

Do you feel any unique sensations in your arms?

Do your arms feel longer?

Do you feel tingling or warmth in your arms?

How about heaviness?

Your arms will feel different after doing this exercise. Most people report a sense of added length in their arms; your arms *are* actually longer because your muscles have relaxed and let go. The feelings of tingling and warmth are the result of increased blood flow; heaviness is experienced because you are more relaxed. This experience may make you more aware of the tension you always hold in your arms. After you practice this exercise for several days, you should notice progressively deeper relaxation and greater sensitivity to subtle levels of tension. If you practice twice a day for several weeks, you should be able to release the tension in your arms and hands completely, and have this relaxation generalize to your shoulders, neck, back, and chest. After two weeks of practice, try tensing and releasing both arms simultaneously.

■ **LEGS AND FEET**

Take a deep breath and relax. Follow your breathing, allowing it to slow and deepen naturally. Remember to exhale fully and completely, releasing any tension with the warm air. Turn your attention to your right foot. Curl your toes, and feel the tension as you progressively tighten them. Hold the tension as tightly as possible for a few moments. Be aware of all the sensations in your toes, foot, and ankle. Release the tension and take a deep, full breath, feeling the difference between tension and relaxation. Exhale, letting go of any remaining tightness. Let your breath become calm and regular. Do this sequence two more times, feeling the deep relaxation in your right foot.

Turn your attention to your left foot. Repeat the exercise three times. Remember to tense completely and relax fully, noticing any difference in the sensations between the left foot and the right. After curling the toes on your left foot for the third time, take a moment and relax even further. Feel the relaxation in both feet.

Now, back to your right foot. Bend your foot backward, toes reaching for the top of the ankle and lower leg. Feel the tension; bend it back even further, stretching as far as you can. Hold for a few moments, and then relax your foot, letting it go limp. Take a deep, full breath, exhaling fully and completely. As you exhale, let go of even more tension; feel the difference between tension and relaxation. Let your breath become calm and regular. Repeat the exercise two more times, allowing your right foot to relax even more with each sequence.

Move on to your left foot. Tighten, and then relax, feeling the tension in your toes, arch, ankle, calf, and knee. Remember to breathe naturally throughout the exercise. Repeat two more times, and then let go for a moment, focusing on the complete relaxation in both feet.

Be aware of your right foot and lower leg. Arch your foot, point your toes, and tighten your lower right leg. Study the tension; tighten even further and then hold for a few moments. Let go of the tension in your leg and foot, and relax even more by breathing away the tension. Let your breath become calm, and release even more tension with each exhalation. Practice the exercise three times. After also practicing the exercise three times with the left foot, feel the relaxation deepening in both feet and lower legs.

Remember to breathe properly, inhaling deeply and exhaling fully and completely. Tense your upper right leg; feel the tightness in the back of your knee and thigh. Tighten it further for a few moments and study the tension. Let go of all the tightness, and notice the difference between tension and relaxation. As your breath becomes even calmer, let your right leg sink deeper into relaxation. Repeat the exercise two more times, each time letting more of the tension fall away. Turn your attention to your upper left leg and repeat the sequence three times.

Next, turn your attention to your buttocks, becoming aware of the feelings there. Pull them in, tightening these muscles as much as you can. Tense the muscles of your buttocks tighter and tighter. Remember to breathe deeply. Pull your buttocks inward and feel the tension in your hips, thighs, and up and down your legs. Contract even further, hold a few moments at the point of complete tension, then relax. Take a deep, full breath, then exhale, breathing away every bit of remaining tension. Repeat two more times, allowing yourself to slip deeper into relaxation with each sequence.

Are you having trouble releasing all the tension?

Are your feet warmer than usual?

Are you more aware of how much tension you ordinarily hold in your legs?

Letting go is always the hardest part. If you are having a lot of difficulty in releasing the tension, perhaps you should use the passive progressive series. Some people tend to go into muscle spasm when they tense too hard or for too long. If your feet feel warmer, or if you are beginning to notice that they are always colder than the rest of your body, this exercise may be very beneficial for you. The feeling of warmth is the sensation of increased circulation to the extremities. The real benefit of these exercises is in making you more aware of the subtle levels of tension you tend to hold in various parts of your body. Perhaps now you will be more able to notice this tension and release it before it causes you pain. Even if you have not become instantly aware of all the places you hold tension, do not despair; such awareness is often cumulative or occurs suddenly after several weeks of performing the progressive series. After two weeks of practice, you will be able to tense and relax both legs at once and be more sensitive to relaxation and increased circulation in the legs and feet.

■ BACK AND TRUNK

Arch your lower back and consider the tension. Do not strain too hard, especially if you have a weakness in your back. Tighten slightly, hold for a few moments, feel the tension, and then relax. Take a deep breath, exhale fully and completely, allowing your lower back to relax. Tense your back again, being careful not to strain, and being aware of the tension in your spine, shoulders, and buttocks. You may even feel tension in your neck, chin, and legs. Study the tension, and realize how back tension affects you and how far this tension can generalize throughout your body. Remember to breathe properly and release any tension on the exhalation. Do not hold this position for too long, as you do not want to create too much tension in your back. Repeat once more.

Tighten your abdomen. Hold the tension and study it. Pull your muscles in even further, and then relax. Feel all the organs move comfortably back into position. Breathe calmly and release more tension as you exhale, allowing your breath to be calm and regular. Take a deep breath and release even more tension with the exhalation. When your breath is calm, repeat the exercise two more times.

Next, tighten your upper back and shoulders. Push back your shoulders, as if you were trying to get them to touch behind your back. Once again, do not strain too hard, especially if you have back problems. Hold; study the tension in your upper back, neck, shoulders, and up and down your spinal column. You may even feel it in your head or face. After holding for a few moments, release the tension and relax. Sink into the chair or bed, and relax completely as you exhale away any tension with the warm air. Consider the difference between tension and relaxation. Let your shoulders drop completely. Allow your breath to become calm and natural and repeat the exercise twice more; with each attempt, allow more tension to flow from your body.

Take a deep, natural breath and exhale fully and completely. Feel your rib cage relax as you exhale, forcing every bit of air from your lungs. Recognize the quietest part of the breath when you are wholly relaxed and free from tension, just before the next inhalation. Stay in this quiet space, and force out even more breath. Repeat twice, relaxing your rib cage more with each attempt.

In tensing your back, did you notice any special weak spots where you feel pain or disproportionate tension?

In tightening the abdomen, did you have a sense of the tension you ordinarily hold there?

Where did you feel the strain when you tightened your upper back and shoulders?

Often, people report feeling more tension in some particular area of their backs—often the same spot where their backaches originate. This may also be the spot hardest to rid of tension during the relaxation exercises. The abdomen is another place where many people hold tension all the time. Tension is held not only in the muscles that can be consciously contracted and released, but also in the smooth muscles that regulate digestive movements. You may find that you tense the abdomen all the time, as if you were waiting for a blow, or that when you feel threatened, your arms immediately go to cover your abdomen as if to protect an especially vulnerable area. People sometimes hunch the upper back and shoulders in a similarly protective gesture or in an effort to pull their heads in from the world and retreat. Sometimes pain in the face, arms, neck, or head is caused by tension in the upper back and shoulders, even though you do not feel the pain there. Try to remember the discomfort of total contraction and the pleasure of complete relaxation. The next time you are standing in line at the bank, or hunched over your desk, or hiding in a corner at a party, ask yourself which of these two sensations you are closer to feeling. Perhaps after doing the progressive sequence for trunk and back, you will learn how to go along with tension for a moment, focus on the place where it is centered, contract as tightly as you can, and then really let go of it.

■ FACE AND HEAD

Open your eyes and mouth as widely as possible, as if you were a fish. Hold this position and study the tension in your forehead and jaw and around your mouth. You may feel tension up the sides of your neck as well. Hold this position for a few moments, and then relax your eyes and mouth, remembering to breathe naturally. Try the position again, this time opening your eyes and mouth even further. Relax and allow the tension to flow out of your whole face. Remember to unclench your jaw and relax completely, letting every bit of tension and any sign of emotion leave your face. Repeat again, relaxing even more.

Close your eyes and focus on your slow, calm breathing. Then, keeping your eyes closed, tense your face by tightening up around the nose as if you were trying to wriggle your nose. Purse your lips, tighten your jaws, and then tense your entire face just a little more. Hold the position for a few moments and then relax, letting all the tension flow from your face.

Breathe away any tension with your calm, even, slow breath. Repeat twice more, remembering to keep your eyes closed throughout the exercise.

Be aware of your forehead; as it relaxes, let it feel smooth and calm. Take a deep, full breath and with the exhalation let your jaw drop, letting all the tension flow out of your mouth, along with the warm air. Feel your face soften into a state of total relaxation. Your eyes are loosely closed, your forehead unwrinkled, your skin smooth. Breathe calmly, slowly, and naturally.

Did you find it harder to relax your face than the other parts of your body? How often is your face totally relaxed?

Many people find it harder to relax their faces than any other part of their bodies. This is because the many muscles of the face are in a constant state of tension, expressing emotion and moving when we speak. Even the act of hiding emotion creates tension. You may not know how many muscles you have in your face until you do this exercise. Most people are never without tension in their faces except while sleeping. If you often get headaches, you may find that they magically disappear once you learned how to relax your facial muscles.

Abbreviated Active Progressive

After you have practiced Active Progressive Relaxation for three weeks and you can relax profoundly, you may be ready for the abbreviated form. Begin by getting into the autogenic sitting or lying position. Be sure that your back and head are supported. Close your eyes gently, and take a few diaphragmatic breaths and begin to relax. Exhale fully and completely, letting all the day's problems leave your consciousness, and allow yourself a moment of peace at that quiet time of the breath, just after exhalation.

Turn your attention to your right foot and any sensations you might be feeling there. Curl your toes. Tighten them even further and be aware of all the tension in your toes, foot, and ankle. Study this tension, and then relax. Be aware of the difference between tension and relaxation. Take a deep, slow breath, and with the exhalation, breathe away any tension you may still be holding in your right foot. Go on to the left foot, repeating the exercise. Be conscious of any difference in tension level between your left and right foot. Let yourself feel the increased blood flow moving through your toes, your feet, and into your legs.

Move back to the right foot and the lower right leg. Arch your foot, point your toes out, and then stretch to point them out even further. Feel the tension, and then relax, letting go of all the tension. Take a deep breath, and as you exhale, allow all the tension in your foot to leave your body with the warm air.

Tighten your upper right leg. Feel the tension in the back of your knee and thigh, and tense your leg even more. Hold the tension for a few moments, and then relax completely. Feel yourself slipping deeper into relaxation as you take a slow, easy diaphragmatic breath. Exhale fully and completely, allowing the exhalation to take every remaining bit of tension with it. Repeat the sequence with your left leg.

Now, direct your attention to your buttocks. Tighten them, pulling the muscles inward. Hold the constriction for a moment and focus all your attention there; then relax. As you relax, notice the pleasure in letting go of tension, the pleasure of just feeling your calm, relaxed body. Take a deep breath and then exhale, relaxing even more. Feel the relaxation deepen in your feet, legs, and buttocks, and spread to the rest of your body.

Tighten your abdominal region. Pull your stomach in, as if your abdomen could touch your back. Tighten it even further, hold this tension for a moment, and then relax. Realize the difference between tension and relaxation in your abdomen. Breathe deeply and then exhale, allowing all the tightness in your abdomen to flow from your body with the warm air. At the end of the exhalation, pause just a moment to appreciate the total peace of this quiet time of the breath.

Tense your shoulders and back. Study the tension, and then relax. Take a deep, full breath, and relax even more deeply, letting all the tension from your back and shoulders move out of your body with the warm exhalation. Sink into whatever surface you are sitting or lying upon. With the next exhalation, become aware of letting go of even more tension.

Contract your arm muscles and make fists with both hands. Concentrate on the tension and squeeze your arms and hands even tighter. Study the tension and then relax, letting your fingers unfold slowly, as you become aware of the tension gradually leaving your hands. Take a deep, full breath and with the exhalation, let go of any tension remaining in your hands and arms. Be aware of the blood flow returning to your hands; feel the warmth and the tingling. Focus on the heaviness in your arms, and allow your arms to sink into the chair or floor. Take another deep breath and exhale, becoming more and more deeply relaxed.

Squeeze your face tightly around your nose. Purse your lips, clench your jaws, and tighten up your entire face. Study the tension in your jaw and forehead, and then relax. Take a deep, slow, full breath and relax even more with the exhalation. Let your jaw drop slightly. Be quiet and still for a few moments, enjoying the feeling of total calmness and relaxation. Realize how good this state of total relaxation feels.

Did you find the abbreviated form as effective as the longer version?

If you had difficulty feeling relaxed with the abbreviated form, return to the longer form. More practice will make you more comfortable with the progression, which will make it easier for you to relax. Releasing all the induced tension is difficult for many people, and you might want to try the passive progressive exercises that follow.

PASSIVE (GENTLE) PROGRESSIVE

The first relaxation exercise I ever tried was a passive progressive sequence. Passive exercises start with the toes and progress to the head, based on the assumption that you first relax those parts of the body that are easiest to relax. I was in a class with a group of other novices, and because it was a warm, early fall day, we moved outdoors. I remember lying in the grass and listening to the voice of the teacher. I experienced a new sense of integration. It was a wonderful sensation to sink into the grass and to feel each set of muscles give up its tension and become part of the balanced wholeness of my body. I hope that the exercises which follow will allow you to have the same sort of deep relaxation.

In the passive form of progressive relaxation, proper breathing and a focus of awareness are combined to induce deep relaxation. The muscles are never intentionally tensed and remain totally unstressed. All tension leaves the body on the exhalation with the warm air. The most important factors in this exercise are the slow progression from one part of the body to another, pausing to focus on the various body parts while in a state of passive rather than agitated attention, and deep breathing to induce relaxation and as the focus of visualization.

Passive Progressive Relaxation

This exercise is available at www.dstress.com. Look for Tape #101.

Begin by sitting or lying in an autogenic position. Try to be very comfortable. To begin, take a few diaphragmatic breaths, exhale completely, allowing yourself to relax. Allow all the tension to leave your body with the exhalation. Let all the daily thoughts, events, and concerns pass through your mind. When you are ready to let go of them, take another very deep breath, and exhale completely, allowing the thoughts to pass out of your mind.

Turn your attention to your feet, for just a moment, and become aware of how your feet feel. Consider the way the skin of your feet feels against the surface of the floor or the bed. Notice the air around you. Is there a slight breeze or does the air feel still? Take a deep, full breath, and then focus completely on your feet. As you exhale, let any tension that you are holding in your feet be released with the exhalation. Then, just appreciate, for a moment, how good this state of relaxation feels.

Shift your focus of attention to your lower legs, and become aware of how your legs feel. If you notice any tension, focus on it. Breathe in, concentrating all your energy on your lower legs, and as you breathe out, let all the tension you are holding be released with the exhalation. If you still notice any tension, take another very deep, very pleasurable breath, and with the exhalation, blow all the tightness away.

Consider your knees and upper legs. Focus on any stress you notice there, any discomfort or tension. Inhale, focusing on the tension in your knees and upper legs, and as you exhale, allow this tension to flow from you, leaving your knees and legs totally relaxed. If you perceive any remaining tension, inhale again, releasing that last bit of tension with the warm air.

Feel your hips and buttocks resting against the floor, bed, or chair. As you take a deep, diaphragmatic breath, be aware of any tension in these areas. Focus on this tension and how it feels. Take a full, cleansing breath, and as you exhale, release the tension with the warm air. If any tension still remains, take another relaxing breath, and just imagine all the stress being carried from your hips and your buttocks by the exhalation.

Gently consider your legs, from your hips down to your feet. They are probably beginning to feel heavy and relaxed. If there is any remaining tension, focus on it, inhale, and then let go of it completely as you exhale. You may wish to repeat this if you still feel any tension.

Move your focus to your lower back and any tension you may be holding there. Focus on the tension, and as you exhale, release this excess energy with the exhalation. Allow your back to become completely relaxed; let any burden you have been carrying there be lifted with the next exhalation. Focus on your shoulders and upper arms. Breathe in and consider any excess energy or tension that you may be storing there. Realize that you can let go of it, and with the next exhalation, let this tension flow out of your body with your breath.

Turn your attention to your lower arms and hands. Inhale fully and completely. With the exhalation, let all the tension from your lower arms and your hands be fully released. Let your arms sink into the surface upon which you are sitting or lying. If you perceive any residual tension, take another very deep, very satisfying breath and let every bit of stress in your arms or your hands be carried away with it.

Consider your back, your neck, and your head. Be aware of any excess energy, any stored tension, any stress, you are holding there. Focus on this tension, and then take a natural, diaphragmatic breath. As you exhale, send all the tension away and out of you. Now, focus on the top and sides of your head. If you feel any tightness, just inhale, and with the exhalation, allow the top and sides of your head to relax fully. Feel your head sinking into the surface upon which you're lying. Consider your forehead and the upper part of your face. Become conscious of any excess energy or discomfort there. Take a deep, full breath, and as you exhale, allow this tension to flow through you and out of your body. Pause for just a moment at the end of the exhalation to enjoy the peaceful feeling at the quiet time of the breath. Then, take another deep breath, and as you exhale, let go of every last bit of tension in your forehead and upper face.

Gently consider your mouth and jaw. Become aware of any clenching, any stored emotion you are holding. Allow yourself to breathe it away with the next deep breath. Focus your attention on this tension, and then, with the exhalation, let yourself release all this stored tension with the warm air. Breathe again, and as you exhale, let go of every last bit of tension. And with the next breath, be aware of any remaining tension in your neck, head, or face. Notice how it feels, and then with the exhalation, let it all go.

Move your attention to your chest and your diaphragm. If you are holding any tension there, and you sense yourself holding back just a little when you breathe, allow those areas to completely relax. Take another, very deep, very satisfying breath, and allow every last bit of tension to be carried away with the exhalation.

Become aware of how your abdomen feels. If there is any tension you are saving in your abdomen, where you are not allowing the breath to reach, then take a very deep breath, and focus on that held tension. Exhale and allow the tension to flow freely from your body, and allow your abdomen to relax completely. Take another very deep breath, letting the breath flow freely throughout your abdomen, and if there is any residual tension, let it flow from your body with your exhalation.

Consider your pelvis and your genitals. Focus on any excess energy or tension you may be holding there, and as you take a deep breath, really feel this tension. As you exhale, let go of all the tension. Inhale again, and exhale slowly and peacefully, sending any remaining tension away and out of your body.

Take a very deep, very pleasurable breath, and appreciate the relaxation in your entire body. Feel the heaviness and the warmth. If you can identify any tension anywhere in your body, turn your awareness there and take another deep breath. As you exhale, allow this last bit of residual tension to flow from you and leave you completely at peace. Imagine yourself in this beautiful state of relaxation; your body is heavy and warm. Retain this mental picture, and whenever you start to feel tense, remember it. Focus on it and realize that you can relax completely any time you wish. Take a deep, full breath, stretch, and begin to return to a fully alert state. Inhale again, and become more alert on the exhalation.

Did you find the passive progressive technique as effective as the active?
Did you find it harder to relax some parts of your body than others?

Your relaxation and stress responses are uniquely your own. Some people find the active sequence more effective, others the passive. With either, remember that stress is a habituated response, one that you learned long ago and have been repeating unconsciously, probably for years. To reprogram your body to relaxation also takes time. For a while, it may seem that you are only going through the motions. If you continue, you will notice results. The part of your body that is most resistant to relaxation may be the place where you hold the most tension. For many people, the back, neck, and head are key areas. For others, the pelvis and abdomen are the most difficult to relax. Even if you cannot relax a particular area completely, the passive progressive sequence will make you more aware of how and where you hold tension and how tension feels. This is the first and most important step.

10-to-1 Passive Progressive Relaxation

This exercise is available at www.dstress.com. Look for Tape #103.

This exercise combines counting, breathing, and focusing on parts of the body. Counting provides a rhythm for the exercise and provides the suggestion for relaxation to deepen during the course of the countdown. The exercise lends itself well to taping. If you cannot tape it, you might ask a friend to read it to you for the first few times. Remember to speak slowly and to pause a moment for the first few times. Remember to speak slowly and to pause a moment after each sentence.

Get into a very comfortable position; use either the sitting or lying autogenic position. Allow yourself to begin to relax. Calm and quiet yourself, letting the day's worries leave your mind; you can cope with them later, but for now, just let them go. Gently close your eyes. If you wish, you may open them any time during the course of this exercise.

Begin by taking a deep, slow breath, pausing for just a moment after you inhale, and then exhaling completely. Allow yourself to continue to breathe slowly and naturally. As you sink into this slow, calm pattern of deep, diaphragmatic breathing, imagine that with every exhalation you can release excess energy or tension. You can just breathe it out and away; the warm air that you exhale carries with it all your tension, discomfort, and excess energy. The warm air carries with it anything that is holding you back from complete calmness. Throughout this exercise, continue to breathe slowly and naturally, breathing away tension from every part of your body. As you do this, you will experience a sense of heaviness and increased warmth.

Now, begin to count backwards from *10* to *1*. Picture the number *10* in your mind, or mentally say the word "ten" to yourself. Continue to just breathe very slowly and calmly, and focus on your entire being. As you become aware of any tension or discomfort, gently shift your attention to it, realizing that you can gradually begin to breathe it away. Just let go of all the tension, and allow yourself to drift deeper into a state of calmness and total relaxation.

Notice that the muscles throughout your body are just letting go of their tension, becoming calm, smooth, and perfectly relaxed. Now, as you picture the number *9* in your mind, or mentally say the word "nine," gently turn your consciousness to your arms and to your hands, letting any tension there be released. If there is any stress, any pain, any excess energy in your muscles, just let go of it, and let the exhalation carry it away. Focus on your upper arms, and as you breathe deeply, let the muscles in your arms go loose and limp. Let the exhalation take the tension with it. Feel the increased heaviness in your arms, spreading down into your elbows, causing all the muscles of your lower arms and of your wrists to become heavy and relaxed. Feel the heaviness gently spreading down into your hands and to your fingers, all the way into each fingertip. As you continue to breathe easily, inhaling deeply and fully, exhaling slowly and completely, just let the tension go with each exhalation. Allow every last bit of tension to leave your arms and hands so that they are absolutely, perfectly relaxed. Pause for just a moment after the exhalation and become even more aware of how heavy and warm they feel.

Now picture the number 8 in your mind, or mentally say the word "eight." Gently turn your awareness to your feet and then your toes. Let go of any tension in your toes and in the balls of your feet; slowly let go of it with your next exhalation. Then be aware of the relaxation spreading to your arches and to your heels, as all the muscles in your feet begin to let go. Now feel the relaxation spread to your ankles and then your lower legs. Take a deep, full breath and imagine any residual tension being carried away as you exhale. Breathe away the tightness in your knees, and let the relaxation freely pass into your upper legs. Continue to breathe slowly and calmly, inhaling fully, and exhaling slowly and completely. Notice any tension in your thighs and just let go of it; allow it to easily leave with the next exhalation. Become aware of the pleasant heaviness in your arms and your legs. Feel them sink into whatever surface you're sitting or lying upon. Just let go, and with each breath, allow yourself to relax further, more and more deeply. As you inhale fully and naturally, drift deeper into a state of calmness and peaceful relaxation.

As you continue to let yourself float, picture the number 7 in your mind, or mentally say the word "seven." Gently carry your awareness to the muscles of your back. Focus on any tension you may be holding there, and with the next exhalation, let them relax. Just let go of any tension or discomfort. Consider the muscles in your shoulders, and focus on any discomfort or rigidity there. Let your shoulders drop and relax, becoming loose and limp. Imagine the muscles on either side of your spine. Let them relax, and let the relaxation spread and follow your spine down into your lower back. Very slowly and calmly, drift deeper into a state of complete peace. Let go of every last bit of tension, and feel yourself sinking deeply into whatever surface you are sitting or lying upon. With each and every exhalation, feel the relaxation spread throughout your body and the feeling of complete peace deepen.

As you picture the number 6 in your mind, or mentally say the word "six," turn your attention to your chest. Allow the muscles around your rib cage to relax, so that your breathing becomes even more relaxed and easy. Feel your calm, regular heartbeat, and the calm, regular pattern of your breaths. Become aware of the sense of calmness and relaxation spreading down into your abdominal region, increasing with every breath. Your abdomen feels completely calm and relaxed. Pause for just a moment, and let the very next breath take away any excess energy or tension still remaining in your abdominal region. With the exhalation, allow all the tension to leave, so that the energy flows freely, slowly, perfectly throughout your body. Let yourself drift deeper into a dreamlike state of calmness and total relaxation.

As you continue to drift deeper, become aware of the number 5 in your mind, or mentally say the word "five." Turn your awareness to your pelvis and the region between your lower back and the top of your legs. Just let those muscles relax completely, slowly and calmly letting go of any tightness, discomfort, or constriction. Allow the relaxation you are feeling to spread into these muscles as well. As you continue to breathe, realize that you continue to sink deeper into whatever you're lying upon. Feel the calmness spread to every part of your body. Take a deep, full breath and realize that you can control your own tension, that you can gently and slowly breathe it away. You need only allow yourself to calm and slow your breath, and then focus on the tension and let go of it with the exhalation.

Now, picture the number 4 in your mind, or mentally say the word "four," and gently consider the muscles in the back of your head and the sides and top of your head. Just as with the rest of your body, allow yourself to slowly and gently breathe away the tension as these muscles go loose and limp. Let your forehead relax, becoming calm and smooth, and let the muscles around your eyes relax even further. Just let go. Peacefully drift into a dreamlike state of calmness and relaxation. Allow this peaceful feeling to spread down into your face, around your mouth, within your jaw and your tongue. Continue to breathe slowly, very slowly and calmly, releasing every last bit of tension or discomfort. Just drift into deeper relaxation, letting go of all your tension, breathing it away with each slow and gentle breath, letting it go with each exhalation.

As the number *3* appears in your consciousness, or you hear the word "three" in your mind, gently turn your awareness to your neck. Let your head just sink into the pillow or chair or whatever surface it's resting on. As you continue to breathe, deeply and fully, exhaling slowly and completely, all muscles of your neck become loose and limp, and your neck becomes calm and comfortable. This pleasant feeling spreads gently downward into your shoulders.

As you picture the number *2*, or mentally say the word "two," your shoulders relax completely and just let go, dropping into an easy, natural position and feeling loose and limp. As your shoulders relax, slowly breathe away any excess energy or tension and allow yourself to drift even deeper, into a deep, perfect state of peaceful relaxation.

Finally, picture the number *1*, or mentally say the word "one," and enlarge your focus to your entire being, feeling total calmness and relaxation. Let yourself float further and further, deeper and deeper into relaxation, realizing that you can control your tension any time you wish, just by letting yourself breathe slowly and calmly, and breathing the tension away. This calmness and relaxation will carry over with you throughout the day, the week, and into the future. Pause for a moment, and just appreciate the calmness. Your energies are flowing freely and easily, and the calmness is spreading to every cell of your body. Just feel the slow, easy calmness easing you deeper into a dreamlike state of complete relaxation. Realize that every time you practice this exercise, you will get better and better at it, and relaxation will come more and more easily. This total relaxation is very good for your mind and your body. It restores every cell of your body completely.

When you wish to complete the exercise and return to your normal alert state, take a deep, full breath and stretch. Allow yourself to feel completely rested and alert. Take another deep, pleasurable breath and stretch. Realize once more before returning to your activities, that you can experience this state of deep relaxation whenever you wish. You do not have to be a slave to your stress response, and whenever you need to, you have the right to relax.

Basic Guided Relaxation: Advanced Technique

This is a sophisticated progressive relaxation that many people prefer. It is best when someone reads this to you or you have taped this exercise for regular use. (This exercise is available at www.dstress.com. It can be found on one side of Tape #202, #203, #204.)

When you are ready to begin, start by getting into a comfortable position in a space where you will not be unnecessarily disturbed for at least twenty minutes. As you sit back or lie back, check to see if your arms and legs are in a relaxed and uncrossed position. Let your shoulders release tension and let your neck begin to relax by letting your head just sink back comfortably into the pillow or chair. Check the muscles of your head and face, especially the muscles around your eyes, even your eyebrows, and the muscles around your mouth, including your jaw and tongue.

Before we begin, let me remind you that I do not want you to try to relax too quickly. In fact, I do not want you to try to relax at all! Because, without any effort, you will be able to drift as deeply into relaxation as you wish by just letting go of stress, thoughts, and physical tensions.

To begin, start by taking three deep, slow diaphragmatic breaths, pausing after you inhale; then exhale fully and completely. You might even imagine that as you exhale you begin to release thoughts, tensions, even discomforts with the warm breath that you breathe out and away. (Pause.)

After these first three slow breaths, continue to breathe slowly, but naturally. As you breathe, please turn your attention to the relaxation that is beginning in your arms and down into your hands. You may feel that one of your arms is just a bit more relaxed than the other. It may be just a subtle difference in which one arm feels slightly heavier, as if the muscles in that arm are more loose or flexible. Or perhaps, one arm feels slightly warmer, as if blood and energy are flowing more freely and easily all the way down that arm into the hand and fingers. (Pause.) Or perhaps, both of your arms are equally relaxed. The only thing that matters is that you continue to breathe slowly and naturally, and perhaps you can begin to feel yourself drifting deeper into a dreamlike state where you feel greater calmness and comfort, and where you begin to develop even greater awareness and control.

As you continue to breathe slowly and gently, become aware of the relaxation that is starting down into your legs and feet. You may feel that one of your legs is a bit more relaxed than the other—slightly heavier, as if the muscles in that leg were more loose or flexible. Or perhaps, you may find that one leg feels slightly warmer, as if the blood and energy is flowing more freely and easily all the way down that leg into your foot and toes. (Pause.) Or perhaps, your legs feel equally relaxed. What matters is that you continue to breathe slowly and gently, and allow yourself to drift deeper into this dreamlike state of calmness, comfort, and control.

Perhaps you can feel the control growing stronger as you feel yourself begin to sink back into whatever you are sitting or lying upon. Let the tensions begin to melt away.

The muscles of your back begin to relax even deeper. You feel the muscles there soften or loosen as you slowly breathe away any unwanted tension. The relaxation spreads to the other muscles of your back, even up into your upper back and your shoulders. Let your shoulders drop down into a more comfortable position. Feel the control grow stronger as your head sinks back, completely supported by the pillow or the chair; now your neck begins to relax even more. Even the muscles of your head and face can relax more.

Perhaps you imagine yourself outdoors on a warm and pleasant day. Perhaps you are standing near a pond of water; the water is calm and clear, and the surface is smooth. You feel the warmth of the sunlight and the warm breezes. If you were to drop a rock or a stone into the water, you could watch as the waves or the ripples spread across the surface of the pond in every direction. In much the same way, you imagine that you send soothing and cleansing waves of relaxation down from the top of your head, in every direction, to soothe, heal, and cleanse every muscle and cell of your body. These waves begin to drift down to relax the muscles at the top and sides of your head. Feel the waves drift down to deeply relax your forehead, letting it go calm and smooth. The waves wash down to relax the muscles around your mouth; even your jaw can loosen a bit better. The waves now slowly spread down to soothe and relax the muscles of your neck and shoulders, and now they drift down through your arms, slowly all the way down into your hands and fingers. (Pause.) Now the waves slowly drift down through your back and your chest. Your breathing is more calm and regular. Your heartbeat is more calm and regular. As you breathe slowly and freely, you may even be able to feel your stomach and abdomen begin to let go and relax more freely. Your lower back and pelvic area now relax further. The waves of relaxation begin to spread down your legs, slowly drifting all the way down and out through the bottom of your feet and into your toes.

Now you watch the pond of water once again become calm and still. The water begins to settle and become clear. Even the surface becomes calm and smooth again. You may wish to turn away from the pond and follow a pathway that takes you to perfect place…a place where you can be yourself and feel calm and comfortable. Once you arrive there, you look around to find the most comfortable place to lay down. As you drift over to that spot, you just sink back into whatever you would be sitting or lying upon. As you settle back, you feel the warmth of the sunlight gently shining down on you. You begin to soak up the warmth as the tensions just melt away. You may even be able to hear the sounds that surround you. Like the sounds of running water, birds, or warm breezes. Perhaps you even smell the fragrance of salt air, flowers, grass, or of the woods that may surround you.

Imagine that you soak up the warmth of the sun. You begin to breathe in the sunlight. As you fill with this warming, healing light and energy, remember that as you relax, there will be an increase of blood flowing more freely and easily to every cell of your body. Each cell is bathed in an increased supply of oxygen and nutrients to help heal and recharge itself. As the cells begin to fill with health and happiness, you can continue to drift in this peaceful state of calmness and relaxation. Though you remain calm and comfortable, you begin to see yourself healing fully and completely. You may even be able to see yourself in perfect health, smiling and celebrating in the sunshine on this warm and beautiful day. You see yourself active, smiling, playing, celebrating, dancing….Remember that every time you practice this exercise you will get better at it. You will be able to relax more deeply and more completely. You will be able to let go more quickly. And the effects of the calmness and comfort will last longer, carrying over throughout your day, enabling you to be more calm and efficient with your available time and energy.

If you are using this exercise at bedtime, or if you wish to drift off to sleep now, then you can begin to do so. Continue to breathe slowly and gently. Focus on the relaxation in your arms and your legs, and drift off into a deep sleep where you are able to rest completely. When you awaken, you will be fully rested and alert.

If, on the other hand, you wish to awaken from this deep relaxation now, then begin to see yourself returning to this room, bringing the feelings of calmness and comfort back with you to a more fully waking state. You may wish to feel the bed or the chair beneath and slowly awaken, letting the feelings of calmness, comfort, health, and joy return with you to a fully waking state. Take a deep breath and slowly release it. You may wish to take another deep breath and stretch, becoming wide awake, feeling refreshed and alert.

Chapter 5
Visualization

Imagine ...

URING THE COURSE OF THIS BOOK, I have often asked you to imagine a hypothetical situation. You have even tried to envision impossible occurrences. In the Three-Part Breathing exercise, you visualized your lungs filling with air; when you did the Autogenics and Deepening Visualization, you pictured your thoughts as bubbles just floating away and later imagined yourself on a slow-moving escalator. Visualization is the use of positive suggestion through visual imagery to change a mental and/or physiological state. When you create a mental picture, your body can actually respond to the visualization as if it were a real experience. This technique can aid in relaxation and healing, or in changing destructive habits; used preventively, it can maintain your good health. It is often used as an adjunct to other relaxation techniques.

With visualization you attempt to affect unconscious processes (the stress response, immunological defenses, conditioned responses) with a conscious suggestion—a mental picture of the desired change. Although it is not understood exactly how a mental image can affect a physiological process, research shows that visualization can change your body's functioning. *Especially dramatic in the treatment of illness, visualization has successfully helped people suffering from terminal diseases.* Carl and Stephanie Simonton are leading researchers on the effect of positive visualization on cancer. Dr. Carl Simonton discovered that tumor visualization (in a relaxed state of mind) in conjunction with traditional therapies, such as radiation, seems to have a much greater success rate than traditional therapies alone. The Simontons have had remarkable success in treating cancer patients with visualization.

Others have used their techniques with great success. A colleague worked with a six-year-old boy whose cancer had metastasized throughout his body. His parents were undergoing a lot of marital problems, and the boy felt responsible. He was always trying to reconcile his parents; when his efforts failed, he felt helpless and guilty. He was undergoing chemotherapy which had painful side effects; naturally he was resistant to the therapy. The chemotherapy was only moderately successful; his life expectancy was estimated to be about one year. The child began visualization therapy in conjunction with his chemotherapy. He imagined his cancer as a monster and his natural defenses as white knights. This was his own imagery; the therapist helped him to develop this imagery into a systematic visualization program. At the same time, the child and his parents began family counselling. This helped him to feel less responsible for his parents' problems and less helpless to control his own life.

The child's disease began to show signs of remission. In his visualization sessions, he reported seeing the monster weakening and the knights growing stronger. He told his visualization therapist that the monster would be conquered by the white knights by his next birthday. His objections to medication grew more vehement and the chemotherapy was discontinued. By the time of his birthday, he informed his therapist that the cancer wasn't there anymore—the monster was dead. His perceptions were accurate: the remission was complete and he showed no signs of cancer.

A sense of helplessness and the fear of losing his parents' love preceded the boy's disease. This is not at all uncommon, as helplessness and the loss of a loved one often seem to generate cancer—cancer often occurs six to eighteen months after the death of a loved one. Any significant emotional trauma that seriously impairs one's will to live can prefigure cancer. Visualization can rally the natural defenses and raise the spirit and positive energies.

Certain factors contribute to the success of visualization therapy. You should:

- Want to get better, or remain healthy. Ambivalent feelings or attachment to secondary gains may interfere.

- Be relaxed. Tensions seem to block the success of the visual suggestion.

- Use a positive visualization. A negative visualization will achieve negative results. Think in terms of becoming completely healthy, not in terms of becoming less sick.

- Visualize immediate results. The visualization must be phrased in the present tense.

First mentally picture your ailment. In the case of the little boy, his picture was not an accurate representation of the disease, but since the image of the white knights was real for him, it was very effective. *If you have a very powerful sense of the configuration of your illness, you should use that in your visualization.* You may wish to consult a medical text or your doctor. Some therapists feel that the more medically accurate your visualization, the more successful you will be. But if it is easier for you to imagine your disease as a weed eventually removed by a beneficent gardener than as a diseased cell being attacked by antibodies, then trust the stronger image. Don't use visualization as the only method of healing. If something is seriously wrong, do not ignore it, or put off getting professional advice. Use visualization as an adjunct.

Visualization can be used to maintain health. See yourself in perfect health, exactly as you wish to be. See yourself doing something active, smiling and celebrating feelings of perfect health. You may know people who get a cold every four months; three and one-half months go by, and they begin to wonder when the next cold will strike. They are programmed for the next cold. By programming continual positive health, you can reprogram yourself from the sickness model and prevent illness.

Just as visualization is effective in the control of disease, it can be useful in removing tension and stress from your daily life. *The same factors which influence the success of healing apply to relaxation visualization therapy.* You might want to imagine the tension in your body and the release of that tension, just as you would picture your disease and its cure. By visualizing relaxation, you are programming future relaxation and giving up the image of yourself as a tense person.

Habits and fears can be changed or reversed if you visualize the desired behavior. If you want to lose weight, picture yourself enjoying healthful, nonfattening foods. See yourself as a thin, attractive person wearing a particular garment in a smaller size than you now wear. If you have had negative sexual experiences, picture yourself having a joyous, mutually satisfying sexual relationship. If you are attempting to learn a new skill, picture yourself proficient.

VISUALIZATION EXERCISES

Tape the following exercises, or have someone read them to you. This will facilitate your involvement and make your visualization easier. You can change the visualization to fit your needs. Mentally phrase your objective in a positive way, leading to the desired response. If you wish to control your eating habits, do not think, "I will not eat junk food." Instead think, "I feel full and satisfied eating natural, healthful foods." Be sure you state the suggestion in the present tense. Remember, you are reprogramming your unconscious mind to achieve what you would like; you need to demand action now. Let the unconscious find a way to make it happen. People with inflammations should use cool colors (blue and green) instead of warm colors (yellow, gold, and red) in the following exercises.

Visualization for Relaxation

This exercise is available at www.dstress.com. Look for Tape #104.

Use the sitting or lying autogenic position. Gently close your eyes. Take one deep, slow breath. After you inhale, hold for a moment, and then exhale fully and completely. Allow yourself to continue to breathe slowly and naturally. Imagine that with each and every breath, you can breathe away tension or anxiety and allow yourself to relax more and more. As you continue to breathe slowly and naturally, imagine that any thoughts or memories that are running through your consciousness appear as bubbles, about to float up and out of your consciousness. Be aware of these thoughts, but do not hold onto any of them. Just watch them as they float by.

Imagine that you are watching a glass of carbonated water and all the bubbles are rising to the surface. See these bubbles float up to the surface, and as they burst, let go of any thoughts still in your consciousness. Watch the glass of carbonated water, and see the bubbles gradually decrease in frequency, slowly, slowly, until the water is clear and calm. Watch as your thoughts flow through your consciousness and gradually slow, as your mind becomes calm and clear, as it peacefully rests in quiet serenity. Let yourself drift even deeper into calm relaxation. Remember to breathe slowly and naturally.

As your mind calms and clears completely, thoughts or distractions leave you and you can focus on the various parts of your body. Allow your muscles to relax fully and completely, and as you become more and more deeply relaxed, your muscles just let go. Your muscles become heavy, flexible, and calm. With each and every exhalation, you breathe away more and more tension from your muscles.

Picture yourself at the top of a very slow-moving escalator. As you step onto the long escalator, begin to slowly ride down.

Hold on to the side, and slowly drift down, down, down. Deeper and deeper you drift into a calm and relaxed state of mind and body. As you ride the escalator down, count backwards from *5* to *1*. Imagine the number *5* in your mind, and say the number to yourself. Breathe slowly and calmly, and allow the tensions to flow out and away from you. Let yourself drift deeper into relaxation. Focus on relaxing your arms and your hands, letting the muscles go completely loose and limp. Relax your upper arms, and then your elbows, your lower arms, your wrists, your hands, down to the tips of your fingers. Feel the heaviness gradually increase in your arms and in your hands, as your muscles just let go and relax. Breathe calmly and naturally, exhaling fully and completely, while you slowly ride down the escalator. Feel the increased blood flow and warmth spreading down your arms and into your hands.

Visualize the number *4* in your mind, and say it to yourself. Gently turn your awareness to your legs and your feet, allowing your legs to relax fully and completely. Allow all the muscles to just let go, and the tension to melt away from your body. Feel your ankles and your feet relax, and allow this relaxation to spread to your knees and to your thighs. Feel your legs sinking into whatever you are sitting or lying upon, as the muscles let go and relax even further.

Continue to breathe slowly and naturally, as you see the number *3* in your mind. Say the number "three" to yourself, and realize that you are more relaxed now than you were at number *4*. Allow your abdomen to relax, feeling all the muscles just let go. Your abdomen is relaxed, as you gently loosen all the muscles in your chest, and just breathe away any excess muscle tension. The muscles in your back relax, going loose and limp, as you just sink back, deeper and deeper into relaxation.

You are slowly nearing the bottom of the escalator. Visualize the number *2* in your mind and say it to yourself. Continue to let go of any remaining tension, and realize that you are more relaxed than you were at number 3. Relax the muscles of your shoulders and your neck, while breathing slowly and naturally. Exhale fully and completely, and feel the tension leave your body with each and every exhalation. Let the relaxation spread to your head and your face, letting your forehead become calm and smooth. The muscles in the back and the sides of your head and neck become loose, flexible, and free of tension. As you breathe slowly and calmly, the muscles around your eyes relax, and you simply let go of the tension in your jaw, your mouth, and your tongue. Let yourself drift deeper into a dreamlike state of calm relaxation. Just let go of as much tension as you wish to, by just breathing it away with each and every exhalation.

Become aware of the number 1, and say it to yourself while visualizing it in your mind. As you continue to breathe slowly and calmly, turn your awareness to your neck and your shoulders, letting your head sink into the pillow or chair. Just let go completely, and let your shoulders drop. Allow your entire body to relax, loose and limp.

As you continue to ride down the escalator, deeper and deeper into relaxation, let go and allow yourself to drift even further into calmness. Picture yourself getting to the bottom of the escalator, and as you step off you are surrounded by your favorite outdoor scene. You are in your favorite outdoor place on a calm and peaceful day. You are there all by yourself, noticing the beauty of the blue sky, the green grass, and the golden sunlight brightening to white light. Pick a very comfortable place, and go and lie down. Picture yourself just letting go, sinking into the ground, and letting the tension melt away, being replaced by calmness and relaxation. Continue to breathe slowly and naturally, and with each inhalation breathe in the warmth of the sunlight. Feel the calmness and serenity of this peaceful, beautiful scene.

Feel the warmth of the sunlight on your arms and hands and the warm breezes blowing on your legs and feet, warming you deep within. This gentle, golden sunlight is peaceful and healing. As you inhale, feel the golden sunlight fill you completely with brilliant golden-white light, warming your body. Your heartbeat carries this energy freely and easily to every cell of your body. Imagine every cell of your body bathed in golden-white light, nourished with oxygen and nutrients. As you continue to breathe in the golden light slowly and peacefully, every cell is able to absorb the healing light and energy, the oxygen, and the nutrients. Every cell becomes strong and vibrantly alive. You can see each cell grow healthy and strong. See each cell as a garden plant, slightly parched, growing robust and strong, healthy and revived, as you water it with golden light.

Health and energy, joy and happiness, well up within you. You feel full of health and happiness, and deeply at peace with yourself and the universe. Any time you wish to relieve yourself of tension and anxiety, and wish to replace these feelings with happiness, calmness, and health, all you need to do is breathe slowly and calmly, allowing yourself to relax. Any time that you wish, you can enjoy this beautiful, healing scene once again, restoring yourself with calmness and relaxation. You have control over the tension. You choose to breathe it away. You may let go of it at any time you wish.

Deep within you, there will remain a core of calmness and light, a being of light that dwells within your heart. It is your soul, your spirit. This being of love and light knows many parts of you. It sees and accepts your strengths and your weaknesses and realizes that they are tools that you can use to learn all of the lessons in life. This golden-white light and being grows brighter every time you practice your relaxation. It allows you to accept yourself even more, because you take the time to do really positive things for yourself, through calmness and relaxation, happiness and health, will carry over with you throughout your day, and throughout your week. Every time you practice this exercise, you will get better and better at it and be able to relax more deeply and more completely, more easily and more quickly. Remember that you have the choice to let go of tension by breathing it away and the freedom to feel calmness and relaxation.

Now gradually allow yourself to become more alert, bringing yourself back to the room you are in. Gently make yourself more and more alert, bringing with you into your completely alert state the feelings of calmness, relaxation, happiness, health, and joy. See yourself coming back to the room, and feel the chair or bed beneath you. Say to yourself: **"I am refreshed and alert. I am refreshed and alert. I am refreshed and alert."** Count to yourself from *1* to *5*. At *1,* feel yourself coming back to the room. At *2,* you are becoming more alive and conscious, feeling your calm heartbeat. At *3,* you are more alert. At *4,* you begin to open your eyes. At *5,* you are fully and completely alert. Take a deep, full breath and stretch. Let the feelings of calmness and relaxation carry over with you to your fully alert state. If you wish, take another deep breath and stretch, letting yourself become fully and completely alert. Remember that you have the choice to let go of tension by slowing and calming your breath.

Did you have any difficulty visualizing the carbonated water?

Did you find the image of yourself on the escalator pleasing?

Did you have to search for an outdoor place, or did one immediately come to mind?

When you ordinarily relax, do certain visual images usually come to mind?

Visualization is more difficult for some people than others. If you had a great deal of difficulty visualizing the carbonated water, you might try doing a breathing exercise first. This will put you in a more relaxed state and may make visualization a bit easier. Some people have difficulty controlling the imagery; for others distracting images may constantly crop up in their minds. If this happens, you might want to give yourself the freedom to explore those images. Perhaps you found that the escalator ride elicited a sinking or falling feeling. If this is the case, eliminated some of the escalator phrases from the visualization. A fantasy of the perfect garden may replace the recollection of a real locale; some people think of a childhood scene that has become idealized in their memories. Sometimes when you are not doing this kind of exercise but are using some other mode of relaxation, you will find that particular images may seem to be associated with the relaxed state. You may wish to incorporate these images into a visualization, or use them to become more aware of your inner life.

Relaxation and Self-Healing Visualization

One of the potentially best uses for visualization is to promote healing or for health maintenance. After initial relaxation is achieved, positive images and sensations can be used to reprogram the unconscious mind to optimum health. Remember that the autonomic functions, which are generated by the unconscious part of the mind, are responsible for maintaining proper metabolic equilibrium and for the not yet fully understood process of healing. The most important part of this exercise is to see yourself in perfect health, not in the future, but right now in the present.

Make yourself comfortable, and assume one of the autogenic positions. Take a deep, slow breath, and gently close your eyes. Exhale fully and completely. Inhale again, and see the number *1* in your mind. Hold your breath for a moment, and then exhale, visualizing the number *2*. Be sure to exhale fully and completely, breathing away tension with the warm air. Inhale, visualizing number *3*, hold for a moment, and then exhale visualizing number *4*. Repeat the exercise until you have established your own natural, slow, calm rhythm. With each exhalation, let go of as much tension as you can, while passively allowing yourself to scan your body for excess tension. Without becoming alarmed, be aware of any place you are holding tension.

Imagine that with each exhalation your tension is being carried out with the warm air. Let your everyday thoughts and annoyances drift through you and out of your consciousness, as if they were credits at the end of a movie. Watch them gradually pass by and leave the screen blank. See yourself on the screen, lying in a meadow on a calm, beautiful, warm day. Gradually shift your perspective, slowly, slowly, so that you are looking down on your body. Watch your body become smooth and quiet, releasing any held tension and conforming to the contours of the meadow. You are completely alone, protected from any intrusion or distraction. Feel the warm sunlight shining gently upon you and spreading to your arms and hands, your legs and feet, your abdomen and your back. Sink deeper into the warm, soft meadow.

Feel the warm breezes blow against you, warming you to the very core of your being. See the beautiful, natural colors, the green of the grass, the soft, rich brown of the earth, and the deep, beautiful blue of the sky. Listen to the wind blowing and rustling the leaves and branches of the trees, and hear the birds' faint melody against the sweet running waters of the stream. See yourself relaxing more and more, drifting deeper into relaxation. Drift deeper into a beautifully relaxed state, becoming calmer and more peaceful. Feel yourself melting into the warm, receptive earth, becoming totally relaxed and at peace.

Become aware of your heart beating, and focus on its regular, even rhythm, pumping blood throughout the body, sending it anywhere that still feels tense or cool. See the lungs expanding with each breath and directing oxygen to each and every cell. Scan your body lightly, looking for any place where you may still hold tension, and gently breathe away the tension. See and feel the blood flowing easily and freely throughout your body, unrestricted to every cell. As the blood flows throughout your body, it carries rejuvenating oxygen and nutrients to each and every cell. The cells become vibrantly alive and healthy with each full and complete breath. Picture increased blood flow to your hands and your feet.

Send increased blood flow to any organ in your body that needs extra support or healing, gradually and slowly increasing the blood flow. See that organ becoming fully responsive and healthy, as the blood carries away the toxins. The organ begins to function perfectly, exactly as it is supposed to, as you help it return to its normal state with your own deep breathing. Visualize yourself in perfect health, smiling and celebrating, doing something active, dancing or walking, or sunning in the beautiful golden sunlight. See and feel yourself in perfect health, completely relaxed and free of any tension or anxiety.

Call upon this feeling of relaxation and health even throughout your day, and feel calm and relaxed once again. Every time you practice this exercise, you will get better and better at it. It will become easier and easier for you to relax, and the deep relaxation will happen more quickly each time. You will relax more deeply each time you practice. Allow this feeling of calmness and relaxation to be with you throughout your day. If you have any illness, each and every breath you take is gently healing you.

Take a deep, full breath, and exhale fully and completely. Gradually become aware of the surface you are sitting or lying upon, while maintaining a feeling of calmness and perfect health. Allow yourself to become fully alert, stretching and getting ready to return to your normal activities.

Was it difficult to watch yourself on a movie screen while feeling bodily sensations?

Did you feel in two places at one time?

If you have an illness, do you feel anxiety when you start to think about that part of your body?

In your dreams you may often observe your behavior from a distance, while also experiencing the feelings and actions associated with the behavior you observe. If you had difficulty with this part of the visualization, try to experience the sensation of being in two places at one time without subjecting it to rational thought. If you have an illness, it is natural for you to feel upset when you focus on that part of your body; but try to maintain the same easy, passive attention that you accepted in the rest of the exercise. After a while you will be able to experience a calm state of mind even when you turn your focus to your illness.

Visualization for the Bath

When you are so anxious that you are tempted to take a pill or have a drink, take a bath instead. In a warm bath, it is difficult to worry or to sustain an anxiety attack. The body feels lighter, muscles are relaxed by the heat and movement of the water, and circulation is increased. Being in warm water for a half hour will lower the blood pressure and slow down your breathing. Though the effects will be the opposite for the first two minutes and you may feel stimulated, the calming properties of warm water will soon soothe you.

This visualization can be used in a bathtub, hot tub, heated swimming pool, or any warm body of water. The temperature should not be over 103 degrees and you should not stay in the water for longer than thirty minutes. If you are alone, ask someone to call you on the phone after one-half hour or set a music alarm to rouse you. Turn out the lights and light a candle or use a small night-light.

Get into a comfortable position, either reclining or sitting. Be sure that your back is supported and your breathing unconstricted. Take a full, deep breath and exhale fully and completely. Slowly close your eyes and feel your heart beating strongly, and then, begin to slow down. Let your thoughts just drift through your consciousness, as you allow them to leave with the warm air. Imagine that with each and every breath, you can breathe away tension or anxiety, as you allow yourself to relax more and more. All the day's burdens, worries, and expectations are leaving your consciousness and evaporating with the hot, moist steam. Feel your arms floating on the water and the warm, soothing water gently lifting and caressing your body. As you continue to breathe slowly and naturally, let go of any thoughts still remaining in your mind. Watch as your thoughts flow through you and out of you, and see them disappear into the air, leaving your mind clear and calm.

Gently turn your attention to your body, and scan your body for any tension that you might still be holding. Allow it to leave with the next exhalation, as the warm water evaporates into steam. As you continue to breathe slowly and calmly, turn your awareness to your feet and to your legs. The water tenderly massages your legs and your feet, as the tension flows through you and out of you. With your next breath, breathe away any tightness still remaining in your feet. Move your attention to your abdomen and your chest, allowing the muscles to just let go and the tension to melt away from your body. Feel your abdomen and your chest relax, as you gently loosen all the muscles and just breathe away any remaining tension. Focus on relaxing your arms and your hands, letting the muscles go completely loose and limp. Relax your fingers and your hands, and let the feeling of deep relaxation spread up into your arms. Breathe away any tension still remaining in your hands and arms, and watch it evaporate with the warm steam.

Now, relax the muscles of your shoulders and your neck, and feel the heaviness gradually increase throughout your musculature, as all your muscles just let go. The muscles in your back go loose and limp, as the water gently supports your whole body. Allow the relaxation to spread to your head and your face and the muscles around your eyes, in your jaw, in your tongue, and in your forehead. Let yourself drift deeper into a dreamlike state of calm relaxation. Just let go of as much tension as you wish to, by just breathing it away with each and every exhalation.

Imagine that the blue water becomes the sky, and the soft clouds gently support you as you drift up above the trees. You no longer feel the weight of your head upon your shoulders, and gravity no longer ties you to the earth. The warm, soft, billowy, pink clouds support you as the sun's gentle heat penetrates through any remaining tension. As you peacefully float through the warm air, the golden sun fills your body with warming heat and light. This golden light penetrates through any tension still remaining in your body. As you free-float in space, your body is becoming lighter and lighter with each full and complete exhalation.

When you have floated as high as you wish, you become still, and the clouds gently cradle you in the warmth of the sun's golden rays. The golden sun finds any tension still remaining in your body and dissolves it in the warm, glowing light. Whenever you are ready, you may return. Feel the warm, pink clouds transform into water, and become aware of the water gently cradling you. Take a few, deep breaths, becoming more and more aware of your surroundings. When you are ready to become fully alert, take a full, deep breath and gently open your eyes on the exhalation. Take a few more deep breaths, and slowly get out of the water, gently drying yourself and feeling the relaxation throughout your body.

Did you find that being in water facilitated the visualization?

Were you able to imagine yourself floating upward?

Was it easy for you to imagine the water becoming sky?

Were you tired after the visualization?

Often people associate the experience of floating in water with the image of floating in the sky. Some people who ordinarily find it difficult to visualize have success when they are immersed in water, since the water's effect on the physiological system is inherently relaxing. Being in water tends to free the imagination. You might want to experiment with any of the other visualizations while in water. Breathing and deepening techniques may also be very effective practiced in water. After you get out of a hot bath, you may feel tired and should spend a few moments relaxing before undertaking any strenuous activity.

Magic Carpet Ride

This exercise enables you to use the creative centers of the mind to create the sensation and scene of flying off for a few moments of vacation from daily pressures and activities. As you use this technique, learn to develop an appreciation for detail and let your mind gently absorb all the beautiful, natural scenes that you may explore. You may treat this as a game, but it can help you to curb the unnecessary buildup of stress.

Get into a comfortable position, and close your eyes. Begin by taking a deep, full breath and exhaling fully and completely, allowing the last bit of air to leave your lungs. Do the breathing exercise with which you are most comfortable, until you are in a state of deep relaxation. Feel the relaxation spreading throughout your body. With each and every breath, feel any excess tension leaving your body with the warm air. Gently scan your body and locate any spot where you may still hold tension, and then breathe it away with an exhalation.

Picture yourself outdoors on a calm, beautiful spring day. The sun shines down and warms your arms and hands, your feet and your legs, your abdomen, your back, and your face. You become as calm and as comfortable as you would like to be.

Imagine that you are lying on a magic carpet, free to travel anywhere without effort. You are in complete control, safe and peaceful. No one is there to distract you or make any demands on you. Drift more deeply into relaxation, just enjoying the sensation of total calm and serenity. Flow freely with the drifting sensation as if you were gently floating on a raft on a warm and beautiful summer day, on a calm, warm, shallow lake. Feel yourself floating gently, deeper and deeper into relaxation. As you sense the feeling of floating, remain calm and sense the magic carpet beginning to float up off the ground. You feel very safe and at ease with your surroundings. The magic carpet rises a few inches above the ground, allowing you to enjoy the floating sensation even more. It is so peaceful that you relax even more and drift deeper into deep relaxation.

You can float as high as you wish to go and control both the speed and altitude of the magic carpet. You can look down and around and see all that surrounds you, as you remain totally calm and relaxed. You are free to fly anywhere you can imagine. If you wish, experiment with flying faster and then slower, higher and then lower. Perhaps you would like to visit some exotic locale or just get a different perspective on your daily environment. Feel the warm air currents blowing gently against your body and the warm sun shining down upon your magic carpet. Travel this way for a few minutes, noticing any detail that attracts you. Leave all your worries and thoughts behind you, and enjoy this brief vacation from your daily life. When you are ready, slowly return to the point of departure. Touch down gently, sinking into relaxation.

Calm and relax yourself, savoring any special moment you may have experienced in your ride. Remember as much of your trip as you wish to and bring this feeling of calm relaxation to mind whenever you feel tension or anxiety. Gradually bring yourself to a state of alertness; take a deep, full breath and stretch. Take another breath and become fully alert.

Do you associate the floating sensation of the magic carpet ride with relaxation?

Do you ever have dreams or fantasies about flying or swimming in air?

Some people find it natural to associate deep relaxation with the sensation of floating or flying. Others feel more comfortable with the sensation of sinking or descent. If you found the ride anxiety-provoking, try increasing the size of your rug or imagine yourself floating on a soft, billowy cloud. If you often dream or fantasize about flying, this visualization may be easy for you to imagine; if you are always earthbound, consider what the freedom of flight might represent for you. You can use this exercise for a few moments during a break in your workday and actually feel as if you had taken a short vacation.

Wiseperson Guide Visualization

Some people have important questions and do not seem to have anyone to help them get answers. This exercise enables you to consult with your own innermost self (intuition, if you want to see it that way). You may wish to just enjoy this exercise to see what questions come up. People sometimes become conscious of problems they had not realized were causing mental or emotional distress. You may use this for personal growth, rather than for problem solving. Whatever you choose to explore, let this be a pleasant way to relax and learn to make better connections with the subtle, but powerful parts of your unconscious mind.

Get into a comfortable position and begin to relax. Inhale deeply, filling your lungs completely with air. Exhale, forcing every last bit of air out of your lungs. Picture your lungs as being divided into three parts. Take another deep breath and visualize the lowest part of your lungs filling with air. Then, imagine the middle part of your lungs filling, and finally the upper part. Your lungs are completely expanded, your shoulders back, your abdomen slightly pushed forward. Begin the exhalation. Visualize the air leaving your upper lungs as your shoulders drop slightly. Feel your rib cage contract as the air leaves the middle portion of your lungs. Pull in your abdomen to force out the last bit of air from the bottom of your lungs. Repeat the lung visualization twice. Continue to breathe calmly, at your own natural pace.

As you relax more deeply, picture yourself outdoors on a calm, gentle day. You are all alone, feeling very relaxed and at peace with yourself and the universe. Feel the warmth from the sun, healing your hands and your feet, penetrating to the very core of your being. You are relaxing more and more and slipping into deep relaxation.

You are in a clearing in a wooded area. Begin to become aware of your environment. Notice the colors, the smells, and the sounds. You are totally safe and comfortable in this special place. You are safe from outside distractions or interruptions. You belong here and can come back to this place any time you need to feel deeply relaxed.

A path appears leading up and away from your resting space. Slowly and gently get up and follow this path upward, until you come to a very sheltered, protected, peaceful clearing. A warm, bright fire burns in the center of the clearing. Gently become aware of your wiseperson sitting on the other side of the fire. The wiseperson sits calmly and peacefully, receptively awaiting your arrival. You are calm and relaxed as you approach to place another log on the fire.

Greet your wiseperson guide warmly, and sit together for a few moments. Look at your guide's face and gently become aware of the wiseperson's all-knowing presence. Breathe slowly and naturally and with each breath become more conscious of the safeness of your surroundings. When you feel totally relaxed, ask the wiseperson the question that you have brought with you. Listen carefully to the answer, letting it become clear and meaningful.

Rest for a few moments and absorb the wisdom that has come to you. Thank your guide, who embraces you gently and lovingly and gives you a special gift in remembrance of this occasion. Remember that any time you wish you may return to meet with your guide. You walk back down the path to your original resting place, feeling calm and satisfied. You are relaxed and happy, and your heart is full of joy and love.

Sit down in your resting place and focus again on your natural, slow breathing. Take a deep, full breath, exhale, and then stretch. Take another breath and begin to bring yourself back to a fully alert state. Carry with you the memory of this experience and the feelings of calmness and relaxation.

Did your wiseperson guide look as you expected?

Did your wiseperson guide undergo any transformation as you sat together?

Did a question come to mind immediately?

Did you understand the answer?

When I first did this exercise, I expected my guide to be a wise, old, bearded fatherly figure. To my surprise, though the guide was a man, he was middle-aged, clean shaven, balding, and appeared to be wearing a pharmacist's smock. Because my expectations had been so different, it took me a moment or two to accept this guide. Don't be stunned by, or try to repress, the nature of your wiseperson guide. This visualization is not to reinforce what you already know, but to provide insight into your life. For some people, the wiseperson guide appears in one form and then undergoes a transformation right before their eyes. A man may become a woman, a woman may become a man, or the guide may become a person who has been important in your life. If a question did not come readily to mind, don't worry. Sometimes there is one crucial question which you must ask and other times the question is of less importance. The answer you received may be ambiguous, or it may not have directly addressed the question you posed. Each time you do this visualization, the appearance of the wiseperson may become more definite and the answer more coherent.

DEEPENING RELAXATION

These abbreviated visualizations can be used to induce relaxation or to deepen relaxation when combined with another technique. Used alone, they will be most effective once you have become adept at the longer exercises and your body is accustomed to relaxing on cue.

10-to-1, 5-to-1 Count

The most basic and probably the most widely used deepening technique is counting backwards slowly from *10* to *1*. As you count, visualize each number, release more tension, and relax more deeply with each exhalation. You may combine counting with a short progressive relaxation, viewing and feeling the major muscle groups with each descending number, relaxing them more and more. Start at your neck and shoulders and work down to your toes; then go back to your face. You may also abbreviate this technique by counting backwards from 5 to 1. Remember to focus on the number, seeing it in your mind and relaxing more deeply with each descending number.

50-to-1 Count

Another counting technique that works well for most people is counting backwards from 50 to 1. As you count each number, insert the sequence 1, 2, 3, between each number. For example: 50, 1, 2, 3, 49, 1, 2, 3, 48, 1, 2, 3, and so on. If you actually visualize each number and let yourself be totally occupied with the exercise while you count backwards, your mind will take a nice vacation from extraneous thoughts or problems. Remember to let all the tension melt out of your body with each and every exhalation. **This breathing technique is great for getting to sleep!**

Escalator Ride

This exercise is often combined with autogenics or a longer visualization, but you can use it alone or combine it with any other relaxation technique. Imagine yourself riding down an escalator which is slowly moving downward, deeper and deeper into relaxation. See and feel yourself slipping more deeply into relaxation as you ride gently downward. Combining this visualization with counting backwards is particularly effective. Hold onto the moving escalator rail so that you feel secure. You may also imagine that you are riding down in an elevator, watching the floors descend and relaxing more deeply as you pass each floor. Walking down stairs can be used in a similar manner.

Melting Relaxation

Imagine yourself lying in a calm and comfortable place. Watch as the various parts of your body relax more and more. Feel them relax more than they ever have before, melting into whatever you are lying upon. Let your body melt completely into relaxation.

Watching the Clock

Imagine a clock with one hand moving backwards. As it moves counterclockwise, relax more and more as it passes each number. When it gets to *11,* you are more relaxed than you were at *12.* When it reaches *10,* you are more relaxed than you were at *11.* When the hand eventually reaches *12* again, you are deeply relaxed and at peace with yourself. The clock hand should move very, very slowly. An alternative to watching a clock is to watch a pressure valve. Imagine that as the valve moves counterclockwise, the pressure is released and with it, your own tension.

Bubble Visualization

If you are having trouble with mental distractions, imagine that all your thoughts or problems are bubbles, floating up to the surface of a glass of carbonated water. As the bubbles reach the surface they burst and all your worries are released into the air. See and feel the word "calm," as you watch the bubbles slowly rise to the surface. Watch the bubbles until the water is completely clear and your mind is no longer distracted. This exercise can be inserted in any other technique if you are having trouble maintaining passive concentration.

Chapter 6
Meditation

East Meets West

WHILE MEDITATING ONCE, I saw myself as a drop of water in a stream. The stream was flowing from the mountains to the sea. I experienced the stream as a symbol of life; all the other drops of water were people and objects moving through life. I felt that I was everywhere in the stream at once. I saw the fast currents, the slow currents, and the eddies of the stream, as stream grew into river and swirled toward the ocean. I was one with all the drops of water in the stream; I was one with all the people and things in the world. I felt great joy. All of this happened in an instant, and yet I can recall this powerful experience, see it again, and describe it at any time. The impact of the symbols etched the vision indelibly into my mind.

Most of the relaxation techniques covered in this book originated in Europe or North America and grew out of a Western scientific and philosophical tradition. Meditation, which is thousands of years old, developed in Eastern cultures which predate Western civilization. I emphasize Western approaches because I find that readers can more easily relate to their philosophical bases. *For our purposes, meditation will be viewed as a relaxation technique outside of the various religious and ideological contexts in which it developed.* For many, meditation is only one part of a life philosophy.

Proponents of the diverse schools of meditation believe that different states of mind can be achieved with different meditative practices. Some forms of meditation seek to free "energy flows" throughout the body. These energy flows have not been recognized by Western medicine or scientific measurement. Inconclusive evidence does not mean that energy flows do not exist; it only means that a way to measure or explain them in Western scientific terms has not yet been found. In the same way, Western science may not be able to quantify subtle changes in state of mind that occur with different meditation practices.

The beneficial effects of meditation which can be measured are those associated with deep relaxation. These effects resemble the benefits of sound sleep, but in meditative states the mind remains awake and alert. (Most teachers of meditation warn against falling asleep during practice.) Meditation has been shown to relieve stress-related disease. Meditators show a substantial reduction in the frequency of such stress-related complaints as headache, gastritis, and insomnia. In blood pressure studies, it has been found that meditation significantly reduces blood pressure during the practice and enables the subjects to maintain lower blood pressures.

Skilled meditators develop a heightened awareness of their own autonomic functions and a heightened capacity for self-regulation. Elmer and Alyce Green studied yogis who were famed for their ability to control their own bodies and withstand extreme stress—such as pain—without manifesting a stress response. The results of the study are amazing. These holy men could slow their own heart rates to three or four beats a minute and warm one hand to a temperature 10 degrees higher than the other hand. This sort of control is only achieved after years of practice. In an interesting cross-cultural exchange, the yogis took biofeedback equipment back with them to India. In their work with the Greens, they realized that such equipment could reduce the learning times of their own students. The Western measurement devices provided instantaneous feedback of success rate in mastering the ancient Eastern techniques.

In *The Relaxation Response,* Herbert Benson reports on his exploration of the physiological effects of meditation. Benson began his research by investigating Transcendental Meditation (TM). TM was brought to the United States in the 1960s by Maharishi Mahesh Yogi, as a readily accessible meditation for uninitiated Westerners. In TM, an instructor selects a mantra, a particular Sanskrit word or sound, for each student. This sound is then repeated mentally while sitting still in a quiet place. The initiate is instructed to concentrate completely on the mantra, letting distractions simply pass over and through the consciousness. Subjects report that after repeated practice "the mantra seems to disappear from mind," they "fall into a space of rich darkness," and "the mind becomes blissfully quiet." They often report a loss of the sense of time passing while remaining fully awake.

In studying TM meditators, Benson found that the subjects were in a state of deep relaxation while repeating the mantra. Their oxygen consumption was markedly lowered; heart rates were slowed; galvanic skin resistance was raised; and blood pressure was lowered. *Benson went on to discover that these positive effects were not exclusive to TM and that individually selected mantras were unnecessary.* He devised his own modified mantra-repeating meditation and achieved similar physiological readings. Certain crucial factors, isolated by Benson, induce relaxation during meditation. They are:

- A quiet environment. At least when beginning to practice, the fewer external distractions the better. More advanced meditators may be able to shut out distractions despite the environment.

- An object to focus attention on. This can be a word, sound, physical object, an area on the floor or a wall, or a physiological function which can be monitored, such as breathing. It is important to concentrate on one thing only and cut down on the usual mental noise.

- A passive attitude. A willingness to let go of all distractions and troubling thoughts and an avoidance of ordinary linear thinking are most important. Refrain from considering the meditation as a performance.

These factors are usually stressed by most schools of meditation for those just beginning practice. They can be taken as guidelines for the meditations included later in this chapter.

All meditations direct attention and alter states of awareness. In our usual thinking, we progress quickly from thought to thought— the mind races and attention is scattered. We usually think in words and then become inundated by our own continuous string of verbalizations. We seldom attend to only one thing at a time or concentrate wholly on the action we're performing while performing it. *In meditation, attention is focused and we become wholly engaged in a single behavior.* Attention is cleansed of preconceptions, abstract beliefs, and distracting input so that phenomena are perceived more directly. Most practiced meditators speak of getting in touch with a self outside of thought, outside of social definition and cultural role. In my drop-of-water vision, I experienced a sense of being at-one-with-the-all and of losing my self. This experience is common in meditation. Although meditations work by narrowing the focus of attention, the results are to enlarge the sense of being and eliminate the subjective distinction between self and environment.

The meditations provided here, with the exception of the Candle Meditation, are all twenty minutes long. They can be used once or twice a day, preferably before breakfast and before dinner. Always meditate on an empty stomach and do not meditate when you are likely to fall asleep. Consistency and discipline are important. Allow three to eight weeks to see results. Begin with the basic Yogic Mantra-Repeating meditation, Zen Breath-Counting, or Shavasana. You can use the Candle Meditation concurrently to help develop your powers of concentration.

Your first experience with meditation may not be entirely positive. A friend of mine, an attorney, went to a meditation class because he was suffering from recurrent bouts of anxiety. He had recently joined his uncle's law firm and was under a lot of pressure from the senior partners. Many of the clients had known him since childhood and didn't accept him in his new more authoritative role.

The class was held in the local YMCA gymnasium. His classmates were already sitting in the middle of the room as he walked in and across the floor and then realized that everyone else was barefooted, their shoes in a neat line by the door. His every step echoed as he walked back to the door to take off his shoes and pick up a mat to sit on. The teacher explained the breath-counting meditation and then advised the class to "just sit" and count their breaths.

It had been a long time since my friend had just sat still anywhere. He began to feel nervous and a little rebellious. Most of his days were spent pacing, either before his uncle's desk or in his own office, talking into a dictaphone. What good could just sitting still do him? Then the real distractions began. With each breath, the tip of his nose itched. He felt the urge to sneeze but denied it since the room was so quiet. No one else so much as squirmed. Then his back started to itch as well, and the sensation jumped all over his body. The backs of his knees throbbed. The mental distractions were as prevalent as the physical ones. He thought: "*1* (inhale) Did I leave my keys in the car? Someone is probably driving it away right now. *2* (exhale) Why did my uncle make that snide remark this afternoon? If he finds out I'm here, he'll think I can't take the pressure. *3* (inhale) What do I get for dinner if I make it through this ordeal?" At that thought his stomach growled. He repeatedly lost count of his breaths and one thought led to another, and some to whole narratives. But eventually, for only a moment, the rhythm of his own breathing carried him.

ZEN MEDITATION

The meditation which my friend experienced is the most basic form of Zen meditation. In the more advanced forms of Zen, you do not narrow your focus of attention, but open your awareness to all the phenomena around you. You attempt to perceive everything with a clean, unappraising mind. This requires a high degree of discipline and self-regulation. Zen Breath-Counting develops discipline and self-awareness. It is performed while sitting still in one place, as sitting still in one place is an integral part of confronting yourself and shutting down noise. But Zen does not always require that you sit in one place; some Zen meditations are done while walking or even running. I have slipped into a meditative state of consciousness during a long, slow run, when my rhythm was regular and effortless and my mind became calm. After running for several minutes in this state of mind, I came back to ordinary consciousness with a curious, but pleasant blankness.

Zen Breath-Counting

Begin by sitting in a comfortable position. The autogenic sitting position is fine, or if you prefer, use the traditional Zen cross-legged, half- or full-lotus. If you are sitting on the floor, you might want to use a small pillow to help support your buttocks and align and balance your body. Your spine should be erect, your torso perpendicular to the chair or floor, your head straight on your neck. You should feel comfortable, and your body weight should be balanced. Half-close your eyes so that they are unfocused and turned downward. Take a few deep, diaphragmatic breaths and begin to clear your mind. Let go of all the worries and concerns of the day. Allow your mind to slow down.

Focus your attention on the area of your lower abdomen. Imagine that there is a balloon in your abdomen and that with each inhalation the balloon is inflated. As you exhale, the balloon is deflated. Keep your focus of attention on your abdomen and see the balloon being inflated and deflated, filling and emptying. Feel the air move into the balloon. Feel the walls of the balloon expand. See the balloon inflate completely and then slowly deflate until the walls collapse on each other. As your breathing becomes more comfortable and begins to regulate itself, turn your attention from your abdomen to the air coming in and leaving your nostrils.

Begin to count your breaths, beginning with the next exhalation as *1*. Count the next inhalation as *2*, the next exhalation as

3, and so on, up to *10.* Then go back to *1.* If any thoughts come to mind, just let them pass over and through you. Do not hold on to them but do not reject them too vigorously either. Just allow them to come and go. Do not evaluate them, and do not judge yourself for having them. If you lose your focus of attention, relax your breathing and go back to *1.* If you start to lose count for any reason, do not try to pick up where you left off; just go back to the number *1.*

If you begin to carry on long internal monologues or fantasies, just relax and begin to count again. You can always return to the easy rhythm of your own breath, the sound of air entering and leaving your body, the feeling of air at your nostrils. Let your breath carry you and breathe itself. If you begin to breathe unnaturally, to hyperventilate, or to hold your breath, just attempt to relax all the muscles in your chest and abdomen. Return briefly to the image of the balloon to restore the easy pattern of your breaths. Then go back to your counting. Continue for twenty minutes.

What sort of distractions did you experience?

Was there any turning point at which the exercise became easier?

Distractions are the rule, not the exception. The body will resist sitting still and the mind will resist being quieted. Especially since you ordinarily program your body to keep moving and your mind to keep thinking, reversal of this process will not be immediate. In your normal workday you may be in a state of emotional arousal that you are unaware of, until you try to sit still and calm down. Distractions range from the usual string of mental verbalizations to visual fantasies. Thoughts are going to appear in your mind. The important thing is not to hold on to them and not to evaluate them. If a particular thought or image recurs, you might want to take a look at it when you are not meditating. Distractions can be illuminating— sometimes the meditative state can provide insight into what's really bothering you.

Often people speak of a turning point at which the exercise becomes easier. This may not occur for weeks. It is similar to the turning point in acquiring any new skill; the gains in competence may be cumulative but are perceived as sudden. Sometimes you must get through the same hurdles and obstacles each time you sit down to meditate. Don't worry, they will probably fall away after the first few minutes of the meditation.

SHAVASANA

Shavasana (Sanskrit for "corpse pose") is another breathing exercise. It comes from the yogic tradition. Unlike the other meditations provided, it is performed in a reclining position. In research on this meditation and hypertension, subjects could lower their blood pressure an average of eleven points during the exercise, after a period of regular practice.

Basic Shavasana

Lie on your back with your legs slightly spread. Your arms should be separated from your torso, your palms open and upward. Make your body as straight as possible; your spine erect; your neck in a straight line up from your shoulders; your head erect on your neck. You should be comfortable and feel no undue strain anywhere in your body. Your breathing should be unrestricted.

Begin by taking a few deep breaths, and allow all the worries and concerns of the day to leave you. Allow your mind to begin to run down. Continue to breathe deeply and allow your breathing to establish its own easy rhythm. Focus your attention upon your breath. Become aware of the cool flow of air into your nostrils as you inhale, the warm flow of air out of your nostrils as you exhale. Focus on the point of your nostrils at which the air enters and exits your body. Let your body breathe itself. Do not force your breath; do not hyperventilate.

Feel the coolness at the tip of your nostrils, and pause for just a moment after the inhalation. Then exhale, fully and completely, feeling the warmth at the tip of your nostrils as the air passes out of your body. Pause again for just a moment after the exhalation. These pauses are the quietest times of the breath.

If any distractions come into your mind, let them go; you want to be aware of only your breath, of that pleasant flow of air into and out of your nostrils. Watch the thoughts just roll through your mind, remembering that you can choose to return to them at the end of the meditation, but letting go of them for now. Feel the warm air leaving your nostrils, the cool air coming in. After twenty minutes of focusing only on your breath, take another deep breath and stretch. Clench your fists for just a moment, and return to your normal consciousness, saying to yourself: **"I am refreshed and alert."**

How did this experience compare to the Zen meditation?

Did you find yourself getting sleepy in the reclining position?

You will find this experience somewhat different from the Zen meditation. Some people find counting easier but cannot detect the difference in temperature between air inhaled and exhaled. For many people, lying down is associated with sleep and makes them automatically sleepy. If this is true for you, stick with other meditations until you are more acquainted with meditative states.

Shavasana Variation

Lie in the same position used for Basic Shavasana. Begin to take a few deep breaths and let go of the day's worries. As your mind winds down, allow all the muscles of your body to go loose and limp. Spend just a few moments scanning your body from the feet up for any held tension. As you find it, just let go of it, sending it away with the exhalation. If you have not already closed your eyes, close them now. Let any images that crop up in your mind pass over and through you. Do not hold on to any stray thoughts; just let go of them.

Place the fingertips of both hands on the solar plexus. This is the top of your abdomen, about the level of the navel. Feel the air coming in at your nostrils. See it being warmed by your nose and then passing into your lungs and from your lungs into your abdomen. Feel the air filling your abdomen and entering your fingertips. Pause at the end of the inhalation.

Move your fingertips to your forehead. Exhale slowly and completely, imagining that the energy in your fingertips can be directed into your head. This energy of breath is a brilliant golden-white light. It first fills your nostrils, then your lungs, then your abdomen, your fingertips, and finally your head. Let your mind just become filled with the image of golden-white light. Let your mind become a blank screen covered with brilliant white light. Focus only on your breathing, which is filling you with this golden-white light, energizing you with this brilliant white light. The white light comes in at your nostrils, moves into your lungs, moves down into your abdomen, moves into your fingertips, and then is carried by your fingertips into your head. You can take in as much of this golden-white light as you need; it fills you, surrounds you, bathes you, so that all you can see and feel is light.

Did the image of the light make it easier for you to focus your attention?

This rather extensive visualization is easier for some people than simply focusing on their breathing. It is easy to imagine a light so bright that it can overwhelm all distractions. This meditation is founded in a traditional yogic belief in energy flows. You need not believe that energy can be transferred from your fingertips to your head to feel energized by the meditation.

MANTRA-REPEATING MEDITATIONS

Mantra-repeating meditations, like TM and Benson's variation, are common in the yogic tradition. Another form is the chant in which a mantra is sung, sometimes with musical accompaniment. In this case, the sound may be varied with each repetition, by variations in the rhythm or the inflection. This same sort of variation will probably occur in your mind; you may hear the sound stretched out or repeated at varying intervals. The mantra will probably start to sound "different" to you after you have repeated it a number of times.

Yogic Mantra-Repeating

Sit comfortably in a chair or on the floor as in the Zen Breath-Counting meditation. Your breathing should be unconstricted. Begin by taking a few deep, cleansing breaths, and allow all of the day's activities and concerns to wash over you. Just let them pass without allowing them to bother you. Do not hold on to any of them. Begin to focus upon your breath, breathing slowly and naturally. Let your body breathe itself, calmly and slowly. Do not force your breath or hyperventilate. Breathe away any experience of the day that may be distracting or disturbing you. As your mind begins to clear and your breathing begins to take care of itself, sense a greater calmness and relaxation coming over you.

Take a moment to scan your body and become aware of any held tension. Turn your attention to your feet and your legs, up to your abdomen, then to your chest, your arms and hands, shoulders, neck, and head. Let go of any tension remaining anywhere in your body. Just breathe it away and allow everything to go loose and limp. Sink into whatever surface you are sitting on. Continue to breathe slowly, releasing any tension in your back. Your jaw and tongue are relaxed; your face is calm and smooth.

Shift your attention back to your breath, which has established its own regular and even pattern. Begin to focus on a word or sound. Choose a word that does not have a lot of specific associations for you. Benson suggests the word "one." You may use a perfectly meaningless sound if you find the sound pleasant. Concentrate on the mantra, hearing, seeing, thinking, feeling nothing else. Whenever your consciousness wanders from the word, gently bring it back. See it for an instant written before you, or isolated on an otherwise blank movie screen. Continue to focus on this mantra, hearing it over and over again. After twenty minutes of this meditation, picture yourself coming completely out of this state. Make a fist with each of your hands and take a deep breath. Exhale fully and completely and open your eyes. Say to yourself: **"I am refreshed and alert."**

Did you have trouble concentrating on your mantra?

How did this meditation compare to Zen Breath-Counting or Shavasana?

Distractions are the most common occurrence during this or any meditation. Sometimes adding the visual sense, in mentally seeing the word on a screen, helps to clear the mind. Make note of how this meditation differs from Zen Breath-Counting or Shavasana. The overall feeling of relaxation should begin to be familiar.

VISUAL FOCAL POINT MEDITATIONS

The next two meditations utilize a visual focal point for focusing attention. They come from the yogic tradition. The visual focal point replaces a repeated mantra or your breathing as the center for awareness. When you look at an object this way, you may start to feel as if your eyes have become your hands and have touched the object. You may also feel a strange sense of unity with the object, as it fills your consciousness and you seem to merge with it.

Candle Meditation

This meditation is only five minutes long. You may repeat it twice in one sitting. It is designed to help you see more clearly and to develop your powers of awareness, attention, and concentration. It may also help you develop your ability to visualize.

Sit in a comfortable position so your breathing is unobstructed and your spine straight. There should be no undue pressure on any part of your body. Take a few deep breaths to begin to relax and clear your mind. Take just a moment to let the day's worries and distractions wash over you, as your breathing establishes itself in a fine, comfortable rhythm.

Place a lighted candle three feet from you. The room should be semidarkened so that you can see the candle well, but not so dark that there is a lot of glare when you look at the candle. Gaze directly at the flame for several minutes. Try to focus completely on the flame and not on a visual distortion. Then, close your eyes and press your palms against the lids.

See the flame again in your mind's eye. Concentrate on keeping this mental image of the flame as vivid as the sight of the real flame. Examine the image of the flame in your mind. Do not let it fade, become distorted, or disappear. Hold your palms against your eyelids for a few minutes. If the image starts to fade, look at the candle again for just a moment, and then shut your eyes and attempt to hold the image in mind. After a few minutes, move your hands away from your eyes and down onto your knees. Relax completely. Take a few deep breaths, and let the image go.

Did you have trouble holding the image of the flame?

The afterimage of the flame appears on your retina after you close your eyes. Holding onto this image and keeping it bright can be difficult, but the more you repeat this exercise the easier it will become. The image of the flame can be a model for you when you try to visualize brilliant light in the visualization and meditation exercises.

Spot-Staring Exercise

Sit in a comfortable position. Use either the autogenic sitting position or any other position you have found comfortable for the sitting meditations. Your back should be straight and your breathing unconstricted. Keep your eyes half-open, gazing upon a fixed object or a space. Either use a lighted candle's flame, a small object like a stone or shell, or a spot on the floor or wall. Avoid intricately detailed or patterned objects. Your focal point should be about three feet in front of you.

Take a few deep breaths and cleanse your consciousness of all distractions. Release any held tension anywhere in your body and let your breathing begin to carry you. Fix your gaze on your visual focal point and continue to breathe slowly and naturally. Do not force your breath and do not hyperventilate. Just continue to breathe, while focusing your entire consciousness on the point that you are gazing at. There is no room in your mind for anything but that point. If any thoughts or experiences from the day crop up, just let them roll through your consciousness. Watch them as if they are on a movie screen, just drifting by. Remember that you can always choose to return to any thoughts, memories, or impressions that are important.

Breathing slowly and naturally, become aware of any tension in your arms, hands, shoulders, or back. Let all the muscles of your arms, hands, shoulders, and back just let go. All of these muscles become loose and limp, as you continue to breathe. For just a few moments, consider your feet and legs, and if there is any tension there, allow it to just melt away. Allow your entire body to relax completely. Continue to gaze at your point, breathing slowly and calmly. Relax all the muscles of your head and face, allowing your jaw to relax and then your tongue. You face becomes calm and smooth. Let all the muscles of your neck relax, and then your chest and abdomen. Feel the breath coming freely into your chest and then into your abdomen. Then, allow the warm air to leave your body, leaving your abdomen and then your chest. If there is any tension remaining anywhere in your body, just breathe it away as you exhale.

Your body is just breathing itself. Your eyes are on your point, and you begin to lose yourself in it. You can relax deeper and deeper, allowing yourself to find the most comfortable position, settling yourself, stilling yourself, slowing your heart, and breathing in your calm, easy, natural pattern of breaths. Your whole being becomes centered in the point you're gazing at. The only other thing in your consciousness is the sound of your easy, natural breathing, the feeling of cool air entering your body at your nostrils, and the feeling of warm air leaving your body at your nostrils. You are drifting into an ever deeper state of relaxation, becoming more and more centered in that point. You drift into an even deeper state of relaxation, imagining that you can drift to the calmest, most peaceful spot, safe and absolutely peaceful. (Continue to gaze at your visual focal point for about five minutes.)

If you have drifted away from your point, gradually draw yourself back, becoming aware of your slow, deep, natural breathing. Fix your eyes again upon that point and allow yourself to really see it without anything else clouding or distorting your sight. See it as if you were touching it with your hands. Let that point be the center of your being.

Remember now that all of the memories and experiences of this meditation can carry over with you, up and out of this meditative state, bringing them with you to a state of full awareness. Let the calmness and the relaxation carry over with you throughout your day and throughout the coming week. Feel the slow, deep relaxation. You can recall this feeling of serenity whenever you wish to for relaxation. Each time you practice this meditation, you will get better and better at it, more able to relax and more able to concentrate your attention on one point. Your meditative state will grow deeper.

Now tighten your fists. Take a very deep breath and stretch, letting yourself return to a state of normal consciousness. You may wish to write down any of the important thoughts or travels that you have experienced in your meditation. Take another deep breath, stretch, and become fully alert.

How do you find concentrating on a visual focal point as compared to focusing on a mantra or your own breathing?

Some people find it easier to focus on a visual object than on a mentally repeated mantra. The mantra is verbal and may stimulate you to produce other internal verbalizations. It may be easier for you to center yourself on a visual point. By all means try both forms of meditation.

SYMBOLIC MEDITATION

Symbolic meditation comes from the yogic school. Instead of concentrating upon a meaningless mantra, you choose a word, scene, or object that holds some higher, symbolic meaning for you. It was during this meditation that I had the experience with which I opened this chapter. I cannot really explain why I feel so strongly about this experience or why it has had such a profound effect upon my life. But I do know that meditation provides for consciousness growth in a way that other relaxation techniques do not—and I find this particular meditation especially powerful.

The meditation is divided into three parts. In the first part, focus your attention fully upon the object or word you have chosen. This might be a word like "love," "peace," "calm," a specific landscape, or a star, cross, or other symbol that holds some meaning for you. In the second part of the meditation, allow your mind to go blank. Concentrate on keeping your mind as blank as an empty movie screen. In the third part of the meditation, close your hands and visualize pure white light surrounding you and filling your being.

Symbolic Meditation Exercise

Begin by sitting in a comfortable position. Use any of the sitting positions that you have found comfortable for the other meditations. Get into this position, and spend a few moments clearing your mind. Allow any disturbing or distracting thoughts or emotions to wash over you. Just let them pass through your consciousness. If you focus on any of them, just become aware and then let them go. You can always return to them later. As these ideas just float through and away from you, begin to breathe slowly and naturally. Take a few deep, diaphragmatic breaths, and with each exhalation, allow any worries or tension to be exhaled with the warm air. Your mind begins to calm and clear, and you begin to relax. The various parts of your body gradually become heavier and more relaxed. Continue to breathe slowly and calmly, letting your breath breathe itself and carry you.

Now place your hands together, palm to palm, and begin to focus on the word or symbol you have chosen. Hold this symbol in your mind. For the first ten minutes of this exercise you will just concentrate on your symbol, seeing it clearly in your mind. Avoid all distractions, internal verbalizations, or other thoughts. Be aware only of the symbol you have chosen and concentrate all your energies on it. (Allow ten minutes for this contemplation.)

If your mind has drifted, bring it gently back to your symbol. Try to see it clearly and become aware of its essence. Experience it with all your senses. Your breathing should remain calm, slow, and natural. Repeat the symbol over and over again in your mind. If it is a scene, explore it completely. When your mind wanders, just gently bring it back to center on the symbol. Now take a few more minutes to continue to concentrate, focusing all your energy upon the essence and feeling of the symbol you are contemplating. (Allow five minutes for further contemplation.)

Continue to concentrate on your symbol, while becoming aware of your breathing. Focus now on breathing very slowly, very calmly, very deeply. Open your hands and lay them on your lap, palms up. Put your mind into neutral gear so that it is perfectly blank. Imagine that you are staring at a perfectly blank movie screen. Whatever images crop up, whatever pictures come from your consciousness, sit back and watch them float by, as if you were seated in a theater and they were moving by on the screen. Be aware of them but do not hold onto them.

Also be aware of the feelings of calmness and relaxation throughout your body. Start with your legs and work your way up through your torso, to your arms and legs, and up into your head. Gently and slowly make a survey of your body, feeling the total calmness and relaxation spreading. The tension is just melting away. Now just focus on the blank screen, not letting any distractions or interferences get in the way. (Allow five minutes for this contemplation of blankness.)

Clench each of your fists tightly, and then take a very deep breath, and stretch. Picture yourself surrounded by a white, absolutely pure light. Picture yourself standing in an all-white room. Imagine that you are outside in the snow on a beautiful, sunny day and all you can see for miles around you is white snow. You are jumping into a pool filled with milk. You are totally surrounded by white light; it absolutely fills you; you can see nothing but pure, white, brilliant light. Take another deep breath and stretch, becoming fully alert.

How did you find this symbolic meditation as opposed to the other meditations in the chapter?

Symbolic meditation offers individualized experiences. Each time I practice the meditation, my experience is different. Experiment with different mantras, and be receptive to the different experiences you may have. This is a good meditation to practice from time to time as a way of gauging your personal growth and exploring the changes in your psyche.

Chapter 7
Physical Exercise

It's How You Play the Game

H AVE YOU EVER FOUND YOURSELF shaking your hand back
and forth after writing for a long time? Have you ever
jumped up and down because you were so excited that
you just couldn't sit still? Most people have experienced some kind of
spontaneous physical movement. Though the effort was not conscious, you were releasing excess muscle tension through physical
activity. Exercise can be active and strenuous and performed on the
football field, the ski slope, or the beach. But it can also be gentle
motions and stretches done in your office, on the elevator, or in your
car while waiting for a light to change.

Many people hold tension in their muscles. Look around and
you will see wrinkled foreheads and tight jaws. *Everywhere you go
there are people holding tension in their skeletal muscles and wearing
stress on their faces.* We are all surrounded by events that create stress.
Filling out income tax forms is a "pain in the neck"—and so is waiting in line for gas, arguing with the phone company about
long-distance calls you didn't make, and shopping for a Christmas
present on December 24. All of these situations can be stressful, and
if you tend to hold tension in your shoulders and neck, a "pain in
the neck" may be more than an expression of distaste.

Skeletal muscles are commonly used under conscious control
for mobility or action. Chronic muscle tension, even if it affects
only a small segment of the muscle, can cause spasms or constriction

which register as pain. Though spontaneous movement will help reduce excess skeletal tension, it is often not appropriate—or just isn't sufficient. Planned physical activity, gentle or strenuous, can help keep your musculature free from unnecessary tension—and can be good preventive therapy for your whole system. But physical exercise, in itself, is rarely enough for relaxation.

GENTLE EXERCISE

Yogic movement is the foundation of the gentle exercise techniques. Basic to these exercises is slow, conscious movement with an awareness of tension and gentle stretching through the tension. Their value is in increasing awareness of tension and dispelling it, rather than for intense physical conditioning. Gentle movement and stretching, if practiced twice a day, can help prevent tension headaches and neckaches that often occur at the end of a long workday. Substitute an exercise for a cup of coffee—this will give you a real energy boost. These exercises are especially beneficial for people who hold tension in their muscles, but everyone can profit from the health-giving properties of these movements.

Breathe properly while practicing. Inhale deeply and exhale fully and completely, using the breath to help release any tension. While you move, allow the deep, slow breath to fade into the background of your consciousness; focus your awareness on the part of the body you are exercising. Feel the tension and allow it to melt away. Remember that awareness is half the battle for stress reduction. *Never force or strain yourself; practice the techniques slowly.* Be quietly aware of the tension and its release.

These exercises can be utilized before excess muscular tension manifests as discomfort, soreness, or pain. Excellent for prevention, gentle movement can teach you how to be more aware of your body and its needs and help you recognize where you hold muscular tension. If prevention fails and you do suffer a neckache after a particularly aggravating quarrel with your former spouse or after some other equally taxing event, then try one of these techniques. It will help relieve a great deal of your tension.

Begin in a standing position, holding onto a table, chair, or desk for stability. Close your eyes and take a few deep, slow breaths, exhaling fully and completely. Allow yourself to relax and become aware of the places where you hold tension. Do not rush. Do not breathe too quickly. Pause between breaths and become fully aware of how your lungs, chest, rib cage, and diaphragm work together. You may become aware of your heartbeat; focus on its fine, even rhythm. Take your time, and never force or strain yourself.

Shoulder Rolls

Let your arms hang loosely at your sides, gently pulling down your shoulders. Rotate both shoulders, forward or backward, very slowly. Do not forget to breathe, exhaling fully and completely. Be aware of how high you can lift your shoulders before you feel tension. Notice where you feel tension when you move them forward, downward, and backward. Take your time; you cannot rush yourself into relaxation. After several full rotations stop for a moment. Notice what position your shoulders are in. Reverse the direction of the rotation. Feel how good it is to move your muscles consciously and gently, allowing them to release all their stored-up tension. Do not forget to breathe deeply and slowly. With each exhalation, allow tension to flow out of your body.

Are your shoulders more relaxed and resting lower than they were?

Are you able to move them further in all directions before feeling tension?

Your shoulders may be more relaxed, but you may still be holding tension in your neck. If you have time, follow up the shoulder rolls with the neck rotation exercise that follows, as the neck rotation movement flows naturally from the shoulder rolls.

Neck Rotation

Take a deep, full breath. Exhale fully and completely. Let your head drop as far forward on your chest as possible. Slowly move it to the left or right; see how close your ear can come to your shoulder. If you feel any resistance, stop for a moment and take a few full, deep breaths. As you exhale, allow the tension and resistance to flow from your body. Start rotating your neck again, very slowly. Do not forget to breathe. After several full rotations, stop for a moment and feel how differently your neck rests upon your shoulders. Take a moment and feel the relaxation. Begin rotating your neck in the other direction, remembering to breathe deeply.

Did you hold your breath to concentrate on the movement?

Does your neck feel more relaxed?

Do your shoulders and neck feel looser?

Remember to breathe correctly; when you reach a tense spot, use your breath to breathe away the tension. If you still feel a lot of tension in your shoulders and neck, repeat the exercises. Make sure that your movements are slow and deliberate. Breathe fully and completely, and allow the excess tension to flow from your neck and shoulders with each exhalation. Remember that these exercises are not a race, but slow, calm, conscious movements.

Arm Shakes

This exercise is great for dispelling that stiff, cramped feeling that results from driving for hours, or sitting at a desk for a long period of time. Practice it in a standing position.

Notice how your right arm feels as it hangs by your side. Lightly shake your hand and your wrist. Gradually let the movement involve your lower arm and your elbow. Remember to breathe deeply, exhaling fully and completely. Shake your arm more vigorously, and feel it become looser and freer. Allow your upper arm to become involved in the shaking motion, and shake the entire arm for about a minute. Swing your arm back and forth while shaking, and involve your shoulder in the motion. Flail it about loosely, shaking the tension out of your hand, wrist, lower arm, upper arm, and shoulder. After a few moments, stop and let your arm hang loosely at your side. Take a deep, full breath and exhale fully and completely. Feel the sensations in your right arm.

Does your right arm feel different than your left arm?

Does it feel longer?

Does your arm actually look longer?

Does it feel heavy, warm, or tingly all over?

Your right arm probably feels much different than your left arm. Many people think that the exercised arm feels longer than the unexercised one. If you look in a mirror, your arm will look longer. This lengthening and the feeling of heaviness are the result of muscles relaxing and letting go. Increased blood flow caused by the movement and relaxation contributes to that tingly, warm feeling. You may recognize other differences between your two arms, but be sure to be aware of the feeling of relaxation in your right arm versus the tense feeling in your left arm. Take a deep, full breath and repeat the exercise with your left arm. Try shaking both at once after exercising each one. After completing the entire exercise sequence, be aware of the relaxation in your arms and shoulders.

Leg Shakes

If you have time after doing the arm shakes, try the leg shakes; this exercise may also be done alone but works especially well in conjunction with the previous one. If you practice the first four exercises one after another, your body will be free of tension and significantly more relaxed. Since this may not always be possible, pick the exercise that relaxes the body part where you hold the most tension.

Balance yourself by holding onto a chair, table, or desk for stability. Take a deep breath, and exhale fully and completely. Remember to breathe deeply throughout the exercise. Slowly rotate your right foot and ankle. After a few moments start shaking your foot, ankle, lower leg, and knee. Shake very slowly at first, and gradually increase the momentum. Do not forget to breathe properly, and as you exhale, let the tension flow from your entire right leg. Involve your entire leg in the movement, and shake for a few moments. Be sure to shake the upper thigh. Swing the entire right leg loosely for about a minute, shaking the tension out of your foot, ankle, calf, knee, and thigh. Stop, take a deep, full breath, and exhale fully and completely.

Did you remember to breathe properly throughout the exercise?

Can you feel the relaxation in your right leg?

Does your left leg feel different?

You may experience the same feeling of warmth, length, heaviness, and tingling that you felt in your arms after the arm shakes, since your leg muscles react just as your arm muscles do to these gentle movements. This exercise is more difficult than the arm technique, and initially you may not have dramatic results. If you practice a few times it will become easier, and the results will be more obvious. Do what feels most comfortable. Do not struggle to shake your foot independently of your knee; it will become easier with practice. Straining to do the movements "exactly right" the first time will only make you more tense. This tension may not be felt in your leg, but you may be hunching your shoulders or wrinkling your forehead. Also, if it is uncomfortable to start the motions with your right leg, use your left leg instead. It doesn't matter which leg you relax first—just so long as you can feel the difference between tension and relaxation.

Now, exercise the other leg, starting at the foot and moving up to the thigh. Remember to hold on to something for balance; do not forget to breathe properly. After exercising both legs, you might jump up and down in place, loosening the legs and the entire body. Stop and take a deep, full breath, exhaling fully and completely. Feel the relaxation.

Scalp Tapping

For a quick energy boost or a quiet moment of relaxation, a form of scalp massage may be the best technique for you. Try it, and you may find that it can be as simple and helpful as a "sigh of relief."

To get an energy boost, tap your scalp very lightly with your fingertips. Close your eyes and breathe properly. Use both hands and start just above your forehead or at the nape of your neck. Experiment with harder and softer taps to see which feel best. Tap lightly and move your fingers slowly over your entire scalp. Some areas may be more sensitive than others, but do not skip these areas. Just tap very, very gently. After tapping your scalp, move your fingertips to your forehead, and then tap your whole face. When you are done, take a deep, full breath. Exhale fully and completely. Open your eyes, and go back to work or play with renewed vigor and a refreshed outlook.

Scalp Massage

This relaxation technique also stimulates your scalp, while relaxing your facial muscles. Raise both your arms so that your elbows are bent outward at about ear level. Massage your scalp lightly and slowly with your fingertips. Remember to breathe properly. If you close your eyes, the movement may be more relaxing, though this is not absolutely essential. Start massaging on the top of the head. Some people like to keep the thumbs more or less in place while they move the fingers, but find the technique that works best for you. Massage the entire scalp and the nape of the neck. Remember to breathe properly. Move your fingers to your forehead, and then your cheeks, jaw, and chin.

Rub both ears, and stimulate them by gently pulling on the ear lobes. This technique can sometimes make a headache disappear in a few minutes, or make the tension flow right out the top of your head and out of your consciousness. As with all the relaxation techniques, this works better for some people than others. Try it and see how it works for you.

Eye Stretches

Some of the previous techniques may not be appropriate for a public place where there are a lot of people. Eye movements can be done just about any time, in any place. If you have a tension headache and can't leave your desk, then try this exercise.

Take a deep, full breath. Close your eyes, and exhale fully and completely. Lean forward and rest your elbows on a table or desk; cup your hands gently over your eyes, with the heels of your hands resting against your cheekbones. Don't put any pressure on your eyeballs. Don't press down; cup them gently. Remain in this position for a few moments, and take about five deep, full breaths. Remove your hands from your face and open your eyes. Look straight up at the ceiling and inhale; look down at the floor and exhale, allowing the tension to flow out of your eyes and face as the air leaves your body. Look up, inhaling; look down, exhaling. Try and look in both directions as far as your eyes will go without straining them too much. Repeat the up-down sequence five times. Then cup your eyes with your hands again, close your eyes, and take five deep, full breaths. Remove your hands and open your eyes.

Do your eyes feel more relaxed?

Are the muscles around your eyes tense or relaxed?

Most likely this short exercise is not quite enough to relieve you of all your eye tension, but you might be able to feel a slight reduction in tension. If you found yourself hunching your back and shoulders when you bent over to cup your eyes, prop your elbows up with a phone book or typewriter. It doesn't help you very much to be creating tension in your back while releasing tension from your face.

Eye Stretches with Visualization

Inhale, and look into the far left-hand ceiling corner. Exhale, while looking down into the far right-hand floor corner. Do this five times. Cup your eyes and take five deep breaths with your eyes closed; remove your hands, and open your eyes. When you breathe, feel all the tension leaving your body with each exhalation. Inhale, and look up into the right-hand ceiling corner. Exhale, while looking down into the far left-hand corner. Repeat the movements five times. Cup your eyes and take five deep breaths. Feel the relaxation in your face.

Imagine that your body is in the middle of a huge clock face. Open your eyes, and look up as far as you can at number *12*. Inhale deeply, and exhale fully and completely. Move your eyes to number *1* while inhaling; exhale fully and completely. Rotate your eyes around the entire clock, remembering to breathe properly. When you get back to number *12,* cup your eyes and close them. Maintain this position for a few moments.

ACTIVE EXERCISE

Active physical exercise can be very beneficial and highly relaxing, but strenuous exercise is not necessarily relaxing. Imagine you are on the tennis court. Your opponent is a member of your department, and you know he wants your job. You are only playing one set, and the score is four games to three, in your favor. You ace your opponent on the first serve. It's been a long day. Your arm is aching and you feel your pulse throbbing in your temples. Is this exercise good for you? If the exercise you are getting is stressful in itself, how relaxing can it be?

Doctors and other health care experts believe that active physical exercise is beneficial. Regular exercise aids the cardiovascular system and strengthens it by increasing its capacity to supply blood to the body tissues. Vibrant exercise clears the lungs and gives the blood vessels a healthy workout. It burns calories and may aid in weight reduction. It stimulates the skeletal muscles and allows them to tense and relax (progressive relaxation).

This type of behavior adds to your stress level, and if you already have a stressful occupation, you are compounding your problems.

People who hold tension in their musculature can use active physical exercise as a stress-reduction technique, if they keep a few things in mind.

- Pick one of these moderate-to-active exercises: walking or hiking fairly long distances, jogging slowly and steadily, swimming, or bicycling.

- Do it regularly every day, or at the very least four or five times a week. A "weekend athlete" often ends up with sore muscles and gets few long-term benefits from exercising.

- Allow yourself at least a half hour to an hour for exercising. Don't try and fit it in while your steaks are barbecuing.

- Get plenty of fresh air. Exercising in a closed room and breathing stale air don't help your lungs.

- Always remember to breathe deeply and fully. Don't hold your breath.

- Drink plenty of liquids to make sure that you replenish vital body salts.

- When you are really tired—stop.

Another way to derive positive benefits from active physical exercise is to combine your exercise with Zen-like meditation. This form of meditation can be applied to any prolonged physical activity such as jogging, running, walking, swimming, or bicycling. Using it will initially make a difference in how you feel, and over a period of time your actual performance may be improved.

Consider your current attitude and motivation in pursuing active physical exercise. Do you find it a grueling and uncomfortable challenge? Do you feel sore or exhausted afterwards? Try to empty your mind of any competitive interests, either against yourself or the clock. The phantom record-breaking athlete who mocks your hard-won efforts should be banned from your consciousness. If you are running so that you can be seen on Saturday morning in your expensive running shoes and monogrammed sweat suit, or so that your body will be more attractive in the end, even though you find the actual experience nauseating, then this meditation should introduce you to a whole new experience. It is designed to help you enjoy the experience and to be always aware of how it is affecting your body. The exercise does not dominate you; your body extends its own natural pace to the exercise.

Zen-like Active Meditation

During this meditation you will enjoy peaceful, internal reflections as you engage in active physical exercise. For some, running around a track repeatedly or swimming laps in an indoor pool provides a good medium for the meditative state. You are not distracted by the external environment and can focus on the internal process. I prefer to run in one large loop so that I never pass the same location twice. It is possible to keep your eyes open and enjoy the changing colors, smells, landscapes, and architecture around you in a peaceful, nonjudgmental way. Don't hold on to any object—just see everything you look at very clearly. The secret lies in passive concentration; you see and feel everything, but in a positive, easy way. So, as you are bicycling down the road and gaze up into the sky, notice its particular shade of blue, and look closely at the cloud formations. Whatever active exercise you choose to try, start slowly. Pain or overexertion is directly opposed to the passive, reflective state of mind you want to induce.

Take a deep breath, and exhale fully and completely. Stretch, and prepare all your muscles for movement. To clear your mind, allow yourself to think of all the things you have to do, all the nagging obligations, and then either make an actual list and put it aside, or make a mental list and then put it out of your mind. Don't take your worries and concerns with you. Remember to breathe properly, and let all the tension flow out of your body.

If you are running, begin with a comfortable lope. If swimming, get used to the water, and consider how buoyant your body feels. Bicyclers should not start peddling at breakneck speed; start slowly and gradually speed up. Look for your own rhythm, your own natural pace. It is better and easier to speed up to reach your comfortable rhythm than it is to slow down. Be aware of any pain, stress, or discomfort you feel in your body and change your movements to alleviate it.

Pay very close attention to your breath. Follow the rhythm of your inhalations and exhalations. Do not hold your breath; take deep, slow, and complete breaths. Remember the complete diaphragmatic breath and let your abdomen expand as you inhale. Imagine the air flowing freely throughout your body; don't close off any part of yourself from the life-giving breath. Be aware of the cool air as you inhale, and feel the warm air leaving your body as you exhale fully and completely. Coordinate your movements with your breathing. Follow your breath and stay within its rhythm. If you begin to pant, slow down until you are breathing comfortably again.

In running, it may take a quarter to a half mile to find your own comfortable pace and a sense of moving with efficiency and smoothness. Bicyclers must learn to flow with the terrain and change their pace when going up and down hills. Swimmers are more accustomed to pacing with their breath, and it might be easier for them to slip into the rhythm of the meditation. If you are walking, it might be more difficult for you to keep extraneous thoughts out of your mind. Concentrate on your breathing, and see clearly each blade of grass and leaf as you pass by.

Focus on every part of your body. Be aware of how you carry your shoulders, and your neck, back, arms, and legs. Do you feel any tightness in your abdomen? Are you holding excess tension anywhere? Working against yourself? Wasting your own energy? Move your attention to your face. Is your jaw tightly clenched with the effort of running or bicycling? Are you holding your mouth and eyes tightly shut against the water? When you become aware of any part of your body that is uncomfortable or sore, move your attention to that spot. Imagine yourself breathing air into that particular spot, and let your exhalation carry all the pain out of your body. Imagine healing breath flowing into your sore or stiff spot, and then exhale the tension away with the warm air. After you have scanned your body once, continue to follow your breathing, slowly and naturally.

You may then slip into internal contemplation of your thoughts or emotions. If you feel resistance, or immediately think of something troubling, return to your body and scan each part again. Remember to consider all the parts of your body: from neck to shoulder, back, arms, legs, abdomen, hands, legs, and face—any part feeling tension. The essence of the meditation is to be engaged in your physical activity and yet gazing peacefully inward. Try to be in the moment—not in the past or future. Turning inward does not mean mentally reviewing business transactions, or reenacting frantic domestic quarrels; if your mind goes in this direction, refocus your attention on the breath and bodily sensations. If you can lose yourself in your surroundings—the trees, flowers, grasses, water, wind, or rocks—this too would be an ideal meditative state.

Return to your body from time to time. Bring yourself back by focusing on your breath; determine if you are running, jogging, or swimming with your own natural rhythm. If you are bicycling, check to see if your pedaling is erratic, or if you have extended yourself beyond the rhythm of your breath. Swimmers can also check for this by being aware of their breathing patterns. Scan your body for any tension that might have crept in, and wherever you are holding tension, let it go. Breathe it away with the warm air, exhaling fully and completely. Are your shoulders hunched up? Breathe the tension away. Are your legs aching? Feel the warm air leave your body, taking the soreness and pain from your legs. Are your fingers clenching the hand grips? Let the tension go. Breathe it away, and feel it melt from the tips of your fingers.

When your exercise period is almost over, you may wish to use the last lap, the last quarter-mile, the last block, to push beyond your rhythm just a bit. Bring yourself totally into your body by testing it with a short burst of speed, becoming aware of your entire body and its movement as a unit. After you have completed the vigorous part of your exercise, slow down your breath and imagine the toxins circulating out and away from your body. Depending on your active exercise, walking for five to thirty minutes afterward will prevent muscle soreness. Be aware of the natural pace of slowing down gradually, and become aware of any tension still held in your body.

This meditation can be changed to suit the physical activity of your choice. The important things to remember are: follow your breath to find your pace; don't strain or overexert yourself; clear your mind of any troubling thoughts; try to be in the moment, not the past or future; be aware of all the parts of your body; and allow any tension to flow from your body. Using this meditation can change a potentially stress-producing activity into a restful, enjoyable, healthful experience.

Chapter 8
Biofeedback

Conversations with a Machine

I MAGINE THAT YOU ARE A CHILD AGAIN, absorbed in a game of "Hot and Cold" with a friend. You cover your eyes while your playmate hides a piece of candy. When you open your eyes and begin the search, your friend provides clues by calling out the words "hot" and "cold." The object itself is considered hot and the distance from it, cold. You dance around the room, peering over surfaces, scanning the shelves beyond your reach. When you approach the hidden candy, your friend screams, "Warm, warmer, getting hot," and as you take a wrong turn she chides, "Cooling off…brrr, it's the North Pole." Through a series of trial and error moves, always adjusting your behavior according to clues, you narrow down the territory. Taking smaller and smaller steps, making infinitely tinier moves, you finally discover the candy. At that moment your friend yells out, "Burning, burning up…you're on fire!"

"Hot and Cold" is a feedback system in which a measure of temperature provides a reading of proximity. Without consciously thinking about each move, the child alters his or her movements in order to stay "hot" and find the candy. Biofeedback works the same way. Monitoring devices provide a measure (a line on a graph, a blinking light, a buzzer, a tone) of autonomic physiological functions. Through a series of trial and error alterations in behavior, you strive to maintain the desired reading (a fork in the graph line, a blinking rather than a lit light, a sounding buzzer, a sounding tone).

When you control the reading, you are also controlling the automatic process being monitored. The way in which you learn to control these processes is more complex than simply changing your location to find a hidden piece of candy.

Biofeedback training was first used clinically in the 1970s. It has quickly become important to the study of stress and is a popular technique for stress reduction and relaxation training. Biofeedback is the use of any instrument or technique to monitor physiological processes and feed back a measure of their function to the individual being monitored. *The beauty of biofeedback is that it allows systems to be monitored that could not otherwise be measured.* Once given information about these functions, we can learn how to consciously alter their functioning. Learning that we can control processes formerly considered beyond conscious intervention has revolutionized our understanding of the autonomic nervous system and all our beliefs about the nature of the control we can exert over our bodies.

Biofeedback has opened up research into the mind and body relationship and the interactions that produce psychosomatic illnesses. There is still much to learn about the control we can achieve outside of the biofeedback laboratory; relaxation techniques are an excellent way of becoming aware of our own physiological processes and beginning to achieve control over them.

Two separate studies led the way for the new science of biofeedback. Both proved that people can learn to control the electrical activity on the surface of their brains and change their brain waves. Researcher Joseph Kamiya amplified signals from the surfaces of his subjects' brains and fed them back to the subjects as auditory tones. Kamiya found that subjects could learn how to slow their own brain waves to produce the tones associated with slower waves. Barbara Brown translated her subjects' alpha brain waves into blue light. The subjects were able to control their brain activity and produce alpha waves in order to keep the blue light lit. These experiments have been readily duplicated. They proved, for the first time, that feedback provided in a usable, continuous, immediate form can teach physiological skills which had been considered beyond human capacity by Western science and medicine. Eastern yogis have been able to control many of the processes for centuries.

From brain waves, researchers went on to study other autonomic functions. These functions include the movements of smooth muscles (muscles which line the blood vessels and digestive tract, for example), the heartbeat, blood pressure, and enzyme and hormone secretion. The researchers found that not only can brain waves be controlled, but so too can the contractions of smooth muscles, heart rate, digestive functions, enzyme secretion, and perhaps every function of the body, down to the minute secretion of a chemical in the brain. Biofeedback researchers are presently directing their attention to perfecting feedback techniques for brain chemical secretion, blood cell manufacture, and other processes.

How do individuals learn to control their autonomic functions? What sort of effort is involved? How does the control acquired in the laboratory carry over into everyday life? In their first session with biofeedback equipment, most people spend some time just getting used to and playing with the equipment. Heart rate is easily monitored, and heart rate feedback often provides the first biofeedback experience. The subject is usually amazed to see what his or her own heartbeat looks like on a graph. Most people are surprised at how variable heart rate is and soon realize that it is sensitive to even minor changes in posture and very slight movements. Breathing has dramatic effects on heart rate, as it does on other physiological systems; since breathing is easily controlled, subjects soon discover its effects. Further experimentation reveals that mental states have definite effects on the measurements. Thinking about anxiety-provoking incidents increases heart rate; imagining restful scenes slows the heart. A particular sort of thinking—visualizing a special scene, or even a shape or color—may facilitate a particular physiological change.

Even the most adept biofeedback subjects may not be able to describe exactly "how" they control their own physiology. Just because they can affect their autonomic processes does not mean that they can "feel" them; they do not feel the blood coursing through their veins or the moment-by-moment movement of their digestion. But they do come to identify a complex of behaviors that elicits the desired results. *Once they have learned how to control an autonomic process, people usually can duplicate the results outside of the laboratory.*

The mental attitude most conducive to successful feedback work is not determined concentration, but passive attention. It is the same state of mind that we strive to achieve in any of the stress-reduction techniques.

SKELETAL MUSCLE TENSION

Skeletal muscle tension can be measured and monitored in the biofeedback laboratory by the electromyograph (EMG) machine. This instrument registers the very sensitive electrical discharge at the junction between nerves and muscles. In order for a muscle to contract or move, the nerve must electrically stimulate it. The impulse for movement is transferred through the nerve to the muscle, which then contracts in order for movement to occur. Muscles usually contract in groups and move the bones to which they are connected.

The EMG senses the nerve impulses that trigger muscular contraction, amplifies them, and converts the amplified impulses into a form usable by the biofeedback subject. The EMG can take a millionth of a volt discharge, amplify it, and use it to flash a light, sound a tone, or move a meter; such a signal indicates increase or decrease in electrical activity, depending on how the machine is set. The EMG measures changes in electrical activity level. The sensory signal gives the subject an accurate measure of excess tension in resting muscles; this level of tension would be required for movement, but is not normal in resting muscles.

EMG sensors can be placed in proximity to any skeletal muscles so that the subject can learn how to relax tight, tense muscles anywhere in the body. For a tension headache sufferer, the sensors can be placed above the eyes to measure the tension in the forehead. The sensory signal provides instantaneous, continuous feedback of any excess tension building in the muscles. The EMG makes the subject aware of held tension which may not have previously been recognized as tension at all. When using the EMG machine, subjects discover the combination of behaviors that are effective at reducing their muscle tension. Trying to relax the forehead is often ineffective, while deep breathing and daydreaming may produce the desired effect. Only the EMG can measure very low levels of tension and give a direct reading of reductions in those levels, but the following exercises will give you feedback on your muscle tension levels.

EMG Exercise

Other people can be a wonderful source of feedback. In the Eastern tradition, the guru gives the novice student of meditation continuous feedback as to his or her progress. In my stress-reduction classes, students often help one another pinpoint and describe each other's individual stress responses. In this exercise one person acts as the subject and the other as the "EMG machine." At the end of the exercise, reverse roles so you will both have an understanding of how muscle tension feels, subjectively and objectively.

In this exercise, verbal feedback can be provided in short appraisals and directives: "Relax the wrist. Relax the elbow." Or: "Let go of this tension here in your neck. Just let me move your leg." Feedback is most effective when it is short, factual, and fairly impersonal. Do not ask questions for which verbal responses must be made; do not comment on the personality of the subject or overall tension levels. Address all feedback to the area under focus and try to determine where the tension is centered. Is it more in the upper or lower arm? Does it come and go? Is it more present with some movements than others? Are there some movements that frighten the subject and cause a reflex tensing? You might also want to try the exercise without talking, communicating only nonverbally.

Begin by being the subject and have your friend be the EMG machine. Stand, facing one another. Have your friend gently, but securely, support your arm. Attempt to relax your arm completely, employing whatever relaxation technique seems most effective. Remember that relaxation is associated with heaviness and warmth, and strive to feel these two sensations. Your friend, the EMG machine, should consider how heavy your arm feels and how much resistance is encountered when the arm is moved. A relaxed arm will feel heavy, limp, and easily manipulated.

Sit in a chair. Be sure that your body is well supported and that no undue stress is placed on your legs. Allow your friend to hold your leg just above the back of the knee and at the calf. It is usually best to work with one leg at a time, since relaxed legs are very heavy. Have the machine move your leg slowly and gently. The leg should not be pulled or jerked suddenly. Be particularly careful in bending the knee. Tension is often pronounced in the calf and some people automatically tense when the knee is flexed.

Lie on the floor or on a couch or bed, with the EMG machine behind you, cradling your head. Have the machine cup his or her hand under your head and use the other hand to support your neck. Your friend should begin to slowly rotate your neck, moving in an even motion. Movements should be gradual, with the machine slowly rotating the neck in an even motion. The EMG machine should be especially sensitive to any resistance or strain. Be aware of any tension that you feel in the head, neck, forehead, jaw, mouth, or ears. When fully relaxed, the neck will rotate freely and to a degree not possible before relaxation. The machine should be aware of any differences in flexibility from one side to the other and any knots or areas of resistance. The head will feel very heavy, almost as heavy as a bowling ball.

Now switch roles. After you have both been the EMG machine and subject, ask yourselves the following questions. Discuss them together.

Did the EMG's perception of my tension correspond to my own perception?

What resistance to complete relaxation did I encounter?

Did feeling another person's tension help me to become aware of how I carry tension in my musculature?

How did my ability to relax my arms, head, and legs in this exercise compare to my success with other stress-reduction techniques?

If there's a marked difference, does it have something to do with my relationships with other people?

Do I feel particular resistance about letting go of tension in the presence of another person?

Often your perception of tension is much different than feedback provided by another person. Another person's input may be very helpful in pinpointing areas where you hold tension. Feeling another person's tense muscles can bring you insight into your own tension. For some people, this exercise is much more effective than exercises performed alone. For others, an added resistance is associated with entrusting their arms, legs, and head to another person. If you encounter such resistance, begin to examine the connection between your stress response and various social situations. Let your reaction to this exercise provide some clues into your unique response to stress.

SKIN TEMPERATURE

Skin temperature is affected by blood flow. The fight or flight response has a dramatic effect on blood flow, sending blood away from the extremities. The smooth muscles in the walls of the arteries which supply blood to the hands and feet constrict, and the hands and feet become colder than the rest of the body. Some people have cold hands and feet all the time. With relaxation, the arteries to the hands and feet dilate and the increased flow of blood warms them; most people, when relaxed, have a skin temperature reading of at least 90 degrees Fahrenheit in their hands. Those whose habituated stress response includes constricting the smooth muscles of the arterial walls can be greatly helped by temperature training.

The temperature trainer machine senses slight changes in the circumference of the arteries which supply blood to the hands and feet. It lets the subject know when the arteries begin to constrict so that he or she can relax them, and maintain warmth in the extremities. Temperature training is especially effective for people who hold tension in the vascular system and have conditions such as migraine headache, hypertension, and Raynaud's syndrome. We are accustomed to relaxing and tensing the skeletal muscles at will, but learning to control the smooth muscles is very different. You can become aware of differences in temperature, but you probably will not be able to directly perceive the constriction or dilation of the muscles lining the arteries.

Temperature Trainer Exercise

Temperature training at home is not as precise as in the laboratory, since vascular constriction and dilation cannot be measured at home. Hand temperature can be measured by loosely holding an aquarium or photo thermometer. Make certain that the thermometer you use has a wide calibration so you can clearly read each degree; it should go to at least 95 degrees Fahrenheit. Allow a few minutes for the reading to stabilize. If the temperature is under 90 degrees Fahrenheit, then practice temperature control by attempting to raise it. You might want to employ one of the stress-reduction techniques, particularly autogenics, to warm your extremities. A reading of 93 to 95 degrees Fahrenheit feels very warm to most people and indicates deep relaxation.

If you have vascular problems, it can be very useful to take your hand temperature several times during the day under different circumstances. This can help you to identify the situations that cause tension. Once you know what makes you tense, you can begin to perfect a technique for alleviating the manifestation of that tension in your vascular system.

GALVANIC SKIN RESPONSE

Your skin responds to thoughts, emotions, and changes in the environment. Whenever you hear a noise, take a deep breath, think an emotion-charged thought, or react to phenomena around you, your skin responds. When you are tense or stimulated, you sweat more heavily; when you are relaxing or resting, you sweat less and your skin dries. *Becoming conscious of your skin's response to stress and controlling it can be useful in conquering anxiety.*

Galvanic skin response (GSR) is a measure of the skin's resistance to an electrical current. Moisture on the skin increases the electrical conductance between any two points on the skin. When conductance is increased, there is less resistance to an electrical current. A low GSR reading indicates tension: the skin is wet, conductance is high, and resistance is low. A high GSR indicates relaxation: the skin is dry, conductance is low, and resistance to the electrical current is high.

Skin response is an immediate and direct gauge of your emotional state and unconscious feelings. Your skin reacts before you are even aware of feeling the emotion which triggers it. Galvanic skin response is often used in polygraph (lie detector) tests in the belief that lying creates emotional tension. A low GSR might indicate the emotional stress of lying. In biofeedback, GSR is very useful in identifying stress-inducing situations and in helping people become more aware of their emotional responses. Even without using a machine, you can become more aware of your skin's responses to your emotions. What social situations make you perspire more? Do you ever notice that your hands are damp and sticky? When? What other symptoms accompany this response?

STOMACH ACID

The digestive tract responds to stress immediately, just like the skin. Stomach acid feedback can allow you to focus on the specific stress response that is making you ill. Acid secretion in the stomach may be increased with tension, and overproduction of stomach acid can lead to ulcers. Subjects have been able to consciously prevent oversecretion of stomach acid and heal their own ulcerated stomach linings. In stomach acid feedback, a special acid-monitoring sensor is used. You swallow the sensor and it gives instantaneous electronic signals when the acid level in your stomach changes. You can become aware of shifts in acid secretion too subtle to be sensed otherwise.

Most people do not become aware of stomach acid production until it manifests as pain or discomfort. With biofeedback you can recognize and reverse this overproduction before its symptoms are manifested. Factors that contribute to increased acid secretion can be easily recognized. You can identify the mental states and the tension-provoking situations that precipitate an attack and the particular state of mind that wards off attacks. As with all biofeedback training, the object is to take the information out of the laboratory and apply it to your daily life. In this instance, you would attempt to maintain the state of mind associated with decreased acid production and avoid the situations that lead to increased production. Although you probably will not learn to "feel" the acid secretion itself, you will identify the whole complex of feelings associated with it.

ABDOMINAL MOVEMENT

Peristalsis is a progressive wavelike movement of the smooth muscles lining the intestine. It pushes the intestinal contents along. The contractions may be regular and even or spastic and irregular. Rate of movement and regularity of each contraction have a direct bearing on the functioning of the intestine. Slow movement may be associated with constipation and rapid movement with diarrhea. Spastic, irregular movement may cause discomfort and other digestive problems.

Abdominal movement can be monitored with a stethoscope or other amplifier so that you can hear your own bowel sounds. Once you become tuned in to your own peristalsis, you can learn how to regulate it and prevent spasms. You may be able to buy a stethoscope and listen to your peristalsis outside of the biofeedback laboratory, but it would be best to begin training with a physician or biofeedback therapist who can explain what you are hearing. Sometimes just placing your hands over the area where you sense spasm allows you to focus on the contraction and alleviate the irregular movement.

HEART RATE

Heart rate can be quite easily monitored today and often is as a matter of course in the emergency room. Usually the monitor is turned away from the subject's line of vision; many doctors believe that the subject doesn't know how to interpret the reading and will just become more agitated. *Research in the biofeedback laboratory has shown that subjects can learn to regulate their own heart rates.* This is significant for people who suffer from tachycardia (irregular heartbeats). Many people experience palpitations in conjunction with anxiety; heart rate biofeedback can help you control palpitations and curtail the entire anxiety response. You can buy a stethoscope for home use; but unfortunately, hearing your own heartbeat can be disturbing and more difficult to work with than a visual display. If you are using a heartbeat monitor of any kind, always remember to slow your heart by slowing your breath and quieting yourself.

DIRECT BLOOD PRESSURE

Several methods of direct blood pressure feedback are being researched. The sphygmomanometer, an indirect method, is the standard instrument used in most doctor's offices; it may distract or even alarm the subject. Researchers would like to develop a method that does not require the cuff and provides continuous, immediate feedback. If you are suffering with hypertension and would like to be involved in biofeedback study, check with your doctor or the closest medical training institution.

BLOOD CHEMISTRY

Blood chemistry may be directly monitored in the future. The potential of this feedback is very exciting. We may be able to control the metabolic secretion of hormones and antibodies and stimulate our own blood cell production. This would be useful in correcting hormonal or chemical imbalances, as well as in stimulating production of the antibodies needed to fight particular diseases. Biofeedback information could greatly augment self-healing visualization. We would then have immediate feedback as to the effectiveness of healing visualization in releasing the appropriate immunological agents.

BRAIN ACTIVITY

The first application of biofeedback and probably the most well known is brain wave feedback. The electroencephalograph machine (EEG) senses electrical activity on the surface of the cortex. This activity is amplified and translated into a pictorial representation or a set of auditory tones. Given feedback on their own brain activity, subjects are able to alter their brain wave patterns.

The electrical activity of the brain is characterized by general wave patterns which reflect different electrical frequencies. The four major wave frequency patterns are associated with four different states of consciousness. In the course of any day, brain waves fluctuate, and all four patterns probably appear intermittently. The association between particular wave frequency patterns and states of mind is general. Certain patterns do seem to predominate during the mental activities with which they are identified, although other kinds of mental activity occur. Brain waves are measured in Hertz, units of frequency equal to one cycle per second. Beta (13–30 Hz) are usually associated with wide awake, alert, problem-solving modes of thought; theta (5–7 Hz) are associated with dreaming or creative activities; delta (.5–4 Hz) are associated with dreamless sleep. Alpha (8–12 Hz) are the most celebrated and correspond to relaxation and contemplative, meditative states.

Early brain wave researchers were interested in the association between state of mind and wave frequency. They were especially intrigued by the correspondence between pleasurable, meditative states and alpha waves. "Alpha training" came into vogue in the 1960s but had fallen out of favor by the early 1970s. Proponents of alpha training believed that alpha states were beneficial and that by inducing such waves, total relaxation was guaranteed. It is true that for most people, alpha waves are associated with deep relaxation and peaceful contemplation, but alpha waves do not always indicate generalized physiological relaxation. Some people experience alpha in meditative states in which their minds are blissfully blank, though trying to make the mind a blank does not always lead to alpha wave production. The long-term benefits claimed by the alpha wave movement have not been proven. The brain is a very complex organ and does not lend itself to either generalization or complete understanding at this time. Brain wave biofeedback holds unlimited promise.

FEEDBACK AT HOME

Of course you do not have to wait for the results of sophisticated research before you can take advantage of feedback techniques. The average household can become a feedback laboratory. You probably have a mirror, scale, thermometer, and other people at your disposal. A stethoscope and blood pressure cuff can be obtained at a medical supply store without a prescription. Used appropriately, these can provide a great deal of information about your stress levels and your unique stress response. The mirror is the most basic feedback device. It allows you to see your face where emotions and a good deal of whatever tension you are feeling are expressed. The following exercise should provide insights useful in performing every other exercise in this book.

Facing Yourself

Begin by taking a very close look at yourself. Try to forget the preconceptions you have about your own appearance. Look at yourself as if it were the first time you ever looked in a mirror. Where are the stress lines in your face? Are you holding your face in a rigid or strained position? Do your eyes look red, puffy, or tired? Are the pupils dilated or constricted? Is your jaw tight? Your mouth pinched or relaxed? How are you holding your neck and shoulders? Are you trying to burrow into your shoulders and hide? What emotion is expressed in your face? Anger? Fear? Sadness? Contentment? Boredom? Distress? Happiness?

Let your face fully express whatever you are feeling. Then let go of it. Release any tension held in your face, neck, or shoulders. Let your expression reveal relaxation. Use the mirror whenever you feel the need to verify your feelings. Be aware of how your self-image affects the way you hold your head and use your face to express emotions.

Chapter 9
Desensitization

Conquering Your Worst Fear

THE SOURCES OF OUR WORST FEARS are often just ghosts of past experiences. We dread what we think might happen in the future, but usually our fantasies are far worse than the actual events. An interesting, but sometimes disastrous, by-product of our evolved consciousness is our ability to vividly imagine situations that are not real. These conjurings can have just as powerful an effect on our bodies as real events. The mind can fool the body into believing that danger is present. The stress response triggered by our own fears and apprehensions is the same physiologically as that triggered by an actual threat.

Many of our worst fears and phobias derive from early childhood experiences. When young, we cannot always deal appropriately with our problems. We react strongly to uncomfortable or frightening events which we do not fully understand. *The defense mechanisms we build up in childhood become burdens borne by the body in adulthood.* We incorporate reactions until they become habituated. If family dinners were the scene of conflict, then we may always feel a little uneasy when we sit down to eat with others. If a parent directed a great deal of attention to our posture, we may have developed a certain rigidity in the way we hold our bodies. Not all of our fears and phobias have such obvious sources, and it may not be possible for us to discover the reasons for all of our stress responses.

That does not mean that we cannot be relieved of some of our fears and the stress that accompanies those fears.

We grow up and learn to cope more appropriately than we did as children. We try to function rationally. We try to distinguish between real threats and phantoms of our imagination. Unfortunately this may not change the way our bodies react. Just calling our fears "irrational," "silly," or "childish" does not alleviate the pain they cause us or make our bodies act differently. Trying to deny the fear when it manifests itself does not help; this can even add more stress and cause an even stronger fear reaction.

Desensitization is a technique for unlearning the fear response triggered by a particular situation. This approach can work even without isolating the cause of the first instance of the fear. Originally developed by behaviorist Joseph Wolpe, it can be practiced with the aid of a therapist or on your own. It is designed to help you reprogram yourself from a fear response to a more relaxed response to a fear-inducing situation. Desensitization must be directed to one specific fear or phobia at a time. The effects may not generalize to other fearful situations; do not expect desensitization of one phobia to alleviate all your fears.

During the desensitization process you are exposed, in reality (*in vivo* desensitization) or in fantasy, to your own feared situation. The first exposure is to the least anxiety-producing stimulus associated with the dreaded event; you progress by gradual stages to the most frightening stimulus. If severe anxiety results at one step, you may move back one or more steps and then progress forward again.

Relaxation training is a crucial prerequisite to successful desensitization. You must be able to induce a state of deep relaxation. Once relaxed you must be able to sense tension coming back into your body and be able to release that tension and return to the relaxed state. Any of the relaxation techniques that work for you would be appropriate, but I suggest that you use either progressive or autogenics because they allow you to reach a state of deep relaxation most quickly. The experience of profound relaxation must be recognizable and fairly accessible. Once you know how deep relaxation feels and can readily induce it, you are ready to begin the desensitization process.

FANTASY DESENSITIZATION

Identify your fear. Then try to isolate the aspects of the experience that are most frightening, recreating the experience in as much detail as possible. Attempt then to break down the experience into a sequence of gradually more threatening stages. *The steps will progress in order of their power to invoke a stress response.* Once you have devised this hierarchy of anxiety-producing steps, you can employ it while deeply relaxed.

Induce a state of deep relaxation. Visualize the first step in your hierarchy. This step should be the least anxiety-producing step that leads to the feared situation. If you can visualize this step while remaining relaxed, go on and imagine the next step. As soon as you begin to feel anxious, stop imagining the event and concentrate on becoming totally relaxed again. With each session, attempt to advance further in your hierarchy, getting closer and closer to imagining the actual event while remaining calm and relaxed.

Let's use public speaking as an example of a stressful situation. Almost everyone feels some anxiety about speaking in public. In many people, this anxiety is manageable and can be utilized in their own behalf, energizing them for the experience. In others this fear is so crippling that it prohibits performance. Assume that your new job demands that you periodically stand up and address a conference hall packed with people. You find the prospect absolutely terrifying. You have an immediate vision of anonymous colleagues shuffling in their chairs, listening incredulously, whispering while you speak. Some of them even get up and leave. The thought of all those eyes and ears focused on you makes you physically ill. Your body kicks into a fight or flight response at the mere mention of the possibility that you might have to give a speech.

Then the inevitable happens: someone asks you to give a speech. Immediately you experience nausea and stomach cramps, and a lump creeps into your throat that prevents you from speaking or swallowing. Your hands become cold and shaky; muscle tension starts to build in your jaw, back, and neck. You feel an overall sense of impending disaster. This life-or-death reaction is probably inappropriate. The threat of impending disaster is greatly exaggerated. After all, what is the worst thing that can happen when you give a speech? No matter what, it is unlikely that the audience is going to rush the stage and kill you. One speech, even if poorly presented, cannot ruin your career.

Your response is out of all proportion to the reality of the situation. You probably have no idea how it first occurred or when or why the pattern stuck. You do not have to know the how-when-why for the desensitization process to work, but often in the course of desensitization people actually do remember the original trauma. In this case, you can desensitize yourself so it no longer causes you so much pain and anguish. *Begin by isolating your physiological response and what triggers it.* If you can learn to control your unwarranted reaction, you may be able to cope with public speaking. After a few positive, reinforcing successes, you may even learn to enjoy it.

Establish in your mind the hierarchy of steps leading up to the actual presentation of the speech. The first stages will probably be the most hypothetical, with the speech itself placed in the remote future. Later steps will be more specific and detailed. In the final step, you should be able to see yourself successfully giving the presentation. With each session, imagine how many steps as you can before beginning to feel anxious. As soon as anxiety becomes uncomfortable, stop and reinvoke the relaxation response. The object is to be able to imagine in detail the formerly anxiety-producing scene while in a state of deep relaxation. You should come to associate the event with relaxation, and stop associating it with negative feelings. Desensitization does not always proceed in a rapid, progressive fashion. Relapses are common and should not be considered as a sign that the desensitization is not working. You may regress and feel more anxiety at a step that you have already taken in an earlier session. Give yourself plenty of time, and be patient with yourself.

In the case of public speaking, a personal hierarchy might look something like the list that follows. This is a rough idea of the major points, starting with the least threatening.

Sample Hierarchy

1. A possibility exists that I may be asked to give a speech.
2. Someone calls me and asks if I will give a speech.
3. I agree to make a speech.
4. I make the preliminary plans.
5. I write the speech.
6 I rehearse the speech in front of a mirror.
7 The publicity and announcements are mailed.
8. I perform the speech for a few close friends. Their reaction is very positive. I begin to eagerly anticipate giving the speech.
9. I go to the auditorium and rehearse the speech to an empty hall.
10. I am getting dressed to go and give the speech.
11. I am sitting on the stage waiting to give the speech.
12. I see myself confidently and calmly giving my speech. The audience is interested and friendly. I feel happy, calm, and relaxed.

Each of these steps is representative. Your own steps will be more detailed and evocative for you. *The more accurate the visualization of the circumstances, the more effective the desensitization will be.* Control over the stress response is absolutely essential; by the final sessions, you should be able to imagine yourself encountering your phobia and surviving without becoming upset. Do not expect the degree of relaxation you feel in the sessions when actually encountering the situation. There is always a little more tension associated with the real event.

IN VIVO DESENSITIZATION

In vivo desensitization applies to the technique used in fantasy desensitization, but instead of visualizing the situation you actually act out the process. If your fear is public speaking, as in the previous example, you would actually go through the process; the final stage would be making a speech in front of an audience. This technique has been used very successfully in treating phobias.

Masters and Johnson use *in vivo* desensitization in their work with sexual dysfunction. In this case, sexual intercourse is the final step in the anxiety-provoking hierarchy. Masters and Johnson break down the sexual experience into graduated steps leading to the successful performance of intercourse. At each stage, the clients attempt to maintain a state of relaxation while performing formerly anxiety-inducing acts. These acts become manageable when separated from the intense threat of coitus. In each therapeutic session, the client-couple is restricted to a defined set of behaviors. Only when the less threatening steps have been conquered can the couple move on to intercourse.

This technique has been successfully applied to other phobias, such as agoraphobia, the fear of leaving one's home. I treated an agoraphobic woman with desensitization therapy. She was in her mid-thirties and suffering so severely that she had become a prisoner in her own home. She could not go anywhere without experiencing severe anxiety attacks. It took her three attempts to keep her first appointment with me. Every time she left her home, she felt barraged by noise, cars, people, movement, and the threat of unknown events that forced her to turn around and go back. Once she described the distance from her front door to her car as mined enemy territory— anything could happen to her there. In her car she felt safer, as if the car were an extension of herself and her home.

She had always been a very insecure person. For five years, she had been married to a man who has very gregarious and ambitious. His work required that she do a great deal of socializing, and her performances as a hostess were always excruciating. Her irrational jealousy of her husband led her to suspect that he was having affairs with other women or that he would leave the house one day and never return. She would often call her husband's office three or four times a day and become very nervous if he wasn't there. She imagined his work life to be very exciting and was disappointed when he refused to share his work with her in any detail. He never took her fears or worries very seriously, but continually humored her and laughed off her concerns.

Somehow her jealousy and resentment of her husband's life out in the world turned into an intense fear of leaving her home. An ordinary trip to the supermarket threw her into terror and she had begun to make up all sorts of desperate excuses to avoid any social engagements. She trembled at the thought of having to give a dinner party.

We began working on relaxation, using the 10-to-1 Progressive Relaxation exercise. As soon as she was able to relax and could induce this state at will, she began to actually enjoy some social engagements. We also discussed her self-image; she began to feel less an extension of her husband and more her own person. Soon, other people began to comment on her new frame of mind. This immediate positive feedback was rewarding. It gave her the confidence to forge ahead in desensitization.

I had my client set up a hierarchy. Her first step was to imagine herself simply opening the door of her house and not feeling overwhelmed. I asked her to imagine that she opened the door and heard the various sounds of suburbia: birds singing, cars starting, dogs barking, children crying, muted conversation. Her second step was to imagine herself walking around the perimeter of her house to pick up the newspaper or standing and watering the front lawn without having an anxiety attack. From there we progressed to a simple trip to an uncrowded drugstore to pick up one item, then to a shopping trip to a small boutique to try on clothes, and finally to the dreaded trip to the supermarket to buy a week's worth of groceries. As soon as we had gotten comfortably past a step for several sessions, she would try to enact the step in real life.

My client successfully conquered several steps in real life and then began to realize that there were other issues behind her fear of leaving the house. The more confident she became, the more anger she felt towards her husband and the less irrationally fearful of everything else. We agreed that psychotherapy was necessary and I recommended a therapist. She had gotten to the point where she was not afraid to drive into the city alone, park, and walk the block to her therapist's office. She knew that a number of conflicts surrounded her role in the house, and her relationship to her husband needed resolution.

As the case study demonstrates, desensitization therapy breaks down the phobia into a hierarchy of stages leading to free, open-ended voyages in the outside world. The first step might be a short trip to a neighborhood drugstore, with a very limited task to fulfill. A companion might accompany you on the initial trips; solo journeys only occur when anxiety has been reduced. With a severe phobia that greatly restricts your life, it may be best to work on desensitization with the help of a therapist.

Desensitization can extend your experience of relaxation to even the most upsetting encounters of your life. Relaxation is not something to be experienced only recreationally and only under optimum conditions. *In order for your stress-reduction practice to really affect your life, you must be willing to perform the exercises even when you feel the most unnerved and incapable of sitting down and doing them.*

Sometimes people fear that they will become so relaxed that they will not respond appropriately to a real threat in their lives. If anything, learning how to control your anxiety level will allow you to respond more appropriately in a genuinely threatening situation. Relaxation does not mean that you are numb or out of touch with your body—it means that you are more aware and more in touch with yourself, other people, and your environment.

Chapter 10
Specific Ailments and Stress Reduction

Helping Yourself

EIGHTY TO 90 PERCENT OF ALL DISEASE is directly or indirectly related to stress. Stress reduction, practiced on a regular basis, can help prevent, modify, or eliminate the sources and symptoms of your physical complaints. Certain factors influence the rate of success: motivation, practice, and the willingness to "let go."

Dr. Carl Simonton's results, in his treatment of cancer patients, revealed that success rates were partially determined by the patient's attitude. Simonton found that a patient with a positive attitude toward the treatment, and an overall positive attitude toward life, had a better chance of positive results. People with negative feelings about the treatment, and life in general, had a lower rate of success.

In my own experience, I have found that people are not always motivated to continue a stress-reduction program, even when they know that the program works. A young woman, who was already an acquaintance, came to see me. Mutual friends had encouraged her to try stress reduction for her migraine headaches, but she was skeptical from the beginning. Migraines had plagued her for fifteen years; they were debilitating and often accompanied by nausea. I was determined to help her because I had had so much success with migraine patients, but I knew that motivation and willingness to give in, to go along with the technique, were all-important. Her lack of such willingness was a definite obstacle.

In our first session I taught her the basic autogenic training, and she went home to practice on her own. In our second session she reported a reduction in the frequency of her headaches, even though she had been inconsistent and resistant to her practice. The two headaches she did experience were shorter in duration and less intense than usual.

At our next session, I reiterated the importance of regular practice, and because she was a friend, spoke strongly to her of the need to perform the sequence regularly. She heeded my advice and, at our fourth and final session, reported relief and control over all her migraine symptoms, after instituting a daily program of autogenics. I reminded her to keep up the practice; she reassured me of her great pleasure at being relieved of her symptoms and left.

Several months later, I learned from mutual friends that her motivation had dropped. She had become negligent in her practice, and the headaches had recurred. For whatever reason, she had not been able to maintain a program, even when the alternative was pain.

My friend's success with autogenics was immediate, but this isn't always the case. *Relaxation is not a magic cure and is not a drug that can be taken for instant results.* It must be utilized on a daily basis and incorporated into your life. The body has disease and pain habits; stress-reduction techniques are helping you to reprogram the body. It is easy for you and your body to slip back into old habits.

Practicing once or twice a day, every day, is absolutely necessary for results. Relaxation and self-regulation come with practice, and for most, the changes are subtle; allow eight to ten weeks for the results to become noticeable. This doesn't mean that for some people the results won't be more immediate, but it is important to persevere even if you don't notice drastic changes right away. Remember again that trying too hard just creates more tension. You have to learn to "let go," and as difficult as that may be, "letting go" is the key.

WARNING: If you are suffering from any of the stress-related symptoms discussed here, it is advised that you seek the diagnosis of your physician to rule out serious physical symptoms which

may be disguised as less dangerous stress-related disorders. If you are currently taking regular medication, please discuss your use of the following behavioral techniques with your doctor. Revisions to your medication regimen may be needed when using these powerful techniques. This caution is designed not to scare you, but is offered to allow for the very best treatment to help minimize if not eliminate your symptoms of stress and anxiety.

MIGRAINE HEADACHES

Migraine headache is a severe and often debilitating vascular complaint that is relatively common. The cause of a "true migraine" is the constriction of the carotid arteries in the neck which supply blood to the head, followed by a dilation of these arteries. During the constriction, the prodrome characteristic of a true migraine occurs, followed by the severe, usually one-sided, pain of the dilation.

Most migraine patients know when a headache is coming on by the prodrome. Prodromes (presymptoms) range from flushing, dizziness, and visual aberrations to just a queer but unmistakable feeling. When you pick up the prodrome signal and respond quickly with the appropriate relaxation technique, you can often prevent the migraine.

In my practice, I have found that a regular regimen of relaxation can prevent migraine, even in people who have suffered for years. But you must set up a regular program, regardless of your symptoms; if you practice only when you already feel a headache coming on, you will find the technique less successful.

Migraine headache can be devastating, but it can also be controlled. *Eighty-five percent of the migraine patients I work with respond positively to stress-reduction practice.* The people who do not get better usually are not practicing consistently, because, for their own reasons, they are not quite ready to give up their migraines and discover a headache-free existence. I strongly recommend that migraine sufferers study the secondary gains they get from migraines and evaluate their lives to determine what needs are not being met appropriately.

Migraine Control Program

I recommend using the autogenic training phrases. Since migraine is a vascular problem, autogenics is the logical choice. By commanding blood flow to the extremities, you decrease the flow to the head and scalp and break the constriction-dilation pattern. *Control of blood flow can reduce, if not eliminate, the migraine's intensity, length, and frequency.*

Autogenics, combined with visualization, is particularly effective for migraine sufferers. Visualize an outdoor location that is calm, pleasant, and warm. Try to feel the sun shining down on your arms, hands, legs, and feet. Picture blood flowing freely and easily through the arms and legs, into the hands and feet. Warming the hands and feet is essential, and it takes time and practice to learn how to quickly feel warmth. I have included an exercise for vascular problems which you may find more effective than your own visualization. Remember to practice the exercise for at least six to twelve weeks. It can be found following Raynaud's syndrome in this chapter.

Until you can demonstrate control over blood flow, you may find an additional exercise helpful. When the prodrome occurs, stop whatever you are doing, if at all possible. Place a cold towel over your head and neck, or use an ice pack on your neck. Run warm water over your hands and feet, while breathing slowly and calmly, encouraging the warmth to circulate to your extremities. Let go of fear and tension, and allow yourself to relax.

KEYS TO CONTROLLING MIGRAINES:

- Learn slow breathing techniques to minimize stress.
- Know what conditions trigger your migraines and avoid them (if possible).
- Learn what presymptoms you experience and use these to prevent or minimize your headaches.
- Avoid being perfectionistic.

- Use biofeedback temperature monitoring for deep relaxation regularly.
  - Use a relaxation tape regularly (like *Stress Management for High Blood Pressure*).
  - Learn to warm your hands and feet to prevent headaches.

Using breathing techniques regularly will prevent stresses from building.

Breathing techniques that relax you and reduce stress in your circulatory system often can help to minimize headache activity when you catch the process early, in the prodromal stage. These techniques can also help to reduce the intensity of your headaches if they cannot be prevented.

Know your migraine triggers.

Most migraines are triggered by specific conditions such as bright lights, noise, allergic responses, certain emotions, etc. If you experience these triggers, minimize your exposure by removing yourself or shorten your stay in these environments. If you experience any prodromal symptoms, remove yourself and begin to practice your relaxation strategies and your hand/foot warming techniques (including visualizations and physically warming your hands and feet while cooling your neck and head). If you can catch your headaches early or before they start, your chances of preventing them or minimizing them are greatly improved.

Learn what your presymptoms ("prodromes") are.

Many people experience certain "feelings" that are commonly perceived before the onset of their migraine headaches. These might be visual cues, certain "odd" feelings, or even pressures in their head or face. If you have identified these patterns (not every migraine sufferer has these), you can use them to stop or to minimize your headache pattern from developing. Stop when you feel these symptoms occurring and take preventive measures like relaxation and hand/foot warming to reduce possible headaches from occurring or becoming worse.

Use the *Stress Management for High Blood Pressure* tape one to three times per day for eight to twelve weeks.
You can order this tape from the Stress Education Center; see the contact information in the back of this book. These relaxation strategies will assist you in developing the skills necessary to prevent or to lessen migraine headaches. Use temperature training biofeedback to learn to warm your hands and feet. It requires repetition and time to learn how to "let go," enabling you to warm your hands to 93 to 95 degrees and then learn to warm your feet to 90 degrees. This mastery over blood flow will offer you the ability to control vascular migraine headaches when you catch them early. Used preventively, this skill will help you minimize the risks that allow the onset and development of your headache pattern.

Regular exercise will help you work off the effects of life's stresses.
Try to elevate your heart rate for fifteen to forty-five minutes three to five times per week. Check with your doctor before beginning an exercise program if you have been inactive for a long while. The release of tensions and the strengthening of your cardiovascular system will have great benefits. This improved circulation will assist you in preventing migraine headaches or offer learned responses that will minimize headaches in duration and intensity.

Eat regular meals.
Proper nutrition can prevent the body's response to stress. Avoid foods that might trigger your headaches.

HYPERTENSION (HIGH BLOOD PRESSURE)

Hypertension is not just a disease of aging. Young men and women can suffer from its damaging, sometimes deadly, effects. Please do not take this condition lightly. Get it treated as soon as possible before it creates lasting damage and adversely affects your life as you age.

Standard medical procedures today are being accompanied by relatively new behavioral approaches for treating conditions such as chronic pain and essential hypertension. These problems frustrate traditional medical practices and are expensive in both money and time lost from work.

High blood pressure, also called hypertension, is potentially fatal. Every year high blood pressure kills 60,000 people. It can lead to other serious health problems such as heart disease, stroke, kidney and liver disease, and arteriosclerosis.

High blood pressure is a dangerous, widespread disease affecting at least 15 percent of the adult population in the United States. *It is rarely caused by any single organic condition and is more often attributable to a whole complex of emotional and physical factors.* Hypertension is not to be treated lightly; medical attention and opinion cannot be replaced. Chronic hypertension can be asymptomatic and still damage the heart, liver, kidneys, and other organs. Untreated, it can precipitate stroke and heart attack. Consult your doctor; even get second and third opinions about your health. Whatever you do, don't drag your feet.

The need for treatment of this condition is an absolute necessity, and, unfortunately, physicians have problems treating this symptom effectively. Only about 30 percent of hypertension is caused by permanent physical factors such as hardening of the arteries (arteriosclerosis) or kidney damage. Because such physical problems offer little possibility of reversal, treating this disease before it creates permanent damage is essential.

The cause of 70 percent of high blood pressure is much less definite. Emotional, unconscious responses usually cause elevations in blood pressure. To understand the mechanism that occurs to elevate blood pressure because of emotional responses requires that the fight or flight response be understood. When excited by a stressor, the body will do several things which can raise the blood pressure. First, certain hormones are released, such as epinephrine and norepinephrine, which causes an elevation of heart rate and the constriction of many blood vessels. The sympathetic nervous system which controls the fight or flight response is responsible for the release of these hormones, and also will elevate the heart rate, therefore elevating blood pressure itself through direct nervous stimulation.

Seventy percent of all hypertension is diagnosed as "essential" hypertension, meaning that the doctor cannot find any organic cause. Some patients say, "I'm not worried. My blood pressure only goes up in the doctor's office." The situation, particularly that of the doctor's office, and your fear and apprehension can raise your blood pressure. It has been estimated that blood pressure rises as much as thirty points in the doctor's office, but it is unlikely that visiting the doctor is the only event that merits that response. The elevation in blood pressure you experience while trembling in the pressure cuff indicates that you respond to stress with an elevation in blood pressure. It also indicates that you hold tension in your vascular system. Holding tension in any physiological system on a regular basis can only weaken it.

It is important to remember that the blood flow patterns of the body are changed when responding to stress. For many people, the blood is redirected away from the extremities and abdomen into major muscle groups and to the central nervous system. As this redirection occurs, the vasoconstriction to the extremities can be monitored and can have direct bearing on the elevation of blood pressure. For this reason, tranquilizers, muscle relaxants, diuretics (to reduce blood volume), and a new series of chemical agents called beta blockers are often prescribed for treating and reducing hypertension. (Beta blockers are drugs that act to reduce the heart's output or to reduce resistance in blood vessels of the extremities. This is chemically induced stress reduction for the cardiovascular system.)

The problem with any of these medications is that they can create negative side effects, and these can be so unpleasant that the patient may stop taking the medication altogether and let the high blood pressure go unchecked. This is dangerous!

Another treatment for high blood pressure is the patient-responsibility approach that encourages change in lifestyle and change in personal response to emotional situations. Proper diet and physical exercise are key factors in conquering heart disease and have long been recognized as the best long-term remedies for treating hypertension. The use of stress management strategies to control the stress response is a technique gaining wide support. Awareness, relaxation, and response management are parts of a good stress control program.

People under a doctor's care for high blood pressure should inform their doctors that they are following a relaxation program. Since doctors often prescribe medication for this type of dysfunction, they must be informed so that medication levels can be periodically checked.

Hypertension Control Program

Since hypertension is a vascular problem, autogenics is a good technique. The special Relaxation for Vascular Complaints (found later in this chapter) works especially well. Progressive relaxation is also valuable; tension in your musculature probably contributes to your vascular dysfunction. Many people have had remarkable success using meditation. Zen-like active meditation combined with a long walk may be helpful; begin with short distances and increase your distance over time. While performing the combined autogenic and visualization exercise, focus on the blood flowing freely and easily throughout your body. Picture your blood vessels dilated and unobstructed. Generating warmth in your extremities will help, as will imagining yourself totally calm, peaceful, and relaxed.

Hypertension often responds to deep breathing exercises. Try to slow your rhythm of respiration. Do not starve yourself of oxygen or hold your breath; just slow and deepen your normal breathing rhythm. The 1-to-4 Count exercise in the chapter on breathing will slow your breath to four or five complete breaths per minute. Five to twenty minutes of this type of breathing can reduce your heart rate, and quite possibly, significantly lower your blood pressure.

If your high blood pressure is linked to particular situations that are unavoidable, then desensitization to the experience may be worthwhile. Read the chapter on desensitization and try following the program, changing it to meet your specific needs.

A relatively recent additional therapy has also been given much credence in the fight against hypertension. This is the use of biofeedback along with regular blood pressure checks, in the home, and the practice of relaxation techniques on a regular daily basis. Biofeedback is the use of instruments or techniques to monitor the changes within the body that are usually related to the stress response pattern. After these responses are monitored, the information is then offered to the individual, who learns to control these responses in a more positive way.

Temperature training, which is used to measure the changes of temperature of the skin of the hands and feet, is a simple but powerful tool to combat hypertension. When relaxed physically and emotionally a person should have a hand temperature above 90 degrees Fahrenheit. When you are completely relaxed, this can go up to 93 to 95 degrees in the hands and 90 degrees measured at the feet below the big toe.

If this can be done consistently by practicing relaxation techniques, then chances are excellent that blood pressure can be controlled. Remember that this control indicates that blood flow is not restricted by the stress response, so the blood pressure will drop and medication can be reduced—and often eliminated—under the care of a physician.

The difference between this new technique and the ones discussed earlier in the book is that specific criteria for both hand and foot warming are requested for true vascular control. Additionally, the regular daily monitoring of blood pressure and modification to lifestyle such as reducing time consciousness (self-pressuring) helps to increase awareness and control.

It sounds very simple, but it can take twelve to fifteen weeks to master the skill of relaxation so that the hands and the feet indicate a relaxed state of even blood flow. The patient learns to control the sympathetic nervous system's response to stress. Relaxation then can generalize to control of the internal mechanism that creates the high blood pressure.

As an example of this technique, Bob was referred to me by his slightly skeptical physician. The idea of biofeedback and behavioral changes controlling his blood pressure problem were not entirely the doctor's idea. Bob had pressured his doctor because of poor results with medication and its negative side effects.

Bob's high motivation to get off the medication definitely worked in his favor. He began regular relaxation practice on a daily basis, as well as self blood pressure checks and home temperature biofeedback. After experimenting for several weeks to determine the best relaxation format, he settled in to consistent practice. Bob discovered that he did not have to get so uptight at work or at home about the little things that had plagued him. He noticed that his blood pressure readings began to drop and his hand and foot temperatures began to climb during the relaxation practice.

In eight weeks he returned to his physician to show his progress of homework forms reflecting reduced blood pressure. Even his blood pressure taken in the doctor's office had dropped significantly. So he discussed reducing his medication needs with his doctor, and together they decided on a gradual highly monitored plan for withdrawal from medication. With the help of his doctor and continued daily relaxation and home monitoring, he worked his way off all medication.

Bob called me some months later to tell me of his pleasure with living medication and side effect free. This is not a random case, for with the additional parameters of specific training criteria the success rate reaches close to 90 percent with the motivated person.

KEYS TO CONTROLLING HIGH BLOOD PRESSURE:

- Breathe slowly.
- Use biofeedback temperature monitoring for deep relaxation regularly.
  - Use a relaxation tape regularly (like *Stress Management for High Blood Pressure*).
  - Learn to warm your hands and feet.
- Exercise aerobically and regularly.
- Avoid caffeine and other stimulants.
- Remain in the present, in your body, and in a positive frame of mind.
- Taper your high blood pressure medication after you have mastered the relaxation-biofeedback under your physician's care.

Learn to breathe diaphragmatically.
Place a hand over your upper abdomen. Push your abdomen out as you inhale. Let your abdomen move in as you exhale. Let your chest, shoulders, neck, and back relax as you breathe. Only on a very deep breath should these parts move in the breath. This may be the most important hypertension technique you can learn!

By linking one deep breath to a reoccurring work event like a telephone ringing or checking the time, you remember to take these slow deep breaths throughout your work schedule to avoid letting tensions build to painful or distracting levels. The secret is to check in with your body in the present moment, relax your major muscles, and slow and deepen your breath. This simple exercise can have miraculous results.

Other breathing techniques involve a short series of deep slow breaths, where you count as you breathe. Try counting slowly *1* to *4* as you inhale, pause and hold your breath as you count *1* to *4* again, and then release slowly, but completely, as you count *1* to *8*. After four of these breaths you will be breathing easier and better able to control your body's pattern of holding tension. This process can in turn help you to control your hypertension.

Use the *Stress Management for High Blood Pressure* tape one to three times per day for eight to twelve weeks.

You can order this tape from the Stress Education Center; see the contact information in the back of this book. This relaxation exercise has been especially created for controlling stress-related high blood pressure. It is taken from the basic formula created for the chapter on aging in *Stress Passages: Surviving Life's Transitions Gracefully* (my second book from Celestial Arts). Use the StressDots or any other temperature training biofeedback device to learn how to warm your hands with relaxation. When you can consistently get above 90 degrees Fahrenheit (93 to 95 degrees is ideal), then you can begin to master warming your feet to 90 degrees. When you can let go by relaxing and warming your hands and feet, you will be able to control, if not prevent, your stress-related high blood pressure episodes. Then you must develop confidence in your control so the high blood pressure does not control your life.

Regular exercise will help you work off the effects of life's stresses. Try to elevate your heart rate for fifteen to forty-five minutes three to five times per week. Check with your doctor before beginning an exercise program if you have been inactive for a long while. The release of tensions and the strengthening of your cardiovascular system will have great benefits. This can improve circulation and so can help to reduce your blood pressure.

Eat regular meals.

Low-fat and complex carbohydrates are better than fast foods with lots of sugar. Avoid caffeine and other stimulants. Caffeine is found in coffee, black teas, cola drinks, chocolate, some over-the-counter pain medications, and other foods and drugs. Read labels. Eat lots of fruits, vegetables, whole grains, and other natural foods.

Live in the present.

Many people with high blood pressure have trouble maintaining their thoughts in present time for focusing on their bodies in positive ways. Fears or angers from the past or apprehensions about the future seem to take up too much of their consciousness. Living in the present, letting go of negative emotions, and letting life's daily dramas roll off you are all important skills to develop.

Taper your high blood pressure medication after you have mastered the relaxation-biofeedback, under your physician's care.

After you have learned to let go through relaxation and biofeedback training, you can monitor your blood pressure at home. When you have developed the skills of hand and foot warming, you will find that your blood pressure drops down to more normal ranges. Write these home blood pressure measurements down regularly to show to your doctor. In the doctor's office your blood pressure may still be higher than you like. Many people have "white coat syndrome" where their blood pressure will be ten to fifteen points higher in the doctor's office than it is at home. With your doctor's agreement and assistance you may be able to begin reducing your high blood pressure medication(s). Any changes to your normal medication may elevate your blood pressure, so reduce these medications slowly, in gradual steps.

Insomnia or problems with sleeping may affect your high blood pressure as well. If this is an issue for you, you may want to read the section on sleeping disorders and use the special tape at bedtime to help you get to sleep and so rest better.

You may also want to read the chapter on meditation from this book. The exercise entitled Shavasana, taken from yoga, has been researched and proven helpful in reducing blood pressure over twelve to twenty weeks.

RAYNAUD'S SYNDROME (COLD HANDS AND FEET) AND VASCULAR COMPLAINTS

Raynaud's syndrome is a relatively new name for a condition that has troubled people for years, increasing in occurrence with the stress in our society. Unconscious constriction of the blood flow to the extremities causes cold hands and feet; in some cases, red, white, or blue discoloration of the skin may occur; severe cases may result in gangrene. Some sufferers of Raynaud's experience pain, numbness, and a tingling sensation. The arteries that flow to the extremities, and occasionally the abdomen, are constricted; as in other vascular dysfunctions, tension plays a large role in Raynaud's syndrome.

I treated a high school chemistry teacher suffering from Raynaud's. The condition had come on rather suddenly. Cold hands especially bothered her in the morning when driving to work; her hands often became numb on the steering wheel. During class lectures, she had trouble holding onto the chalk, her hands were so cold. When she came into my office one morning, she seemed calm and poised. Her tension was only discernable in her hand temperature, which I measured at 66 degrees.

We started with the autogenic training phrases, emphasizing the sensations of warmth. As we went over the phrases, her hands began to get warmer. She was hooked up to a biofeedback thermometer so she could see her own degree of success. By the third time through the phrases, her hands were warmed to a temperature of 95 degrees, almost a 30-degree increase in just one session. She continued to work with me and greatly alleviated the condition. Of course, the initial, intense session with biofeedback helped.

Raynaud's Syndrome and Vascular Complaint Control Program

I recommend autogenics, visualization, and temperature-training biofeedback as relaxation therapy for this complaint. Always focus on warmth. Generating warmth is difficult for most people, and all the more difficult for those who manifest stress in restricted blood flow. Some Raynaud's patients have acquired considerable control over the temperature of their hands and feet. They even learn a sort of physiological gymnastics, by which they can warm one hand and cool the other, or even cool one side of the hand, and warm the other by as much as 10 degrees. Maybe someday an Olympics of Physiological Control will be held. Try the exercise that follows, and you might be competing for the gold medal.

You probably don't have a biofeedback device at home, but you can still measure and monitor your own temperature. Hold a photo or aquarium thermometer loosely in your hand. Wait for the temperature to stabilize. Keep track of your temperature before and after completing a warming exercise. Try this with the relaxation exercise that follows.

Relaxation for Vascular Complaints

This exercise is available at www.dstress.com. Look for Tape #203.

This exercise is a combination of autogenics and visualization, especially designed for people with migraine headaches, high blood pressure, Raynaud's syndrome, and other vascular complaints. It may be beneficial to have someone read you the exercise for the first few weeks, or you may wish to tape it. You should eventually learn to do the exercise by yourself, without any outside assistance.

Begin by getting into a comfortable position. It is crucial that there is no pressure or strain on your head or neck. Allow yourself to begin to relax by taking one deep, slow breath. Pause for a moment after you inhale, and then exhale, fully and completely. Now, just continue to breathe, slowly and naturally. Imagine that with each and every breath, as you exhale, you release more and more stored tension, and allow yourself to relax even more.

As you continue to breathe slowly and naturally, begin to relax all the muscles throughout your body. Allow them to let go, to go loose and limp. Begin by focusing on your arms and hands. Become aware of your upper arms, and breathe away the tension, as you let your upper arms go loose and limp. Relax your elbows, and let the relaxation spread down into your lower arms and wrists. Remember to breathe slowly and naturally. Slowly breathe away the tension, and now relax your hands and your fingers. As you continue to breathe calmly and slowly, experience the increasing heaviness of your arms and hands, as you just let go of the tension, and allow your arms to relax more fully and completely.

Gently turn your attention to your feet and legs. Allow your feet and your legs to relax, and let the muscles go loose and limp. Become aware of your toes, and let them relax more and more, with each and every breath. Allow the tension in the balls of your feet and in your arches to just flow from you as you exhale, fully and completely. As the tension melts away from your feet, let the relaxation spread up into your ankles and lower legs. Let go of the muscles around your knees and your upper legs. Breathe slowly and naturally, feeling the muscles relaxing, going loose and limp. Experience the sensation of sinking into whatever you are sitting or lying upon. The muscles of your feet and your legs relax even further. Let yourself drift deeper into relaxation, controlling the tension by slowly breathing it away and just letting it go out of your body with each exhalation.

Let the relaxation spread up into your pelvic area, up into your back. Allow all the muscles of your legs and your pelvic area to relax completely, just letting go, sinking in as the tension melts away. As you continue to breathe slowly and naturally, the relaxation spreads into your back, allowing the muscles around your shoulder blades to go loose and limp. The muscles on both sides of your spine relax, all the way down into your lower back. Let your shoulders relax by allowing them to drop into a comfortable position, just letting go of the tension and allowing these muscles to go loose and limp.

Slowly and gently turn your attention to your chest and your abdominal region, while breathing calmly and naturally. Let all the muscles of your rib cage relax, letting that sense of calmness and relaxation spread into your abdomen. Realize that your heartbeat is calm and regular, and your breathing is calm and regular. As you continue to breathe slowly and calmly, your whole being sinks deeper into the chair or bed, as the tension melts away, being replaced by calmness and relaxation. Allow yourself to drift deeper into complete, calm relaxation.

Allow your neck and shoulders to relax even more, letting your head just rest on the pillow or chair. As the muscles go loose and limp, your head sinks in, and the muscles of your neck stretch gently and completely into total relaxation. This relaxation spreads to the muscles in the back of your head, as you slowly breathe away the tension from the muscles in the top and the sides of your head. As your forehead goes calm and smooth, you let go of the tension in your eyes. The relaxation spreads to your mouth, and your jaw and your tongue drop. Just let them go completely loose and limp. Become aware of the calm relaxation that is spreading to every cell in your body, with each and every breath.

Say to yourself: **"My right arm is heavy."** Just let your arm become heavy as you let go of the tension. Now say to yourself: **"My left arm is heavy. My right leg is heavy. My left leg is heavy. My neck and shoulders are heavy."** As you continue to breathe slowly and calmly, say to yourself: **"My right arm is warm."** Imagine blood flowing, freely and easily, through your arm and into your hand, and say to yourself: **"My right arm is warm."** Feel the pulsations of your heart in your fingertips, as the blood flows freely and easily into your hand. Say to yourself: **"My**

left arm is warm. My left arm is warm." Allow the relaxation and warmth to spread throughout your arms and into your hands.

Say to yourself: **"My right leg is warm."** Completely relaxed and wide-open blood vessels carry the blood freely and easily into your legs and into your feet, while you just let go and allow the warmth to spread. **"My right leg is warm. My left leg is warm."** Feel the pulse spreading down into your legs and your feet and your toes. Let go, and feel the blood flow freely and easily, saying to yourself: **"My right leg is warm; my left leg is warm."** Breathe slowly and naturally, allowing your breath to spread warmth with each and every inhalation.

Relax the muscles of your neck and shoulders, and say to yourself: **"My neck and shoulders are warm. My neck and shoulders are warm."** Now say: **"My heartbeat is calm and regular. My heartbeat is calm and regular."** Become aware of the calm warmth that is gently spreading throughout your body, slowly and easily spreading to every cell of your being. Say to yourself: **"My breathing is calm and regular. My breathing is calm and regular."** Allow yourself to drift deeper into a state of calmness and relaxation; feel what it's like to completely let go. Allow yourself to breathe the tension, completely and slowly, away and out of your body.

Imagine yourself outdoors on a calm and beautiful day. You are in your favorite locale, all alone, and not influenced by any distractions. Pick a comfortable place to lie down, and as you slowly drift over to that spot, make yourself completely comfortable. Feel yourself sinking into the earth, floating in a sea of calm relaxation as the tension melts away. Let yourself drift deeper into a dreamlike state of calmness and relaxation.

Feel the warmth of the golden sunlight as it gently shines down on your arms and hands. Feel the warm rays of the sunlight sinking deep within you. Let the warm breezes warm your feet and your legs, as the sunlight and warmth sinks into your feet, deep within the muscles. Imagine that you can breathe in the golden sunlight and warmth; slowly the warmth spreads freely and easily to every cell in your body. With each breath, feel the energy flowing freely and slowly throughout your being, easily and gently spreading to every cell of your body.

Remember that any time you wish to, you can relax deeply and completely by slowing your breath and breathing away the tensions. By allowing yourself to let go and relax, you are healing and restoring yourself. Every time you practice this exercise, you will be able to do it better and better, be able to relax more deeply, be able to relax more easily and more quickly. Allow yourself to feel the relaxation and the warmth in your arms and hands and in your legs and feet, more and more, every time you practice. Take just a few moments and feel the calmness and relaxation, as you continue to focus on breathing slowly and calmly.

Now, begin to bring yourself back from this state of deep relaxation. Gently bring yourself up and out of relaxation, and let the calmness and relaxation carry over into a fully alert state. Let the relaxation carry over throughout your day and throughout your week. Gently bring yourself away from your visualization and back to the feeling of the chair or the bed beneath you. Say to yourself: **"I am refreshed and alert. I am refreshed and alert."** When you wish to be fully alert, take a deep, full breath and stretch, letting yourself become wide awake. Allow the feelings of calmness and relaxation to carry over with you into a fully alert state. Take another deep breath, stretch, and become completely alert.

KEYS TO CONTROLLING RAYNAUD'S AND VASCULAR COMPLAINTS:

- Learn slow breathing techniques to minimize stress.
- Use biofeedback temperature monitoring for deep relaxation regularly.
  - Use a relaxation tape regularly (like *Stress Management for High Blood Pressure*).
  - Learn to warm your hands and feet to lessen your Raynaud's.

- Regular exercise can help prevent these complaints.
- Reduce your emotional triggers if these are a factor in your symptom activity.

Using breathing techniques regularly will prevent stresses from building.
Breathing techniques can relax you and reduce stress in your circulatory system. These techniques can also help to reduce the intensity of your symptoms if they cannot be prevented.

Use the *Stress Management for High Blood Pressure* tape one to three times per day for eight to twelve weeks.
You can order this tape from the Stress Education Center; see the contact information in the back of this book. These relaxation strategies will assist you in developing the skills necessary to prevent or to lessen your Raynaud's. Use temperature training biofeedback to learn to warm your hands and feet. It requires repetition and time to learn how to "let go," enabling you to warm your hands to 93 to 95 degrees and then learn to warm your feet to 90 degrees. This mastery over blood flow will offer you the ability to control vascular challenges. Used preventively, this skill will help you minimize the risks that allow the onset and development of your vascular complaint.

Regular exercise will help you work off the effects of life's stresses.
Try to elevate your heart rate for fifteen to forty-five minutes three to five times per week. Check with your doctor before beginning an exercise program if you have been inactive for a long while. The release of tensions and the strengthening of your cardiovascular system will have great benefits. This improved circulation will assist you in preventing vascular problems.

Eat regular meals.
Proper nutrition can prevent the body's response to stress that can make your vascular complaints worse.

Reduce your emotional triggers if these are a factor in your symptom activity.

Perfectionism, repressed anger, and anxiety can all be potential triggers that either create vascular symptoms or make them worse. Get help in identifying these issues and seek out support as you work through them to find more appropriate ways to respond when these emotional states are triggered.

TENSION HEADACHE

Turn on your television set, and you will be besieged by commercials extolling the benefits of over-the-counter medications. One will combat the effects of fatigue; one will stop the "heartbreak of psoriasis"; and yet another will stamp out acid indigestion. Yet, far more patent headache medications are advertised than any other nonprescription drug.

Tension headache is the most common symptom of stress in our society. Muscle tension in the neck and shoulders, around the eyes, and in the jaw, often results in a throbbing tension headache. Tension may begin affecting you subtly; most people are not even aware that an energy-robbing headache is in the making. People start holding tension in their musculature as soon as they get out of bed in the morning, and by the beginning of the afternoon they have a worrisome, nagging, creeping headache. By evening they are holding their heads and looking for relief.

I usually buy my office supplies at the same store and often from the same salesperson. One day I noticed that he seemed irritable and asked if there was some way that I could help. He then told me that he had been getting excruciating tension headaches almost every day. Since I happened to have a tape of the 10-to-1 Passive Progressive Relaxation exercise with me, I suggested that he practice it daily and explained that it was important to become aware of the tension and learn to let go of it. Two weeks later, I returned to buy more office supplies. He was very pleased with the tape; control of tension headache had become possible for him. Any time he felt a headache coming on, he would take a few moments to relax. If possible, he would put on the tape and listen to it, even if he only had a few minutes. Awareness, letting go, and practice had worked for him.

Tension Headache Control Program

Knowledge of what triggers your stress response and where it manifests itself, and the realization that you can control muscle tension, is half the battle for stress reduction. The other 50 percent is learning to reduce or release the tension. Prevention is the best remedy. If you practice stress reduction for about twenty minutes a day on a regular basis, the number of headaches you get should decrease radically. For some people, this is enough to wipe out any tension headache problem. This may also be sufficient to alleviate other muscle tension complaints, such as back pain, muscle spasms, or tics.

Progressive relaxation deals directly with your muscles; some form of this exercise is recommended if you are commonly afflicted by muscle tension pain. Autogenic training phrases are also powerful control tools, and in combination with progressive relaxation and visualization, can be the most beneficial exercise of all. Breathing exercises will make you more aware of building tension levels, while continually releasing excess stress. The gentle movement exercises can be practiced just about anywhere and are excellent for reducing excess muscle tension. Just remember that stress-reduction practice will not only help you prevent or control your headaches; it will positively affect your emotional state as well.

KEYS TO CONTROLLING TENSION HEADACHES:

- Learn slow breathing techniques to minimize stress.
- Use EMG biofeedback monitoring for deep relaxation of your muscles regularly.
  - Use a relaxation tape regularly (like *Stress Management for Chronic Pain* or *10-to-1 Countdown*).
  - Learn to relax your jaw, forehead, and neck/shoulders.

- Regular exercise can help prevent these complaints.
- Reduce your emotional triggers if these are a factor in your symptom activity.

Using breathing techniques regularly will prevent stresses from building.
Breathing techniques can relax you and reduce stress in your muscles. These techniques can also help to reduce the intensity of your symptoms if they cannot be prevented.

Use the *Stress Management for Chronic Pain* tape one to three times per day for eight to twelve weeks.
You can order this tape from the Stress Education Center; see the contact information in the back of this book. These relaxation strategies will assist you in developing the skills necessary to prevent or to lessen your tension headaches. Use EMG training biofeedback to learn to relax the muscles of your jaw, forehead, and neck/shoulders. It requires repetition and time to learn how to "let go," enabling you to relax these muscle groups. Used preventively, this skill will help you minimize the risks that allow the onset and development of your tension headaches.

Regular exercise will help you work off the effects of life's stresses.
Try to elevate your heart rate for fifteen to forty-five minutes three to five times per week. Check with your doctor before beginning an exercise program if you have been inactive for a long while. The release of tensions and the strengthening of your cardiovascular system will have great benefits. This improved circulation will assist you in preventing the building of stresses that may trigger your tension headaches.

Eat regular meals.
Proper nutrition can prevent the body's response to stress. Avoid caffeine when you are stressed or susceptible to headaches because caffeine can trigger the muscle tension that leads to headaches and

increased levels of pain. Caffeine also will prevent you from sleeping deeply and restfully, which can trigger headaches.

Reduce your emotional triggers if these are a factor in your symptom activity.

Perfectionism (or needing to control most situations), repressed anger, and anxiety can all be potential triggers that either create tension headaches or make them worse. Get help in identifying these issues and seek out support as you work through them to find more appropriate ways to respond when these emotional states are triggered. Look for the issues that cause you to be "uptight" and can lead to you holding tension in your jaw or neck/shoulders.

BACK PAIN

After tension headache, back pain is the most common form of tension pain in this country. Lack of exercise, or underexercise, can be a contributing factor in persistent back pain, and a combination of stress-reduction techniques and appropriate exercise can be most beneficial. Often specific muscle groups may not be strong enough to support your body weight; the addition of environmental and emotional stress which tenses these weak muscles results in pain. A stiff neck, pain between your shoulder blades, lower back pain, and even a tension headache can result from stiff and weakened back muscles. Weakness in other parts of your musculature can also be a contributing factor. If your abdominal muscles are weak, which often occurs after pregnancy, you may suffer lower back pain. Compounded by the tension of taking care of an infant, this back pain may become excruciating.

I once treated a bank executive for persistent lower back pain. His doctor had checked him thoroughly, and after ruling out a disc problem, sent him to me for relaxation therapy. As the pain was located only on his right side, I questioned him about his work habits and discovered that he always kept the phone on his right side; he was right-handed and always answered the phone with his right hand. I suggested that he switch the phone to his left side and always pick up the phone in his left hand, for the time being. I also requested that he take one deep, full breath before answering the phone. The physician had recommended a specific exercise program, and I combined this program with autogenics and progressive relaxation. I instructed him to start switching his telephone from side to side after one week of keeping it on his left. He religiously followed the program and, after one month of practice, was rarely experiencing any lower back pain. Then, he had a setback. Since he had been doing so well and was obviously practicing the exercises, neither his doctor nor I could understand what had triggered his relapse. Upon questioning, it all became quite clear.

Before he had started having trouble with his back, he had played tennis three or four times a week. Under a lot of pressure at work, he had played tennis for relaxation. After his back pain subsided, he started playing again; it was after only three days of tennis that his back started to hurt again. We talked about his tennis partners, when he played, and for how long. Flabbergasted, he realized that the tennis was adding to his tension, not reducing it as he had originally thought. His partners were all co-workers, and they often discussed work after they played; he often had a match on days when the tension at work was the worst. He was not a young man, but prided himself on consistently beating younger men who had been playing for longer than he had. I asked him if he stopped when he was tired or continued playing to the point of exhaustion. He laughed and said he played until the game was over, tired or not. I recommend that he stop playing tennis for three months and continue with his exercise program and relaxation techniques. Once again, the pain subsided. After three months he started playing tennis again; now, he played with his wife or children and stopped when he became tired. The back pain only rarely occurred, and only when he was under extreme pressure.

Back Pain Control Program

If you are suffering back pain, always make certain that you check with your physician before instituting any physical exercise program. Not all kinds of exercise may be beneficial. Some sports, such as football or golf, which may add stress to your life, may actually be harmful. Read the chapter on physical exercise for more information. *Backache, Stress and Tension,* by Dr. Hans Kraus, outlines a complete exercise program for people who suffer back pain. Included is the Kraus-Weber self-test, which will help you determine if any part of your muscle system is too weak to support your body weight. Specific exercise plans are keyed to specific problems and will help you develop or exercise any weak area.

Practice autogenic training, combined with progressive relaxation in conjunction with physical exercise. Concentrate on heaviness in your limbs and muscles while doing autogenics. Use passive progressive, since active progressive may tighten your muscles even more. Once again, motivation is a key factor in your success at eliminating back pain. Backaches are controllable, but it's up to you to exercise that control.

KEYS TO CONTROLLING BACK PAIN:

- Learn slow breathing techniques to minimize stress.
- Use EMG biofeedback monitoring for deep relaxation of your muscles regularly.
  - Use a relaxation tape regularly (like *Stress Management for Chronic Pain* or *10-to-1 Countdown*).
  - Learn to relax your lower back and neck/shoulders.
- Regular exercise can help prevent these complaints.
- Reduce your emotional triggers if these are a factor in your symptom activity.

Using breathing techniques regularly will prevent stresses from building.

Breathing techniques can relax you and reduce stress in your muscles. These techniques can also help to reduce the intensity of your symptoms if they cannot be prevented.

Use the *Stress Management for Chronic Pain* tape one to three times per day for eight to twelve weeks.

You can order this tape from the Stress Education Center; see the contact information in the back of this book. These relaxation strategies will assist you in developing the skills necessary to prevent or to lessen your back pain. Use EMG training biofeedback to learn to relax the muscles of your lower back and neck/shoulders. It requires repetition and time to learn how to "let go," enabling you to relax these muscle groups. Used preventively, this skill will help you minimize the risks that allow the onset and development of your back pain.

Regular exercise will help you work off the effects of life's stresses.

Try to elevate your heart rate for fifteen to forty-five minutes three to five times per week. Check with your doctor before beginning an exercise program if you have been inactive for a long while. The release of tensions and the strengthening of your cardiovascular system will have great benefits. This improved circulation will assist you in preventing the tensions from building that may trigger your back pain. Learn to relax and stretch the muscles of the backs of your upper legs.

Eat regular meals.

Proper nutrition can prevent the body's response to stress. Avoid caffeine when you are stressed or susceptible to back pain because caffeine can trigger the muscle tension that leads to increased levels of pain. Caffeine also will prevent you from sleeping deeply and restfully, which can trigger back pain.

Reduce your emotional triggers if these are a factor in your symptom activity.

Perfectionism (or needing to control most situations), repressed anger, and anxiety can all be potential triggers that either create back pain or make it worse. Get help in identifying these issues and seek out support as you work through them to find more appropriate ways to respond when these emotional states are triggered. Look for the issues that cause you to be "uptight" and can lead to you holding tension in your lower back or neck/shoulders.

Develop a sense that you do have control of your back pain.

This is not easy in the beginning, but the behavioral techniques can help you to minimize the intensity of your back pain, if not eliminate it. Many people feel "out of control" when their pain becomes chronic. This can make the intensity of the pain worse because you have fear and anxiety regarding these ongoing challenges. Temperature training biofeedback can help you to learn to relax and to "let go" of the anxiety that can intensify your complaints.

CHRONIC PAIN

Chronic pain ailments are very expensive and difficult to treat. The expense is both in quality of life and interference with productivity. The difficulties arise from the frustrations of dealing with a physical problem that does not seem to go away and the medical/insurance system that does not deal in a positive, productive way with a lot of chronic pain problems. In most cases, chronic pain has real physical origins that do not show up as clearly as some other physical complaints in typical medical testing. Broken bones can be discovered by X rays, MRIs, or CAT scans and treated by physical medicine including surgeries. But soft-tissue injuries that often comprise chronic pain complaints are frustrating for doctors and patients alike. They do not heal well or quickly for reasons to be discussed. And the frustration experienced by patients, doctors, and the insurance companies creates stress that can actually perpetuate chronic problems rather than help solve them.

Chronic muscle-contraction headaches, neck/shoulder pain, low back pain, and pain/tightness of the jaw are the most common, devastating, and expensive of these problems. There are others that certainly fit in here such as peripheral pain in the arms and legs, intercostal-muscular chest pain, and pelvic pain; however, these are not as common.

The most common reason that these problems do not heal easily relates to the nature of the injury and the healing process. If you were to cut yourself, what would you do? You would clean the wound and bandage it. The bandage helps to protect this location from added abuse and it helps to hold the wounded skin in place so that it may heal by a knitting together of the skin cells. However, in many low back or neck/shoulder injuries, after an accident that pulls or strains these muscles, tendons, or ligaments, it is unlikely that you have the luxury of just lying down and waiting for these injuries to heal. By moving in normal daily activities, you use these important muscle groups, and using these muscles groups is similar to pulling at either side of a cut. Movement and unconscious muscle tension keeps the deeper muscle or soft tissue injuries from healing. The catch-22 is that immobility will produce physical therapy problems as well. A "frozen shoulder," for example, can be a nightmare for people who avoid movement in that joint for a long period of time while trying to protect it from further injury.

The frustration experienced by chronic pain sufferers can also exacerbate their symptoms. The lack of progress and the sense of loss of control of their bodies and their lives often leads to an emotional state of tension that can intensify pain and slow the healing process. All of the muscles involved in these pain complaints are subject to unconscious tension from the major survival mechanism known as the fight or flight response. This automatic response prepares the body to defend itself from a perceived life-threatening situation by preparing to fight or to flee. When the muscle groups tighten to get ready for the action of fighting or fleeing the pain or emotional upsets, these muscle groups, if injured, can increase their own fatigue and go into the spasms that create pain or make existing pain or injuries worse.

I treated a construction worker whose leg had been grazed by a falling I beam. Though the accident had happened five years earlier, the man was still suffering severe pain. The original pain was a direct result of the accident, but the subsequent chronic pain was aggravated by several emotional problems. Since he could not work, he was deeply depressed and his self-esteem was low. His relationship with his family had deteriorated, and his wife was asking for a divorce. For the first session he limped into my office and gingerly sat down. All his complaints were neuromuscular: tension headache, low back pain, and leg pain. We worked on breathing techniques and autogenic training.

The second session I guided him through a pain visualization, in which he left his problems beneath a tree next to a fast-running brook. We also worked with progressive relaxation. After only one month of practice he informed me that his wife had agreed to try again with their marriage; his rapid and radical personality change had renewed her hope. He eventually learned how to control his neuromuscular tension; the backaches and headaches completely disappeared. After I worked with him for nearly three months and taught him how to take control of his life by practicing relaxation, he finally walked into my office without limping. Eventually he began vocational retraining and made significant progress in the relationship with his wife. He led a normal, pain-free life.

Though not all people who experience chronic pain have such emotional problems, many will find that their pain is intensified by anxiety and stress. Some people who suffer chronic pain and discomfort could find some, if not total, relief through mind control and stress reduction. Many doctors have become interested in pain management, and entire programs have been established to help people combat pain. Not all pain clinics are the same, but most are based on a combination of relaxation training, physical therapy, exercise, psychotherapy, and personality adjustment. Some clinics stress one type of therapy more than another, yet the basic philosophy is always the same: to help people find relief from pain. Check with your physician or hospital for the location of the center nearest you. Pain clinics may not be as plentiful as local drugstores, but they are located all over the United States.

Chronic Pain Control Program

Pain is a warning signal—a signal that something is wrong. Don't mask or medicate the pain before finding the source: is it caused by tension, anxiety, or even a psychological need? Secondary gains can be met by illness or pain; pain originally generated by an organic dysfunction can continue long after healing is completed. If you have this type of pain, you must ask yourself some questions which are often difficult to answer.

- Am I using my illness to get care and attention that I wouldn't normally receive?
- Do I enjoy not having to deal with people and situations I dislike?
- Am I extending my illness for this reason?
- If other people have high expectations for me, am I using my sickness to avoid dealing with failure? Or even success?
- Am I using my illness to avoid dealing with my own expectations?
- Do I feel like a victim?

If your answer to these questions is yes, then you need to make a decision. You need to decide to get better. Relaxation techniques which teach self-control, such as autogenic training, can help you get out of the pattern of being a victim, can help you take control of your life, and teach you how to take a more active role in your own healing.

Practice relaxation techniques daily, preferably twice a day. Use progressive relaxation or autogenic training to reach deep relaxation, or when the pain is severe. Use a long visualization with a deepening technique, stressing a pain-free existence. Such positive programming can be very beneficial. To increase circulation to the painful spot, use colored light in the visualization; warm colors like yellow, orange, red, and gold encourage warmth and increased blood flow. Blues and greens are cooling, soothing, relaxing, and comforting. Do not use warm colors if you have an inflammation.

When working with people referred for chronic pain, I often recommend that they start with gentle passive progressive relaxation to help control their stress and pain. The 10-to-1 Passive Progressive Relaxation is very effective when practiced regularly. This exercise not only helps to increase awareness and reduce muscle tension, but it can help to give much needed rest and sleep. When a person lacks sleep, a much lower threshold to pain and depression exists.

It is not surprising that chronic pain can lead to drug dependency problems. To treat these effectively, a program of supervised lifestyle adjustment is often needed. Inpatient and local outpatient facilities are springing up around the country to aid sufferers. Proper motivation of the patient is critical for this new pain clinic approach. Treatment is designed to help create awareness and positive alternatives to minimize the pain but cannot work without the positive desire of the patient.

Biofeedback and stress management are important parts of this work. The ability to control anxiety can give individuals more control over their energies and indeed over their lives. This sense of control is often missing from the sufferer of chronic pain, and this in turn can lead to more anxiety and depression. Breaking old patterns and substituting new control really help turn things around.

Many other unconscious factors can contribute to the creation or intensification of pain. Headaches, jaw pain, neck/shoulder pain, and back pain can all be made worse by habits such as poor posture and poor breathing. A potential factor in all of these chronic pains can be head position. We are unconsciously taught to be aggressive and many of us keep our heads or chins stuck out in front of us, as if to "lead" with our jaws/chins. This aggressive, attacking posture can put a major postural strain on the neck, shoulders, jaw, and lower back. Improper breathing can put an unnecessary, inappropriate workload on your shoulders and upper back. Diaphragmatic breathing should be learned to avoid headache, neck/shoulder pain, and back pain.

Motivation and the help of your family are the most important ingredients for conquering debilitating chronic pain. People who do not really want to get well have less success with these techniques. I have seen motivated individuals use stress-reduction techniques to overcome severe back pain and spasms, and return to a normal working life. Many people can successfully use stress reduction to eliminate, or at least reduce, discomfort and pain.

Offering any control over stress and pain gives the chronic pain sufferer a new lease on hope and future control by reducing symptoms even further with practice. This does not always work to reduce pain completely, but can help to get the person back to a more normal lifestyle and often back to work.

Marsha is a chronic low back pain patient who was referred to the pain clinic where I consult. Her depression and anxiety were very close to the surface. She had been suffering for a year with pain that had not responded to any medication or physical therapy. Her doctor did not believe that surgery was an appropriate option. Marsha did not realize how much her injury and lifestyle changes had influenced her level of stress, anxiety, and tension.

We discussed this and introduced her to biofeedback, so she could see for herself how tension was being held in her musculature when she waited for her sharp pains to recur. In fact, her anticipation at an unconscious level was bringing on a large measure of her tiredness, then spasms and pain.

Relaxation training was initiated, and Marsha was able to increase her awareness and control over the pain. She understood that her posture needed to change. Her patterns of communication were examined and slightly changed so that she did not withhold emotional stress as much, finding more appropriate outlets.

As her pain lessened, her activity increased. When last seen, she had begun taking classes to retrain herself for a more productive and physically easier job. Marsha's mood had changed dramatically from depression to optimism. And although she still needed to be careful and not overdo things, she was living a normal lifestyle.

KEYS TO CONTROLLING THE STRESS THAT CREATES OR INTENSIFIES YOUR PAIN:

- Breathe slowly.
- Use relaxation techniques regularly.
  - Use a relaxation tape regularly.
  - Learn to relax your jaw and neck/shoulders.
- Exercise aerobically and regularly.
- Avoid caffeine and other stimulants.
- Vent your emotions.

Learn to breathe diaphragmatically.

Place a hand over your upper abdomen. Push your abdomen out as you inhale. Let your abdomen move in as you exhale. Let your chest, shoulders, neck, and back relax as you breathe. Only on a very deep breath should these parts move in the breath

Diaphragmatic breathing throughout your day should make relaxing at bedtime easier. By linking one deep breath to a reoccurring work event like a telephone ringing or checking the time, you remember to take these slow deep breaths throughout your work schedule to avoid letting tensions build to painful or distracting levels. The secret is to check in with your body in the present moment, relax your major muscles, and slow and deepen your breath. This simple exercise can have miraculous results.

Other techniques involve counting as you breathe through a short series of deep, slow breaths. Try counting slowly *1* to *4* as you inhale, pause and hold your breath as you count *1* to *4* again, and then release slowly, but completely, as you count *1* to *8*. After four of these breaths, you will be breathing better and more in control of your body's pattern of holding tension. This simple technique, if done regularly, can help teach you how to control your chronic pain.

Practice relaxation techniques.

Relaxation of the major muscle groups is very helpful for rest and sleep enhancement. And good sleep is necessary to manage pain. You are encouraged to use the *Stress Management for Chronic Pain* audio-tape during the day (one to two times or more) and at bedtime to help you relax and to fall asleep. (You can order this tape from the Stress Education Center; see the contact information in the back of this book.) You may need to practice with this tape for four to twelve weeks to develop the skill necessary to help you relax and drift off into a restful state that can help control your pain.

Remember, the jaw and neck/shoulders are often the areas of the body that are tight and can distract you from falling asleep. These are also the most difficult parts of the body for most people to learn to relax.

Relaxation is easier in a quiet, comfortable space. You may want to be warm, but not too warm for restful sleep. If you have a lot on your mind, write out a list and prioritize it so you can begin to work on these items in the morning.

RELAXATION TECHNIQUES FOR SPECIFIC SYMPTOMS

Headache: Muscle contraction headaches can develop from muscle tension in the jaw, spreading to the sides of the head or to the fore-head. Headaches can also develop from tension coming up from the neck and shoulders. This can create headaches at the back of head or at the base of the skull. This neck/shoulder tension can be related to improper head position (posture) or inappropriate shoulder breathing. Biofeedback monitoring of this muscle tension can help create awareness and can help you to develop the skills to relax these specific muscle groups.

Jaw Tension/Pain: Tension held in the muscles of the jaw around the temporomandibular joint (TMJ) is the cause of headaches and dental pain. Jaw and head position can affect this pain. Relaxation of this tension is essential and yet can take a surprising amount of time and practice. Use your regular breathing check-ins to reduce tension in the jaw and save lots of pain later in your day.

Neck/Shoulder Pain: Neck pain or tightness is very common. We have expressions like "pain in the neck" when we describe a difficult person or activity because this is where we habitually store our tension. The neck is a relatively poorly designed structure so it can be injured fairly easily over time. People will psychologically guard themselves in stressful situations by tightening their neck and shoulders to brace against trauma or stressors. Being aware and learning to let go of such guarding is very helpful for controlling pain.

As with headaches, neck/shoulder tension can be related to improper head position (posture) or inappropriate shoulder breathing. Biofeedback monitoring can help to create awareness and help you develop the skills to relax these specific muscle groups.

Low Back Pain: Back problems are very common and extremely painful. The low back is not a well-designed structure and so can be injured easily. Soft-tissue injuries in this area of the body are often overlooked but can contribute to the cause or increased intensity of low back pain. Look for muscle tension in back of the upper legs to create tension and pain in the lower back. Lower back pain can be related to improper head position (posture) or even inappropriate shoulder breathing. Biofeedback monitoring of this muscle tension can help to create awareness and can help you develop the skills to relax these specific muscle groups.

Exercise regularly.

Regular exercise, during the day, can help you handle physical stresses that build in your body. Exercise can also help to fatigue you so you will sleep easier. There are many exercises to strengthen and stretch you out that can be learned from a good physical therapist, trained physician, chiropractor, or chronic pain clinic. These exercises can help you with range of motion, posture, strengthening weakened muscle groups, and release of stored muscle tension.

Eat regular meals.
Low-fat and complex carbohydrates are better than fast foods with lots of sugar. Avoid caffeine and other stimulants. Caffeine is found in coffee, black teas, cola drinks, chocolate, some over-the-counter pain medications, and other foods and drugs. Caffeine can intensify your stress/anxiety and your pain. Read labels. Eat lots of fruits, vegetables, whole grains, and other natural foods.

Vent your emotions.
Frustration, anger, resentment, anxiety, and depression are normal by-products of coping with injury and pain. An appropriate and supportive way of discharging this potentially damaging emotional energy can be very helpful. Your church, pain clinic, psychological counselor/therapist, even your physical therapist may be able to help you vent your frustration. Getting this support from family and friends can be useful but may wear thin over time. You may need to search out the appropriate groups or professionals who are equipped to help you handle your frustrations.

Communication tools can help you vent your emotions safely and can save you wear and tear on your injured systems. Make a point of finding the best, most therapeutic method for you—this will be an extremely important key to managing your chronic pain.

RHEUMATOID ARTHRITIS

Though no one really knows the cause of rheumatoid arthritis, one thing is certain: stress and tension play a major role in the onset and recurrence of this disease. Young adults, at an average age of thirty-five and three times as many women as men, are stricken with this form of arthritis, the most widespread form in our country.

A severe emotional or physical shock often precipitates the onset of this disease. A death in the family, a business calamity, or a difficult operation may precede the first symptoms. Prolonged physical or mental stress may also be a factor. Heredity plays a role, as at least 50 percent of rheumatoid sufferers have the rheumatoid factor in their blood; often this factor is also found in their close relatives. Having this factor does not necessarily mean that you will get rheumatoid arthritis, but it does increase your vulnerability. Certain personality traits are associated with this dysfunction, and psychiatrists have compiled a list of traits culled from studies of rheumatoid sufferers. The following are typical: shy, inhibited, masochistic, self-sacrificing, anxious, depressed, resentful, and repressed anger. People who possess these characteristics along with the rheumatoid factor are the most likely candidates for this disease; *people who have a healthy psychological balance and the factor rarely suffer from the disease.*

Rheumatoid arthritis is an autoimmune illness. The body turns against itself and destroys healthy and unhealthy tissue indiscriminately. For example, if you had an infection in your joints, the antibodies would attack the infection, and under normal conditions, destroy the unhealthy tissue. In rheumatoid arthritis the antibodies cannot distinguish between healthy and unhealthy cells, and destroy both. Healthy cells, in an attempt to heal the system, begin to divide rapidly and more tissue is created than is necessary. This tissue creeps in between the joints, causing the swelling endemic to this form of arthritis.

Though this disease responds well, at first, to chemical treatment, often this treatment does not effect a cure. If the patient is subject to stress, the symptoms often flare up. Complete rest, with some form of exercise, is often prescribed; for many people this is financially infeasible, and the strain of an additional financial burden may create more excess tension. Climate also seems to have some effect, and in some cases a change from the northern part of the temperate zone to a hotter climate brings about a remission or slows down the progression. But once again, this treatment is not possible for most sufferers and doesn't always work.

Rheumatoid arthritis commonly affects the joints of the body: the shoulders, elbows, hips, wrists, fingers, knees, ankles, and feet. In some people the disease may progress rapidly, while in others there may be flare-ups every few years, with little pain for years at a time. *Some cases have a complete remission, others are stabilized, and others progress over the years to severe debilitation.* Interestingly, the people who respond the best to stress-reduction therapy are those who have chronic, severe cases. People with sporadic, unprolonged attacks often lack the motivation necessary to follow the exercise program.

The onset of this dysfunction may be sudden, but usually it is gradual. The first sign is swelling and pain in the joints; the symptoms are often migratory, moving from joint to joint. Often the symptoms will abruptly disappear. After an indeterminate period of time, the pain and swelling reappear. Certain prodromal symptoms may be noticed, such as weakness and fatigue, loss of weight, anemia, and a tingling sensation in the hands and feet. The collagen fibers of the connective tissue are the most affected parts of the body; the cartilage may eventually be destroyed, and in severe cases, the bones themselves destroyed. Scar tissue forms and the joints become immobilized and deformed.

A woman who had tried just about every possible treatment for rheumatoid arthritis was referred to me for stress-reduction therapy. Her doctors had prescribed cortisone treatments, gold injections, and a combination of codeine and aspirin for pain. Though she had been temporarily relieved, the symptoms had always reappeared. Her parents had been missionaries, and she had had a very strict and structured upbringing. She was very guilty about not practicing Christianity, tended to be self-sacrificing to assuage her guilt, and had difficulty in recognizing and expressing anger. As she lived out of town, it was necessary for me to see her for an intensive two-week session. We worked on autogenics and visualization, and then she returned to her home and continued to practice on her own. After one month she had dramatically reduced her medication needs, which surprised her physician very much; but more importantly, she began to notice a reduction in the stiffness of her fingers. There was a noticeable difference in the amount of discomfort and pain, and the woman felt more positive about her condition and its effect on her life.

Rheumatoid Arthritis Control Program

I recommend autogenics and visualization for rheumatoid sufferers. Though you may not have a complete remission of the disease, the progression can be slowed down, and at the very least, your attacks can be reduced. Autogenics will work well because the suggestion of increased blood flow to the extremities eases pain and promotes healing. Visualizations which picture increased blood flow are also beneficial for the same reason, and visualization of the joints healing themselves can be valuable when used after a deep relaxation state is achieved. A warm bath stimulates the circulation and reduces severe pain.

If you plan to institute a stress-reduction program for rheumatoid arthritis, please check with your physician. Your medication needs may radically change as a result of stress management, and your doctor should monitor your progress. Do not expect any magic cure, but a positive, stress-free existence can only help your condition.

KEYS TO CONTROLLING RHEUMATOID ARTHRITIS:

- Learn slow breathing techniques to minimize stress
- Use biofeedback temperature monitoring for deep relaxation regularly.
  - Use a relaxation tape regularly (like *Stress Management for High Blood Pressure*).
  - Learn to warm your hands and feet to lessen your stress.
- Regular exercise can help prevent these complaints.
- Reduce your emotional triggers if these are a factor in your symptom activity.

Using breathing techniques regularly will prevent stresses from building.
Breathing techniques can relax you and reduce stress in your circulatory system. These techniques can also help to reduce the intensity of your symptoms if they cannot be prevented.

Use the *Stress Management for High Blood Pressure* tape one to three times per day for eight to twelve weeks.
You can order this tape from the Stress Education Center; see the contact information in the back of this book. These relaxation strategies will assist you in developing the skills necessary to prevent or to lessen your rheumatoid arthritis. Use temperature training biofeedback to learn to warm your hands and feet. It requires repetition and time to learn how to "let go," enabling you to warm your hands to 93 to 95 degrees and then learn to warm your feet to 90 degrees. This mastery over blood flow will offer you the ability to control vascular challenges. Used preventively, this skill will help you minimize the risks that allow the onset and development of your rheumatoid arthritis.

Regular exercise will help you work off the effects of life's stresses.
You may need assistance from a physical therapist to learn the proper activities to avoid unnecessary stress on your inflamed joints, if this is possible. Try to elevate your heart rate for fifteen to forty-five minutes three to five times per week. Check with your doctor before beginning an exercise program if you have been inactive for a long while. The release of tensions and the strengthening of your cardiovascular system will have great benefits. This improved circulation will assist you in preventing vascular problems.

Eat regular meals.
Proper nutrition can prevent the body's response to stress that can make your rheumatoid arthritis worse.

Reduce your emotional triggers if these are a factor in your symptom activity.

Perfectionism, repressed anger, and anxiety can all be potential triggers that either create rheumatoid arthritis or make it worse. Get help in identifying these issues and seek out support as you work through them to find more appropriate ways to respond when these emotional states are triggered.

Develop a sense that you do have control of your rheumatoid arthritis. This is not easy in the beginning, but the behavioral techniques can help you to minimize the intensity of your pain, if not eliminate it. Many people feel "out of control" when their pain becomes chronic. This can make the intensity of the pain worse because you have fear and anxiety regarding these ongoing challenges. Temperature training biofeedback can help you to learn to relax and to "let go" of the anxiety that can intensify your complaints.

ALLERGIES AND STRESS-RELATED RESPIRATORY PROBLEMS

One of the main manifestations of the stress response's range of physical symptoms is the effect upon normal respiration patterns. Asthma, chronic bronchitis, chronic respiratory infections, and even some allergic respiratory response can be irritated or prolonged by your response to life's changes. These conditions are not always created by stress, but can be made worse in stressful situations. People inherit characteristics both physically and emotionally that increase the possibilities of these types of symptoms. However, this does not mean that you are predestined to suffer from these complaints. You may need to change your lifestyle with behavioral techniques that can help you to get back in control of the way your body responds to stress and major life changes. (Respiratory symptoms that are created or made worse by stress can be confused with serious, sometimes life-threatening physical disorders. Please consult your physician to determine the source of your symptoms.)

Not all allergies are directly caused by stress, but stress and allergies are intrinsically related. *Stress heightens your sensitivity to allergens because the immunological system is unbalanced when you are stressed.* When you have an allergic reaction, your entire body is thrown into a stress response as strong as the fight or flight response; every time you have an allergic reaction, more stress is put on your system. This continued state of stress response makes you more susceptible to future attacks. Also, since allergic reactions perpetuate immunological disequilibrium, you become more susceptible to stress. During prolonged stress you are more prone to infection, which in turn may trigger an allergic response. This vicious cycle eventually weakens your entire system. Though drug therapy can help modify the allergic response, drugs also place stress on your system; though in many cases drugs are necessary, a stress-reduction program can help you reduce your need for medication.

When you have an allergy, your body overreacts to a foreign substance, an allergen, and responds as if that substance were a toxin. Allergies are usually characterized by an inflammation of the mucous membranes in the eyes, nose, and throat. You can be born with an allergy, it can disappear during adolescence, or an allergy can first occur during adulthood. There is no hard and fast rule about allergic responses. Some people respond immediately to an allergen, and others have a delayed reaction which may not occur for as long as twenty-four hours. Contact with an allergen may give you a slight reaction; the next contact may cause a severe attack. If you are constantly undergoing an allergic response, you may become more sensitive to other substances because you are placing added stress on your immunological system.

One manifestation of allergy is asthma, a reaction in which the bronchial tubes constrict, the breathing becomes labored, and a characteristic wheezing sound accompanies the exhalation. Emotional stress is a contributing factor and can often precipitate an asthma attack. Asthmatics not allergic to a particular substance often have an attack solely as a reaction to stress. If you have asthma, you can see how much of a role emotional stress plays in asthma; when you get more upset your attack often becomes more severe. Try to correlate your attacks with life events to discover what triggers them. You may notice a pattern of attacks occurring during certain kinds of emotionally upsetting situations.

Allergy and Respiratory Complaint Control Program

Meditation, biofeedback, progressive relaxation, and autogenics can be helpful in combating allergic reactions and asthma. Progressive relaxation and autogenics can be used for a long-term program for reducing the amount of excess stress in your life. Deep breathing and Zen Breath-Counting will help you move the focus of breathing from your chest to the abdominal region. Concentrating on releasing muscle tension in progressive relaxation will help you release muscle tension from your chest when you are experiencing an asthma attack. Visualizing blue and green colors, or cool blue water, will help reduce the inflammation of the mucous membranes associated with these dysfunctions.

A lifetime asthma sufferer that I worked with found that visualization gave him the most relief. He was not able to completely cure himself, but he was able to minimize the attacks. He was in his late twenties, and his barrel-chested, round-shouldered physique was typical of asthmatics. Though he was definitely allergic to smoke and specific chemical substances, his attacks were often triggered by visits to his dying mother. His job as a counselor of the emotionally disturbed also placed him in upsetting situations. We worked with a visualization of the complete dilation of his respiratory system, first picturing his bronchial tubes expanding and allowing for free air flow. Then he pictured himself as completely calm and relaxed, breathing easily and fully. He used this visualization as soon as he started wheezing and found that he was able to reduce the severity of the attack.

KEYS TO CONTROLLING STRESS-RELATED RESPIRATORY COMPLAINTS:

- Breathe slowly.
- Remain in the present, in your body, and in a positive frame of mind.
- Avoid being perfectionistic and controlling.
- Use positive self-talk; avoid negative expectations.
- Use biofeedback temperature monitoring for deep relaxation regularly.
  - Use a relaxation tape regularly.
  - Learn to warm your hands and feet.
- Exercise aerobically and regularly.
- Avoid caffeine and other stimulants.
- Get support or professional counsel in confronting and then desensitizing yourself to fears/phobias related to your symptoms.

Learn to breathe diaphragmatically.
Place a hand over your upper abdomen. Push your abdomen out as you inhale. Let your abdomen move in as you exhale. Let your chest, shoulders, neck, and back relax as you breathe. Only on a very deep breath should these parts move in the breath. (Use the other exercises from the chapter on relaxation through breathing.)

Use any of the stress management exercises or tapes from this book one to three times per day for eight to twelve weeks.
You may want to try the prepared tapes for high blood pressure or chronic pain available from the Stress Education Center; see the contact information in the back of this book. After achieving a state of deep relaxation, encourage slow, regular diaphragmatic breathing with increased control and maintain a present and positive mental awareness. Use the StressDots or any other temperature

trainer biofeedback device to learn how to warm your hands with relaxation. When you can consistently get above 90 degrees Fahrenheit (93 to 95 degrees is ideal) then you can begin to master warming your feet to 90 degrees. When you can let go by relaxing and warming your hands and feet, you will be able to control, if not prevent, your difficult breathing episodes. Then you must develop confidence in your control so the fear of breathing problems does not control your life. This skill can teach you how to minimize, if not eliminate, your symptoms.

Regular exercise will help you work off the effects of life's stresses. Try to elevate your heart rate for fifteen to forty-five minutes three to five times per week. Check with your doctor before beginning an exercise program if you have been inactive for a long while. The release of tensions and the strengthening of your cardiovascular system will have great benefits.

Eat regular meals.
Low-fat and complex carbohydrates are better than fast foods with lots of sugar. Avoid caffeine and other stimulants. Caffeine is found in coffee, black teas, cola drinks, chocolate, some over-the-counter pain medications, and other foods and drugs. Read labels. Eat lots of fruits, vegetables, whole grains, and other natural foods. You may want to get checked for allergies to common refined foods, even dairy or wheat, which can add to respiratory symptoms.

Develop skills of control through positive expectations.
Do not let your fears escalate into losing control of your body and mind. By breathing slowly and staying in your body, in present time, you avoid falling into the negative pattern of fear and panic which can intensify if not create breathing symptoms.

The more you practice these relaxation techniques and practice the preventive lifestyle suggestions, the better your results will be in the near future. The key will be preventing the breathing difficulties. Early detection and positive actions during a respiratory flare-up will be the next best step. This will work most effectively after you have mastered diaphragmatic breathing and relaxation, and have the confidence to use these techniques even in the panic situation that accompanies breathing difficulties.

Remember that just as with other stress symptoms, respiratory difficulties are warnings to pay attention to our lives. We are being given an opportunity to examine our stresses and alleviate if not eliminate them.

Good luck! Remember to give this program enough time and practice so that you may gain the control you need to have for better breathing.

ABDOMINAL DISORDERS

A "knot in the stomach" can be the first sign of stress for some people. In most people the emotions are intimately linked to the digestive process, and doctors have long known that a number of digestive disorders originate in emotional distress, rather than in any organic dysfunction. Pre-ulcer, ulcer, gastritis, and colitis are among the digestive disorders considered psychosomatic.

The term psychosomatic has negative connotations which are ill deserved. To many people, a psychosomatic illness is "all in your head," created to get out of an unpleasant situation, or the manipulation of a person "too lazy for his own good." In some sense, all illnesses are psychosomatic, since the mind and body cannot be separated. Psychosomatic diseases have an emotional or psychological origin, manifesting in physical dysfunction. *Psychosomatic illnesses are really diseases of stress.* These illnesses are not imaginary and do not magically disappear. Since the mind causes these malfunctions, the mind can be the most powerful tool in reversing the disease process and creating better health. Research continually validates the power of the mind in positively affecting psychosomatic disorders.

A chronic stress response can cause increased production of digestive enzymes, leading to stomach distress and ulcers, and can affect peristalsis in the digestive tract, leading to colitis, constipation, and diarrhea. Emotional distress also alters eating patterns, which may further contribute to abdominal dysfunctions. There may be a very complex relationship between emotional stability, diet, personality traits, and environmental influences which contribute to any stress-related disease. Hereditary tendencies may also play a role. People inherit characteristics both physically and emotionally that increase the possibilities of these types of symptoms. However, this does not mean that you are predestined to suffer from these complaints. You may need to change your lifestyle with behavioral techniques that can help you to get back in control of the way your body responds to stress and major life changes. Stress reduction, practiced on a daily basis, can relieve the symptoms and help cure gastritis and colitis, prevent or heal ulcers, and help control eating patterns.

I once treated a restaurant owner for pre-ulcer. His condition had been diagnosed by a physician, who had referred him to me for stress-reduction therapy. Trained as a French chef, the client had recently purchased a restaurant business and was attempting to manage as well as function as the main chef. We discussed the difficulty of playing a double role and the added stress this placed on him. He was aware that it was a stressful situation, but until the restaurant was well established he could not afford to hire additional help. He first noticed his condition when he experienced severe pain and a burning sensation in his abdomen after eating a filet mignon. During the day, he drank a lot of coffee and cola; he began experiencing the same discomfort he had felt after the steak dinner when he drank either of these beverages. He had steak one more time with the same result before going to the doctor.

In the first two sessions I taught him autogenic training phrases and how to use this technique for inducing deep relaxation. After practicing twice a day for three weeks, he was able to deeply relax. We also discussed his diet, and I explained that coffee and cola placed added strain on his physiological system, while also causing an overproduction of hydrochloric acid which was irritating his stomach lining. Coffee and cola were banned from his diet, as were fried foods and, temporarily, steak. After about six weeks of practicing autogenics and staying on his diet, the symptoms radically decreased in severity. The last part of the treatment employed autogenics combined with a visualization, to aid in deepening relaxation and encourage a calmer overall state. He imagined himself outdoors, on a beautiful day, riding his bicycle down a coastal highway. Totally absorbed and lost in this experience during the visualization, he was cleansed of any emotional stress or anxiety. He spoke to me after the first time we used the exercise and stated that it had been highly calming and relaxing for him; he planned to practice the visualization once a day, during a break in his work.

The program of autogenics, visualization, and diet control was very effective. He reported very little discomfort in his stomach region after eight weeks, and after three months he was no longer considered a pre-ulcer patient. He still continued to watch his diet, and practiced stress-reduction techniques once a day, even though his symptoms had virtually disappeared.

Another case demonstrates the effectiveness of visualization for abdominal pain sufferers. I was seeing a client, again referred by her physician, who had severe gastritis. She had first come to me for back pain. She worked in a factory, assembling computer parts. Bending over a counter eight hours a day had been too much for her back to handle. Recently divorced, she had only been working a few months before her back began to give her discomfort. She was in her early thirties and was raising two children alone; this in itself was creating a lot of emotional stress. There was no question in my mind that the gastritis was a result of stress; her system had been so weakened by her chronic stress response that it was out of balance.

The phone rang in the middle of the night; it must have been about 2 A.M. Groggy, I answered the phone. A hysterical voice told me that she had no one else to call, and I realized that it was my gastritis client. She had apparently been in severe pain for over twelve hours, and after attempting to reach her doctor, with no success, she decided to call me. She was panicking due to the extreme pain. Realizing that she needed help immediately, I suggested that we do deep breathing together, and after the first few deep breaths her hysteria abated. Unfortunately, she was still suffering severe pain. I slowly incorporated progressive relaxation into the breathing exercise; this still wasn't sufficient, though it did decrease the pain level slightly. Finally, we tried a visualization. She imagined that she was breathing sky blue, soothing, cooling light directly into her abdomen. After almost twenty minutes of this visualization, with me constantly guiding her, I realized that she had practically fallen asleep.

Abdominal Disorder Control Program

I recommend autogenic training and visualization for abdominal disorders. Substitute the word "calm" for the word "warm" in the autogenic exercises, particularly if you have a bleeding ulcer or diabetes, are in the third trimester of pregnancy, or experience any discomfort when using the suggestion of warmth. Inform your doctor that you are practicing stress reduction, as any medication levels must be monitored. Progressive relaxation, meditation, and breathing exercises may also be effective, but autogenics is a good technique with which to learn control and take charge of your body. The control you strive for is not rigid control in which you repress emotions and turn negative emotions against yourself. It just means knowing your body and not turning destructive stress against it.

Your body is not your enemy. When your body signals you with abdominal pain, stop and try to change the situation or the emotional state that is generating the disturbance. Your body's warning signals can be used to your advantage, to guide you around some of the pitfalls of life. The way you respond to these signals is an important indicator of your self-awareness. To control your distress, you must get to the source of your problem, not just mask the symptoms. Relaxation and self-regulation can often help you find peace of mind, which will minimize, if not eliminate, the upsetting sources of abdominal discomfort. (Digestive and abdominal symptoms may point to serious, sometimes life-threatening physical disorders. Please consult your physician to determine the source of your symptoms.)

KEYS TO CONTROLLING ABDOMINAL COMPLAINTS:

- Breathe slowly.
- Remain in the present, in your body, and in a positive frame of mind.
- Avoid being perfectionistic and controlling.
- Use biofeedback temperature monitoring for deep relaxation regularly.
  - Use a relaxation tape regularly.
  - Learn to warm your hands and feet.
- Exercise aerobically and regularly.
- Avoid caffeine and other stimulants.
- Engage in positive self-talk, not negative ruminations.

Learn to breathe diaphragmatically.
Place a hand over your upper abdomen. Push your abdomen out as you inhale. Let your abdomen move in as you exhale. Let your chest, shoulders, neck, and back relax as you breathe. Only on a very deep breath should these parts move in the breath. (Use the other exercises from the chapter on relaxation through breathing.)

Use any of the stress management tapes one to three times per day for eight to twelve weeks.
You can order a copy of any of these tapes from the Stress Education Center; see the contact information in the back of the book. Any of the deep relaxations in this book can be helpful, but especially recommended are the autogenic training exercises, visualizations, or the high blood pressure tape. After achieving a state of deep relaxation, encourage slow, regular diaphragmatic breathing with increased control, and maintain a present and positive mental awareness. Use the StressDots or some sort of temperature training biofeedback device to learn how to warm your hands with relaxation.

When you can consistently get above 90 degrees Fahrenheit (93 to 95 degrees is ideal) then you can begin to master warming your feet to 90 degrees. When you can let go by relaxing and warming your hands and feet, you will be able to control, if not prevent, the panic/anxiety episodes that can contribute to your digestive complaints. Then you must develop confidence in your control so the fear of digestive and/or abdominal disorders does not control your life. This skill can teach you how to minimize, if not eliminate, your symptoms.

Regular exercise will help you work off the effects of life's stresses. Try to elevate your heart rate for fifteen to forty-five minutes three to five times per week. Check with your doctor before beginning an exercise program if you have been inactive for a long while. The release of tensions and the strengthening of your cardiovascular system will have great benefits.

Eat regular meals.
Low-fat and complex carbohydrates are better than fast foods with lots of sugar. Avoid caffeine and other stimulants. Caffeine is found in coffee, black teas, cola drinks, chocolate, some over-the-counter pain medications, and other foods and drugs. Caffeine is an irritant to your digestive track. Read labels. Eat fruits, vegetables, whole grains, and other natural foods. (Some people cannot tolerate raw fruits and vegetables; however, when slowly integrated into the diet, these may be very healthful over time.) You will want to avoid spicy foods and eating late in the evening to help control digestive symptoms.

Practice positive self-talk.
Accept that you, along with everyone else, have imperfections which offer an opportunity to develop in yet more positive ways. Learn from mistakes, but do not beat yourself with these flaws. Do not let your fears escalate into losing control of your body and mind. By breathing slowly and staying in your body, in present time, you avoid falling into the negative pattern of fear and panic which can

intensify if not create digestive symptoms. People who have insecurities that make them control others will encounter long-term difficulties in the quality of their life and health.

Abdominal symptoms are not always your enemy. They are designed to protect you and teach you something about the stresses and transitions you are going through. Denial of these challenges only creates a more stubborn set of symptoms which can be more debilitating.

Remember, this program works best preventively and takes time to master. Be patient! Your skills will develop and you will learn to control the stress-related components of your digestive disorder. You will be able to minimize if not eliminate these symptoms through awareness and confidence in your developing relaxation skills.

INSOMNIA AND SLEEPING DISORDERS

Sleep dysfunctions are as common in our society as headaches. Difficulty getting to sleep, staying asleep, and resting during sleep are all forms of insomnia. Sleep remedies have become big business for the drug industry; they do not cure the problem. Drugs may induce a dreamless sleep that leaves you groggy in the morning, and regular use creates dependency.

Nearly everyone, at some point in their lives, is affected by sleeping difficulties—getting to sleep, staying asleep, or getting true rest while sleeping. For many people, these problems are inherited or learned in childhood. For others, they may be related to trauma or habit changes that have happened later in life. For still others, they may be related to physical changes that interrupt normal restful patterns of sleep. Such problems can become chronic unless you take action and develop the appropriate strategies to regain control.

To begin, insomnia is often related to the body's distraction and unconscious preoccupation with hypervigilance or hyperarousal. This often takes the form of unnecessary and inappropriately high levels of muscle tension, especially in the muscles of your jaw, face, neck/shoulders, back, and legs. With this habitual muscle tension as a distraction, it is difficult to relax and drift off into a restful state of sleep.

Usually insomnia has no organic cause, beyond protracted and chronic tension, though your diet may influence your sleeping patterns. Worrying about not being able to sleep well creates more tension, and it is not unusual for the condition to perpetuate in a snowball fashion. Ordinary daily tension can create enough anxiety, pain, and discomfort to keep you awake at night. If you have insomnia, institute a daily stress-reduction program. Stress-reduction techniques should be practiced before bed; you should also practice earlier in the day, since your anxiety about going to sleep will make it more difficult for you to relax at night.

Insomnia Control Program

Books have been written which are entirely devoted to sleeping disorders. This section is designed to get you started on a behavioral program for controlling the stresses that contribute to, if not cause, your sleeping problems.

Start your program with progressive relaxation, or the Visualization for Relaxation found in the chapter on visualization. Any autogenics, meditation, visualization, or breathing exercise may also be useful. Even if practicing relaxation does not completely stop insomnia attacks, relaxation can prevent the fatigue which often accompanies sleeplessness. *Twenty minutes of relaxation a day can take the place of two hours of sleep at night.* Your need for sleep may drop from nine to ten hours a night to six or seven hours. Mine did when I began to practice daily. This radical change is not at all unusual, and I recommend that people keep a diary of their sleeping habits so that they can become aware of any changes.

If relaxation cannot control the thoughts keeping you from sleep, maybe you should give in to them completely. Get up and take out your tape recorder. Speak all your thoughts, fears, worries, and irrational concerns into it. If some of your problems require action, record plans as to when, where, and how to act. Chronic worries or problems that you cannot immediately solve may obsess you; accept that you cannot resolve them. Close the book on these thoughts, return to bed, and try a relaxation technique.

Sometimes your body may just not be ready to go to sleep. Muscle tension may need to be released through physical movement, and a plan of daily physical activity combined with relaxation techniques can be the best "sleeping pill" of all. Check the chapter on physical movement; your activity doesn't need to be aggressive and extremely athletic to be effective. Gentle physical exercise can be even more appropriate and helpful than a set of tennis or handball.

I devised the following exercise to induce sleep, and my insomniac clients have found it very helpful. One client, a middle manager in a large corporation, spent every night awake, thinking about work-related issues. He worried about everything he had left unfinished on his desk; he worried about his relationship with his employees; he worried that he would be phased out by new "talent" in the firm. Because he did not get enough sleep, his work suffered: more and more work was left undone, and relationships with his co-workers deteriorated. His worries became self-perpetuating, and fear of replacement became more of a reality than an unfounded obsession.

He started to practice Relaxation for Sleep using my tape that is based on the progressive relaxation technique. After gaining some perspective on how his state of continual tension affected his health, he began to make definite associations between work events and sleepless nights. Once he consciously understood that he could control his sleeping habits and often positively affect difficult work situations, his behavior became less self-destructive. In a matter of months, his sleeping patterns had altered radically; he was sleeping peacefully every night of the week.

Relaxation for Sleep

**An insomnia control exercise is available at www.dstress.com.
Look for Tape #204.**

This exercise works best if it is taped. Begin by getting into a comfortable position. Allow yourself to begin to calm and relax. Take one, deep, full breath, pause for a moment, and then exhale, fully and completely. Now, allow yourself to breathe slowly and naturally. Imagine that with each and every breath, you can exhale away excess energy or tension.

As you continue to breathe slowly and naturally, your muscles will gradually get heavier, and as you let go of more and more tension, your muscles will go loose and limp. As you continue to allow yourself to relax, focus your attention on your arms and hands. Imagine that the muscles of your upper arms are getting loose and limp as you let go of tension. Allow your upper arms to relax more fully and completely. Imagine that you can breathe away the tension, just exhaling it away with every full and complete exhalation. Remember that you can control tension and gradually you can let your muscles become even more relaxed.

Now, relax the muscles around your elbows, letting them go limp and relaxed. Let the relaxation spread down into your lower arms, while you slowly breathe away the tension, even from your wrists. Just release the tension, and feel it flowing through your hands, and then into your fingers, and out of your body through your fingertips. Let your muscles go loose and limp, and just allow the tension to flow from you, while you drift slightly deeper into calmness and relaxation.

Continue to breathe slowly and naturally, while considering your feet and your legs. Allow them to relax fully and completely, slowly breathing away the tension from the muscles in your toes and feet. Gently release the tension from your arches and your heels, letting the tension spread out of your

es, and breathe away the excess energy slowly and completely. Allow yourself to relax your lower legs, just letting go of
tension. Let the muscles go loose and limp. Relax the muscles
around your knees, and in your upper legs, slowly allow the tension to melt away, as you sink deeper into whatever you are
sitting upon or lying upon. Slowly allow yourself to drift deeper
into a state of complete calmness and relaxation.

Gently turn your awareness to your back, and let the
muscles around your shoulder blades relax. Just let go and
allow these muscles to go loose and limp, allowing yourself to
sink further into the bed or chair. Let the muscles on both
sides of your spine relax, all the way down, down into your
lower back. Allow the relaxation to spread slowly to all of your
muscles, and feel them totally relaxing as all the tension melts
away. Remember to breathe calmly and naturally, exhaling
fully and completely.

Let the relaxation spread down into your pelvic area, down
into your lower back, and down into your legs. Just let go of the
tension, and allow yourself to drift as deeply as you wish to, into
a state of calmness and deep relaxation. As you continue to
breathe slowly and calmly, gently become aware of the muscles
in your chest and in your abdomen, and allow these muscles to
relax. Your heartbeat is calm and regular, and your breathing is
calm and regular. Feel the calmness in your abdominal region,
and allow yourself to relax, letting yourself drift deeper into a
dreamlike state of complete calmness and relaxation.

Now, become aware of the muscles in the back of your head,
on the sides, and on the top of your head. Let these muscles go
loose and limp, while breathing away the tensions slowly and naturally and allowing your forehead to go calm and smooth. Relax
the muscles around your eyes and throughout your face. Relax
your mouth, your tongue, and your jaw. Gently breathe away the
tension, letting yourself flow into a peaceful state of calmness and
deep relaxation.

Become aware of the muscles in your neck, and just let your head sink into a pillow or the chair, as your neck muscles go loose and limp. Relax your shoulders and your neck more completely now, letting your shoulders drop, letting go of the tension in these muscles, and peacefully easing yourself into a dreamlike state of calmness and deep relaxation. As you continue to breathe slowly and naturally, be aware that your arms and legs begin to feel heavier and more relaxed, and that the blood flow and energy flow is free and easy to every part of your body. You can control tension by breathing it away slowly and naturally, letting yourself drift deeper into a state of deep relaxation.

Imagine that you are outdoors on a very calm and peaceful day, in your favorite place, in a beautiful locale where you will not be disturbed by any distractions. Imagine that you can see yourself moving over to a very comfortable spot, and you lie down, just melting into the ground. Golden sunlight and its warmth gently shine down upon you. Feel the warmth on your arms and your hands, and feel the warm sunlight and breezes create pulsating, warming sensations in your feet and your legs. Just allow this feeling of warmth and relaxation to spread to every part of your body. Let your mind drift in a dreamlike state, as you continue to let go and drift peacefully along, deeper and deeper, into a sleepy, calm state of deep relaxation.

Feel yourself slowing and calming, just letting go more and more. Count backward from 5 down to 1, picturing each number, and slowing and relaxing even more, as each number fades from your peaceful, calm mind. As you picture the number 5, remember to breathe slowly and calmly, letting go and sinking deeper and deeper into relaxation. At 4, you are more relaxed than you were at 5, taking a step deeper into relaxation. At 3, you are more relaxed than you were at 4, relaxing and letting go, gently drifting down into deep relaxation. At 2, you can feel your slow, natural heartbeat gently pulsating to every cell in your body. And at *1* you are more relaxed than you were at *2*, gently letting yourself drift even deeper into relaxation.

Drift into a dreamlike state of pleasant, relaxing slumber. As you let yourself drift off peacefully and comfortably, remember whenever you wish you can awake, feeling calm and relaxed. When you finally awake, you will feel refreshed and alert, and realize how much control you have over your tension and excess energy. By breathing it away slowly and calmly, you can let go even further, peacefully drifting into calmness and restful relaxation. Just continue to let yourself drift peacefully deeper into calmness and deep relaxation.

KEYS TO CONTROLLING INSOMNIA:

- Breathe slowly.
- Maintain a regular schedule.
- Use relaxation techniques regularly.
  - Use a relaxation tape regularly.
  - Learn to relax your jaw and neck/shoulders.
- Exercise aerobically and regularly.
- Avoid caffeine and other stimulants.

Learn to breathe diaphragmatically.
Place a hand over your upper abdomen. Push your abdomen out as you inhale. Let your abdomen move in as you exhale. Let your chest, shoulders, neck, and back relax as you breathe. Only on a very deep breath should these parts move in the breath. (Use the other exercises from the chapter on relaxation through breathing.)

Relaxing/breathing throughout your day may make relaxing at bedtime easier. By linking one deep breath to a reoccurring work event like a telephone ringing or checking the time, you remember to take these slow deep breaths throughout your work schedule to avoid letting tensions build to painful or distracting levels. The secret is to check in with your body in the present moment, relax your major muscles, and slow and deepen your breath. This simple exercise can have miraculous results.

Other breathing techniques involve a short series of deep slow breaths, where you count as you breathe. Try counting slowly *1* to *4* as you inhale, pause and hold your breath as you count *1* to *4* again, and then release slowly, but completely, as you count *1* to *8*. After four of these breaths, you will be breathing easier and better able to control your body's pattern of holding tension. This can help teach you how to control your insomnia.

Another breathing/counting exercise that works very well for many people is a technique of counting backward from *50* down to *1*. The unique addition to this countdown is to add counting *1, 2, 3* to every number in your countdown. Example: *50, 1, 2, 3, 49, 1, 2, 3, 48, 1, 2, 3, 47, 1, 2, 3, 46*, and so on. By focusing on these numbers, you will relax enough to drift off into relaxation and sleep.

Maintain a regular schedule.
Make sure that you keep a regular bedtime, if possible. Changes in a regular routine can upset one's normal balance. This may even relate to the place and bed that you sleep in. Eventually you will not be so bound by time and environment, but to get a handle on this problem, it is best not to have too many variables. It is not recommended to schedule vigorous exercise or high-energy activities right before bedtime. A quiet, settling time would be best. Action books, arguments, movies, or even the news on TV may not be conducive to proper relaxation at bedtime. Eating too close to sleep may be another problem. Many people find that eating a heavy meal (with lots of protein or sauces) or spicy foods may interfere with getting sleep.

A warm bath or shower, a massage, or some other peaceful relaxation technique before sleep may encourage better sleeping patterns.

Practice relaxation techniques.
Relaxation of the major muscle groups is very helpful for rest and sleep enhancement. You are encouraged to use the *Stress Management for Sleep* audiotape available from the Stress Education Center (see the contact information in the back of this book) at bedtime to help you relax and fall asleep. You may need to practice with this

tape for four to twelve weeks to develop the skill necessary to help you relax and drift off into a restful state of sleep.

Remember, the jaw, the neck, and the shoulders are often the areas of the body that are tight and can distract you from falling asleep. These are also the most difficult parts of the body for most people to learn to relax. It takes time!

Relaxation is easier in a quiet comfortable space. You may want to be warm, but not too warm for a restful sleep. If you have a lot on your mind, write out a list and prioritize it so you can begin to work on these items in the morning.

Exercise regularly.

Regular exercise, during the day, can help you handle physical stresses that build in your body. Exercise can also help to fatigue you so you will be readier for sleeping. Try to elevate your heart rate for fifteen to forty-five minutes three to five times per week. Check with your doctor before beginning an exercise program if you have been inactive for a long while. The release of tensions and the strengthening of your cardiovascular system will have great benefits.

Eat regular meals.

Low-fat and complex carbohydrates are better than fast foods with lots of sugar. Avoid caffeine and other stimulants. Caffeine is found in coffee, black teas, cola drinks, chocolate, some over-the-counter pain medications, and other foods and drugs. Read labels. Eat lots of fruits, vegetables, whole grains, and other natural foods. You may want to get checked for allergies to common refined foods, even dairy or wheat, which can add to respiratory symptoms.

PANIC/ANXIETY

Anxiety is the most prevalent type of neurosis in the United States and is the direct result of stress; its increase is in direct proportion to the increase of environmental and social problems such as noise pollution, air pollution, urbanization, inflation, crime, decay of the nuclear family, and divorce.

Everyone experiences anxiety. It is the normal reaction to a threat to your body, values, lifestyle, or a loved one. A certain amount is normal and even stimulating; it may provoke you to resolve conflicts and unhealthy situations. An excess amount of anxiety can be debilitating and, at the very least, interfere with your normal functioning. Healthy, normal anxiety usually decreases over a period of time as you become gradually desensitized by repeated exposure to the anxiety-producing situation. Neurotic anxiety increases with repeated exposure to the situation and eventually leads to avoidance or withdrawal from the dreaded circumstances.

Major transitions, trauma, and stress can lead to feelings of little or no control over one's life. As a result, a feeling of panic may ensue. A panic episode can come on suddenly or can awaken you from sleep with an overwhelming feeling of apprehension. Some people believe that they are having a heart attack because often there is chest pain, a shortness of breath, neck or arm pain, major stomach upset, an adrenaline rush, lightheadedness, dizziness, and other unpleasant feelings of fear and apprehension. These feelings can be triggered by specific events such as: driving (getting stuck in traffic); shopping; waiting in lines (at stores, banks, post offices, and so on); feeling trapped (in church, movie theaters, classes, and so on); traveling distances from home (especially by airplane); making a presentation in front of a group of people (or something else which draws attention toward oneself); doing new or unfamiliar things; meeting new people. Anything new or seemingly stressful where you fear losing control can bring on a panic episode.

Loss of control is the main feature of panic attacks. The anticipation of the attacks can be very frightening, and of course the attacks themselves give the feeling of no control. We may not know a panic sufferer by looking at him or her unless we look very carefully to notice the nervousness below the surface.

Fear may be out of proportion to the real threat in an anxiety attack. Some people may know what precipitates an attack, and others may not recognize the cause. The fear itself is always conscious, though the cause may not be. A client of mine exhibited fear and anxiety about going to work on the weekends, but was unable to determine exactly what was causing his attacks of rapid heartbeat and nausea. He felt fearful and always recognized his feeling as fear; he did not know what was directly responsible for the fear.

His work as a lab technician in a hospital was rewarding and enjoyable. Life with his wife was stimulating, and they did not have any serious marital problems. At first he only disliked going to work; eventually his dislike became dread, and he refused to get out of bed and go to work on the weekend. I taught him autogenics combined with passive progressive relaxation. This helped him to partially control his anxiety and tension, and after two weeks of practice he realized what had generated his fear.

During the week he worked with other people and was not solely responsible for interpreting test results. He worked alone on Saturday. The strain of not being able to discuss and compare test results with other technicians made him feel inadequate and on edge. He realized that it had become almost impossible for him to analyze the tests when he worked alone. After eight weeks of intensive practice he no longer had attacks of nausea; going to work on Saturday was still anxiety-producing. He decided that the best thing he could do for himself would be to find another hospital job where he always worked with other people and was not personally responsible for analyzing findings.

Intense emotional reactions to ordinary events may indicate anxiety. Common tasks such as preparing a meal or socializing with friends may create an unnatural fear or dread. A feeling of inadequacy at meeting obligations, despondency, pessimism, and lack of concentration are indicators of an anxiety state. Decision-making becomes difficult and tolerance for frustration is decreased. Inability to determine the relationship between life events and unnatural feelings of fear can cause humiliation; you may view your fears and anxieties as a childish inability to control the functioning of your own mind.

A person suffering from an anxiety neurosis may exhibit certain physical symptoms: palpitations, chest pain, cold and sweaty extremities, bandlike pressure around the head, constriction of the throat, fatigue, lack of appetite, vomiting, and diarrhea. Not all of the symptoms will be present, but all acute anxiety attacks will manifest in some physical dysfunction. Often people suffering from severe anxiety believe that they have a serious illness; symptoms of panic and anxiety can be confused with life-threatening physical disorders. Please consult your physician to determine the source of your symptoms.

Heart problems, chest pain, and respiratory difficulties (hyperventilation and dizziness are common symptoms of panic/anxiety attacks) should be carefully examined by your physician. If no heart-related problem exists, but you are still in great fear of these occurrences of panic, then the following behavioral program, with practice, will greatly aid you in preventing or at least minimizing the episodes of panic. Also, remember that exciting/positive actions or events can raise your heart rate as well. This excitement is not bad or life threatening, and the fear of the physical symptoms of excitement can really hamper your enjoyment of life.

Panic/Anxiety Control Program

Any of the forms of relaxation you use and feel comfortable with can be of aid to you in a time of anxiety. I particularly recommend autogenics, visualization, progressive relaxation, desensitization, and meditation. Practice two to three times daily, and keep a first-aid tape on hand, such as a 10-to-1 Passive Progressive Relaxation tape. Use this tape if things get out of control; listening to and following the instructions will calm you.

A therapist or doctor can help you regain your emotional equilibrium. Empathy, compassion, and the support of your family and friends are very important; it will be more difficult for you to help yourself if your family and friends are constantly reinforcing negative and destructive tendencies. Also, be aware of your diet, and any effect that it might have on your emotional stability. If you find yourself knocked off balance soon after you eat, evaluate what was in your food. Some people are radically affected by hidden chemicals and sugars.

Practiced on a regular basis, relaxation can give you more control over your mind and body, and help you take control of your own life. During deep relaxation, when the mind is calmed and quieted, you may be able to come to terms with what is really bothering you. Relaxation can be a safety valve for releasing excess tension and can keep you on an even keel in the sea of life.

KEYS TO CONTROLLING PANIC AND ANXIETY:

- Breathe slowly.
- Remain in the present, in your body, and in a positive frame of mind.
- Use positive self-talk; avoid negative expectations.
- Use biofeedback temperature monitoring for deep relaxation regularly.
  - Use a relaxation tape regularly.
  - Learn to warm your hands and feet.
- Exercise aerobically and regularly.
- Avoid caffeine and other stimulants.
- Get support in confronting and then desensitizing yourself to your fears/phobias.
- Taper your antianxiety medication after you have mastered the relaxation-biofeedback.

Learn to breathe diaphragmatically.

Place a hand over your upper abdomen. Push your abdomen out as you inhale. Let your abdomen move in as you exhale. Let your chest, shoulders, neck, and back relax as you breathe. Only on a very deep breath should these parts move in the breath. (Use the other exercises from the chapter on relaxation through breathing.) This may be the most important panic control technique you can learn!

Use any of the stress management tapes one to three times per day for eight to twelve weeks.

Or make your own tape from the exercises in this book. You can order a copy of any of the tapes available from the Stress Education Center; see the contact information in the back of this book. The *Stress Management for High Blood Pressure* tape is strongly recommended for panic/anxiety control. If you do not have an audiotape for relaxation yet, use any deep relaxation from this book. After achieving a level of controlled, deep relaxation, repeat suggestions of control, especially control of slow, regular breathing and slow, regular heart rate. Suggestions of "letting go" to help achieve hand and foot warming, along with any visualizations that can encourage this increase of peripheral blood flow, will be very useful as well. Use the StressDots or some sort of temperature training biofeedback device on your hands to learn how to warm your hands with relaxation. When you can consistently get above 90 degrees Fahrenheit (93 to 95 degrees is ideal) then you can begin to master warming your feet to 90 degrees. When you can let go by relaxing and warming your hands and feet, you will be able to control, if not prevent, your panic episodes. Then you must develop confidence in your control so the fear of panic does not control your life.

Regular exercise will help you work off the effects of life's stresses.
Try to elevate your heart rate for fifteen to forty-five minutes three to five times per week. Check with your doctor before beginning an exercise program if you have been inactive for a long while. The release of tensions and the strengthening of your cardiovascular system will have great benefits.

Eat regular meals.

Low-fat and complex carbohydrates are better than fast foods with lots of sugar. Avoid caffeine and other stimulants. Caffeine is found in coffee, black teas, cola drinks, chocolate, some over-the-counter pain medications, and other foods and drugs. Read labels. Eat lots of fruits, vegetables, whole grains, and other natural foods.

Practice positive self-talk.

Do not let your fears escalate into losing control of your body and mind. By breathing slowly and staying in your body, in present time, you avoid falling into the negative pattern of fear and panic.

Get support from your friends, doctor, and a therapist, if necessary.

Check your area for panic/anxiety support or treatment groups. Regular use of antianxiety medications may be better than taking your prescription only after the panic has begun. Reduce your medication in a supervised way after you have mastered the relaxation-biofeedback control techniques.

Remember you can get back in control of your body and your life!

You must make this a priority so you can avoid being a victim to this set of scary symptoms. Panic/anxiety is not always your enemy. This reaction is designed to protect you and may teach you something about the stresses and transitions you are going through. Denial of these challenges only creates a more stubborn set of symptoms that can be more debilitating.

Other good books that can help you:

Psychological Treatment of Panic by David Barlow, Ph.D., and Jerome Cerny, New York: Guilford Press, 1988.

Anxiety & Stress Self Help Book by Susan Lark, M.D., Berkeley, CA: Celestial Arts, 2000.

PRESENTATION ANXIETY:
FEAR THAT KEEPS YOU FROM MOVING AHEAD

The fear of making a presentation is the most common phobia that exists. It ranks with the fear of death as a traumatic experience, probably because people unconsciously fear that the attention directed at them when they are making a presentation will somehow expose them to dangers that could actually lead to death. This unfounded fear (in most normal situations) paralyzes millions of people and keeps them from moving ahead in their careers or in their enjoyment of life. Certainly you can live without taking center stage but, due to fear, the quality of life can even be disrupted by the possibility of being called upon to make a speech or a presentation, lead a prayer, or confront a hiring committee.

Presentation Anxiety Control Program

To overcome this fear, you must grow aware of how you handle stress and anxiety. Awareness is half the battle. The other half is learning how to let go of anxiety so you may take back control of the way you respond in difficult situations. Presentation anxiety can manifest in much the same way as panic/anxiety. Commonly people suffering from this anxiety will change their breathing (short shallow breaths or held breath), tighten their muscles, tighten their gut (slowing or stopping digestion and reducing normal reproductive activity), reduce blood flow to the surface of the skin in their hands and feet, increase heart rate, increase stress hormone secretion (which increases blood sugar and reduces immune system function over time), and increase sensitivity to all environmental changes. You can learn to control each of these symptoms either directly or indirectly, and, as a result, you can learn to get back in control of your life.

KEYS TO CONTROLLING PRESENTATION ANXIETY:

- Breathe slowly.

- Remain in the present, in your body, and in a positive frame of mind.

- Use biofeedback temperature monitoring for deep relaxation regularly.
  - Use a relaxation tape regularly.
  - Learn to warm your hands and feet.

- Exercise aerobically and regularly.

- Avoid caffeine and other stimulants.

- Use positive self-talk; avoid negative expectations.

- Get support in confronting and then desensitizing yourself to your fears/phobias of speaking in public.

- Taper your antianxiety medication after you have mastered the relaxation-biofeedback.

Learn to breathe diaphragmatically.
Place a hand over your upper abdomen. Push your abdomen out as you inhale. Let your abdomen move in as you exhale. Let your chest, shoulders, neck, and back relax as you breathe. Only on a very deep breath should these parts move in the breath. (Use the other exercises from the chapter on relaxation through breathing.) This may be the most important presentation anxiety control you can learn!

Use a stress management tape one to three times per day for eight to twelve weeks.
If you do not have a relaxation tape, then you can use any of the deep relaxations from this book, provided you emphasize "letting go" to feel hand and foot warming and the use of slow, deep diaphragmatic breathing which can assist you in remaining in present time in your body (as opposed to concentrating on future fears). If you want to order an audiotape from the Stress Education Center, see the contact information in the back of this book.

High blood pressure, autogenic training, or visualization tapes are recommended. Use the StressDots or some other form of temperature training biofeedback to learn how to warm your hands with relaxation. When you can consistently get above 90 degrees Fahrenheit (93 to 95 degrees is ideal) then you can begin to master warming your feet to 90 degrees. When you can let go by relaxing and warming your hands and feet, you will be able to control, if not prevent, your panic episodes. Then you must develop confidence in your control so the fear of panic during presentations does not control your life.

Regular exercise will help you work off the effects of life's stresses. Try to elevate your heart rate for fifteen to forty-five minutes three to five times per week. Check with your doctor before beginning an exercise program if you have been inactive for a long while. The release of tensions and the strengthening of your cardiovascular system will have great benefits.

Eat regular meals.
Low-fat and complex carbohydrates are better than fast foods with lots of sugar. Avoid caffeine and other stimulants. Caffeine is found in coffee, black teas, cola drinks, chocolate, some over-the-counter pain medications, and other foods and drugs. Read labels. Eat lots of fruits, vegetables, whole grains, and other natural foods.

Practice positive self-talk.
Do not let your fears escalate into your losing control of your body and your mind. By breathing slowly and staying in your body, in present time, you avoid falling into the negative pattern of fear and panic.

Get support from your friends, doctor, and therapist, if necessary.
Check your area for panic/anxiety support or treatment groups. Then consider joining a local Toastmasters group to desensitize yourself, slowly, to speaking in public.

Desensitization to your fear can be started after you have mastered relaxation. When you know how to breathe diaphragmatically and can warm your hands and feet, you have the skills to begin the mental rehearsal called desensitization. After getting completely relaxed, maintain this comfort/relaxation, and begin to picture yourself preparing and then giving a presentation to a positive, supportive audience. When you can do this mental rehearsal successfully, remaining relaxed, then you can begin to actually prepare for such an experience. This will take time and practice; however, overcoming your emotional fears through rehearsals will remove much of the fear from the actual event.

The secret to making a good presentation comes in the preparation. Repeated practice adds confidence. Humor or funny stories can help break the ice at the beginning of your presentation, but you need to rehearse even this part. Practice a strong closing that asks the audience for a call to action! You may even want to videotape a dress rehearsal so you can observe your mannerisms and voice tones when you emphasize your main points. This extra work will be well worth the effort when you actually perform. After all this preparation you may even find that the event itself is less stressful than you had expected. Indeed, the anticipation of a future presentation is usually worse than the presentation itself. So live in the present, in your body, and under your own control!

TERMINAL AND SEVERE DISORDERS

If you have a severe or terminal illness you should be under a doctor's care. This does not mean that you should abdicate full responsibility for your cure, as you may be the best healer of your own body. In *Anatomy of an Illness as Perceived by the Patient,* Norman Cousins describes his "miracle cure." Diagnosed as having an incurable collagen ailment, he took an active role as partner with his physician in the healing process. He believes that positive emotions and behaviors, such as joy and laughter, can activate the immunological system's defenses; he maintained a positive attitude despite the prognosis.

Death of a family member or an acute trauma often precedes the onset of cancer or another serious illness by six to eighteen months.

Emotional upset seems to predispose human beings to severe illnesses. If, like Norman Cousins, you can dwell upon positive emotions, your chances of getting well again are much better. When you are in a state of emotional upset, your immunological defenses are weakened; you are more susceptible to illness. People often use this information to blame themselves for having an incurable disease. This creates guilt, which is just one more negative emotion. Nor should you feel bad if you can't instantly mobilize all your positive feelings; it is natural to be angry, desperate, and afraid. It is better to accept these feelings rather than repress them, which just places more stress upon your system.

Carl and Stephanie Simonton have done extensive research with cancer patients. They have discovered that there is a definite correlation between attitude and cure rate. In their program, used as an adjunct to conventional medical treatment, cancer patients use visualization and also explore their attitudes toward their illness. Life drive is examined and patients are helped to determine if secondary gains play a large role in their disease. *Getting Well Again* explains the disease process and also outlines a powerful program for self-healing. The book can be applied not only to a terminal disorder, but to any disease.

A woman in her mid-forties was suffering from ulcerative colitis. Preliminary X rays indicated that about two feet of intestinal damage had occurred. She had severe emotional and family problems and a history of asthma, allergies, and migraine. She constantly worried about everything; even if the mail carrier was late, she worried that something had happened to him or that she would never get the mail. All her anger was repressed, and she never directly confronted anyone who had upset or inconvenienced her. Fifteen years before the onset of the disease, her husband had deserted her, leaving her with a three-year-old daughter. The child had always been overly dependent on her mother and for the two years prior to her mother's hospitalization had been undergoing psychotherapy twice a week. Her biggest fear upon entering the hospital was that her eighteen-year-old daughter wouldn't be able to feed and care for herself.

After her first hospitalization, when the physicians had diagnosed her illness, she returned home to recuperate before the surgery. She still experienced severe pain in her abdominal area; though she was very skeptical, she started attending a pain clinic two nights a week. She practiced a healing visualization twice a day until she returned to the hospital two months later. The doctors informed her that they had only removed a six-inch section of her intestines, as the original damage appeared to be partially healed. She believes that the healing visualization had a great deal to do with the improvement. Realizing that any added stress will possibly cause a recurrence of the disease, she is practicing stress reduction to control her anxiety.

Terminal and Severe Disorder Control Program

A combined program of relaxation therapy and self-healing visualization should be discussed with your doctor. If you are severely ill, I would recommend three relaxation sessions a day. After you have learned to relax, add a self-healing visualization to the exercise. Taping a relaxation-visualization exercise, rather than trying to memorize, would be ideal. In visualizing your ailment, picture your defenses defeating the infection or aberrant cells; use an image that seems most accurate to you. Your medical therapy is a positive agent, helping you to rally your natural defenses and destroy the disease. Use images for your disease that are weak and easily overwhelmed by your natural defenses.

Many people start this therapy with skepticism, and if you feel this way it doesn't mean you shouldn't try. Motivation does play a part in the healing process, but your unconscious is also involved. Listening to the tape over and over again can activate unconscious healing. You may need to revise your visualization as your health changes. If you are going to have surgery, visualize the entire procedure and its positive results. After surgery visualize complete healing of the area.

You may feel as if you have no control over what is happening in your body. To give yourself some hope, read Norman Cousins and the Simontons. Find a doctor or a clinic that will understand and cooperate with a relaxation and visualization program. More and more doctors are beginning to recognize the significance of the patient's atti-tude. *Disease is complicated by many factors, but there are some factors you can control.*

KEYS TO CONTROLLING TERMINAL AND/OR SEVERE DISORDERS:

- Learn slow breathing techniques to minimize stress.
- Use of biofeedback temperature monitoring for deep relaxation regularly.
  - Use a relaxation tape regularly (like *Stress Management for High Blood Pressure*).
  - Learn to warm your hands and feet to lessen your stress.
- Regular exercise can help minimize or prevent these complaints.
- Reduce your emotional triggers if these are a factor in your symptom activity.

Using breathing techniques regularly will prevent stresses from building.
Breathing techniques can relax you and reduce stress in your circu-latory system. These techniques can also help to reduce the intensity of your symptoms if they cannot be prevented.

Use the *Stress Management for High Blood Pressure* tape one to three times per day for eight to twelve weeks.
You can order this tape from the Stress Education Center; see the con-tact information in the back of this book. These relaxation strategies will assist you in developing the skills necessary to prevent or to lessen your symptoms. Use temperature training biofeedback to learn to warm your hands and feet. It requires repetition and time to learn how to "let go," enabling you to warm your hands to 93 to 95 degrees and then learn to warm your feet to 90 degrees. This mastery over blood flow will offer you the ability to control vascular challenges. Used preventively, this skill will help you minimize the risks that allow the onset and development of your symptoms.

Regular exercise will help you work off the effects of life's stresses. (If you have the energy to engage in regular activity, exercise can be very beneficial.) You may need assistance from a physical therapist to learn the proper activities to avoid unnecessary stress on your inflamed joints, if this is an issue. Try to elevate your heart rate for fifteen to forty five minutes three to five times per week. Check with your doctor before beginning an exercise program if you have been inactive for a long while. The release of tensions and the strengthening of your cardiovascular system will have great benefits. This improved circulation will assist you in preventing vascular problems and minimizing pain and anxiety.

Eat regular meals.
Proper nutrition can prevent the body's response to stress that can make your symptoms worse.

Reduce your emotional triggers if these are a factor in your symptom activity.
Perfectionism, repressed anger, and anxiety can all be potential triggers that either create symptoms or make them worse. Get help in identifying these issues and seek out support as you work through them to find more appropriate ways to respond when these emotional states are triggered.

Develop a sense that you do have control of your symptoms.
This is not easy in the beginning, but the behavioral techniques can help you to minimize the intensity of your pain, if not eliminate it. Many people feel "out of control" when their pain becomes chronic. This can make the intensity of the pain worse because you have fear and anxiety regarding these ongoing challenges. Temperature training biofeedback can help you to learn to relax and to "let go" of the anxiety that can intensify your complaints. Eventually, acceptance of your symptoms or illness may prove useful to minimize the anxiety and fears that can make pain worse. Lessening your physical and emotional pains will allow a better quality of life.

Chapter 11
Nutrition

You Are What You Eat

NUTRITION PLAYS A SIGNIFICANT ROLE in your total feeling of physical and mental well-being. In undertaking a stress-reduction program, you should be aware of how foods, beverages, drugs, and food additives may compound your stress level. The food you eat, and the way you eat it, may counteract all the good work you are doing to reduce stress in your life. If you are having difficulty relaxing or feel that you overreact to minimally distressing situations, changing your diet may reduce your susceptibility to stress.

Your eating habits partially determine the amount of nutrients you will be able to absorb from your food. If you are anxious, you will most likely eat more quickly than if you are calm and relaxed. This disrupts the digestive process, which starts with chewing and salivation, and all the nutrients are not absorbed. This also places an additional strain on your gastrointestinal tract. If you eat on the run—while driving, working, or even playing—it adds more stress to your system. It is better for you to sit down and eat your meals slowly, chewing all your food completely and paying attention to only eating. Some people react to tension by not eating. If you respond to stress with increased gastric secretion but are too tense to eat, you may eventually get an ulcer.

People may eat for reasons other than physical sustenance. Boredom, anxiety, and need for oral gratification may force you to eat more, and more often than is necessary. Too much weight is an added stress that is associated with hypertension and heart disease. If you are panicky all the time, you may be out of touch with your body's needs. Panic may be so overwhelming that you don't even know when your body needs fuel. You may be eating pizza at midnight because you know you need to eat something, but not supplying your body with proper nutrition at the proper time will just add to your stress level.

Foods are broken down into six nutrient classes: carbohydrates, fats, proteins, vitamins, minerals, and water. These nutrients interact to perform three basic functions. Proteins, minerals, and water facilitate growth and sustain body structures. Vitamins, minerals, proteins, and water control and coordinate internal processes. Fats, carbohydrates, and proteins provide energy and maintain body temperature. A crucial balance exists between nutrients. For example, when you have excess phosphorus in relation to calcium, you may become calcium-deficient. Since phosphorus must combine with calcium in order to be excreted, calcium needed for maintaining bone structure is lost. If your carbohydrate intake is too low, then your body will have to metabolize protein for energy since there is not enough carbohydrate to supply the energy. This places added stress on your system because it is more difficult to metabolize protein than carbohydrate for energy; also, protein needed for growth and sustaining body structures is depleted. If your body fails to use, or if you fail to eat, the necessary nutrients, then the cells may not function correctly. This will cause excess stress on your system. Conversely, stress may cause improper functioning of the cells so that nutrients are not used completely.

STRESS-PRODUCING FOODS

Some foods are "empty calories." In order to metabolize them, the body must use stored nutrients which are not replaced by these empty calories. Also, the consumption of junk food or overrefined and processed foods may destroy the appetite for more nutritious food. Other foods create excess wear and tear on the body by either kicking it into a stress response or by placing an added burden on its detoxification system. *Sugar and caffeine, both of which precipitate the stress response, are two of the most harmful substances consumed in excess by most Americans.*

I was teaching the first session in my stress-reduction course. During a discussion following a progressive relaxation exercise, one man reported that it had been almost impossible for him to relax. He felt restless, his heart was racing, and he couldn't stop thinking about his work. After almost fourteen years as a desk sergeant on the day shift, he had switched to the midnight-to-eight shift. He had changed his hours because he was bored and restless, and although he found working at night a challenging learning experience, he was having difficulty adjusting. In a midlife crisis, he felt that he needed a radical change in his life and was considering a divorce, a career change, or both.

He asked me to go out for a cup of coffee and further discuss his problem. He seemed extremely motivated and was intent upon controlling his agitation. We went to a local diner where he proceeded to bolt down two cups of coffee and a piece of lemon meringue pie. I asked him if he often drank coffee and if he craved sweets. Since he had just switched to nights, he was using the coffee to keep himself awake and alert. He had always consumed a lot of cake, candy, cookies, and other foods high in refined sugar. I asked him to keep track of his coffee and sugar consumption for the next week and to discuss it with me at the end of the next lecture.

He was surprised to discover that he drank as many as twelve cups of coffee each night and always had at least one candy bar. We discussed the effects of sugar and caffeine upon the body and how they were aggravating his restlessness. He decided to keep a log of his coffee and sugar consumption and to gradually cut down. By the next week he had cut down to four cups and decreased the sugar from two teaspoons per cup to one and a half, and he was trying to substitute nuts for the candy bars. He found it easier to sleep and was less irritated by his wife. Though not all his problems had been solved, it was easier for him to practice relaxation, and he felt more in control of his life.

Caffeine and Refined Sugar

What happens physiologically when you consume a lot of caffeine? Caffeine stimulates the nervous system, the heart, and the respiratory system and also acts as a diuretic. The adrenal glands are stimulated to produce adrenaline; the adrenaline triggers the liver to release glycogen into the blood; the pancreas must work harder to burn up the excess sugar. *The entire stress response mechanism is triggered.* As a diuretic, caffeine washes water-soluble vitamins (C and B complex) out of the body, further compounding the effects of stress by depleting needed nutrients. *Combining caffeine with refined sugar is doubly stressful for the pancreas, liver, and all the other systems involved in responding to stress.*

Refined sugar is absorbed quickly and easily into the bloodstream, elevating the blood sugar level. In the stress response the liver releases glycogen (stored body sugar) into the blood, preparing the body for the work of fight or flight. *When you eat sugar, the body interprets the increased blood sugar as a sign that you are in a fight or flight situation.* All the other characteristic physiological reactions are triggered. This is why the quick energy you get from eating sugar is called the "sugar rush." This rush throws your entire system out of balance; your body struggles for equilibrium. The pancreas produces insulin to burn up the sugar. It may overreact, producing too much insulin, and an overabundance of insulin causes the blood sugar level to drop below normal. You may feel suddenly depressed or lethargic, and to restore equilibrium you crave sugar. Many people are stuck on this roller coaster all day long, from their first cup of coffee and donut in the morning until their midnight snack.

Overconsumption of caffeine and sugar may lead to diabetes and hypoglycemia. In both dysfunctions the body's sugar-insulin regulatory mechanism is out of balance. In diabetes the blood sugar level is too high; in hypoglycemia the level is too low. Though none of the evidence is conclusive, sugar consumption is also believed to be related to the following disorders: atherosclerosis, cancer, diverticulitis, and coronary thrombosis.

Caffeine is almost as pervasive in our diets as sugar and you should be just as diligent in eliminating it. If you drink five ounces of coffee, instant or brewed, you consume about 90 to 120 milligrams of caffeine. The longer you brew tea, the higher the caffeine concentration. Caffeine content is also determined by the type of tea you drink: bagged tea has 42 to 100 milligrams per five ounces; instant tea has 30 to 60; and leaf tea also has 30 to 60. Cocoa and cola drinks also contain caffeine (as well a sugar). You can decrease your caffeine consumption by switching to decaffeinated coffee, a grain beverage, or herb teas.

Maybe you don't think you eat very much sugar. *The average sugar consumption, per person, each year in the United States is 102 pounds.* The only country which has a higher average consumption is the United Kingdom, where the rate is 120 pounds per year. You may say: "I don't eat anywhere near that amount of sugar. My teeth would be rotting if I did." Stop for a moment, and then answer these questions: Do you eat breakfast cereals? What about canned fruits and vegetables? White bread, TV dinners, catsup, tomato sauce, salad dressing, or peanut butter? Do you use mayonnaise in tuna fish salad? This is only a partial list, but it should give you some idea of how many hidden sugars there are in an average American diet. *There is no physiological need for refined sugar.* All the sugar that your body needs for energy can be obtained from more nutritious foods such as fruit, bread, grains, potatoes, and other complex carbohydrates. In fact, refined sugar is a harmful substance that should be completely eliminated from your diet. Honey is not a good substitute because it causes the same rise in blood sugar level.

Start reading labels on all the foods you buy. If sugar is the first or second listed ingredient, avoid that food since sugar makes up a high percentage of its contents. Many breakfast cereals have sugar listed as the first or second ingredient. Wean yourself slowly from the taste of sugar. Start decreasing the amount you use in beverages. If you use two teaspoonsful, cut down to one and a half; next month cut down to one, and the month after use only one-half. By this time you should start noticing the real taste of the beverage and easily be able to give up the remaining sugar.

Alcohol, Additives, Allergens, and Drugs

Alcohol is another stress-producing substance. It is high in calories but offers the body little nutritional value. It places a burden on the detoxification system, taxing the liver, kidneys, and pancreas. Alcohol may be addictive, and with repeated, heavy consumption, the organs involved in detoxification wear out and are unable to perform their function. The liver is the body's main detoxifying organ, and continual exposure to alcohol or other toxins can destroy the liver. Alcohol depletes magnesium, thiamin, and other B vitamins. Overconsumption of alcohol is implicated in blood sugar level imbalances such as hypoglycemia and diabetes. Although alcohol depresses the nervous system, which may make you feel temporarily less anxious, the overall effects are stressful.

Food additives, void of any nutrients, are contained in most processed foods. They function as flavor enhancers, emulsifiers, spoilage retardants, and coloring agents, and have a variety of other uses. These are fairly new additions to the human diet and the long-term effects are generally unknown, though some substances have been tested and shown to be carcinogenic in animals. Monosodium glutamate (MSG) may be found in almost any food; in sensitive people it causes headaches, skin flushing, and a constriction in the chest. Nitrates and nitrites, found most commonly in meat, may also cause headaches. Food additives to avoid are sodium nitrate and sodium nitrite, BHT, brominated vegetable oil (BVO), saccharin, blue #1 and #2, citrus red #2, red #3 and #40, green #3, orange B, and yellow #5.

Allergies to foods are common and difficult to detect. Your body responds to the food allergen as if it were a toxin. The immunological system is especially taxed. Symptoms can manifest in any part of the body, from the respiratory tract, to the digestive system, and even to the brain. Allergies can cause such mental symptoms as restlessness, confusion, and dizziness. To test for food allergies, the suspect food must be completely removed from the diet and reintroduced in a pure form. If an allergic reaction occurs, the food should be eliminated from your diet. Milk, milk products, grains such as wheat, and fruits such as strawberries are common allergens, but you can be allergic to any food, even sesame seeds. Since it is difficult to isolate the troublesome food, it is best to consult a doctor or nutritionist. After the allergen has been established, discuss a stress-reduction program with your doctor.

A variety of drugs have become commonplace in our society. Barbiturates, amphetamines, and tranquilizers are often overprescribed. Like alcohol, they have harmful side effects and can be addictive. They stress the body, especially the detoxification systems. Drugs are alluring in their promise of instant relief from symptoms. If you can resist you may find that stress-reduction techniques are as effective in modifying your emotional and physiological state. If you have been taking drugs, consult with your physician about reducing dosages or eliminating them from your life.

PROPER DIET FOR STRESS MANAGEMENT

What you consume can be a help or a detriment to your health and stress levels. Since time and space do not allow for a complete study of diet's effect on stress, we must simplify in the space available.

A huge amount of new research has been published which begins to prove what some researchers have been saying for the past few decades. We are increasingly bombarded by stresses from toxins in our environment, including toxins within our foods. If our foods are not toxic, they are generally depleted in nutrients, especially the micronutrients and trace minerals that are essential for normal health and life functions.

Research has also been done on the workings of antioxidants and their effects on free radicals. Free radicals, very simply, are molecules (usually oxygen molecules) created in our bodies that are unstable. They lack a paired electron in the outer orbits of their atomic structures. This instability is created by environmental facts like sunlight (ultraviolet light), smoke, and toxins in food, air, and water. Physical stress from excessive exercise can generate free radicals. Emotional stresses may also trigger the development of these dangerous molecules. To quench their need for an extra electron, they can cause a destructive chain reaction which steals available electrons from necessary body molecules. This can destroy molecules, cell membranes, and cells, and can even cause damage to the DNA structures resulting in improper cell divisions (which may be linked to cancer). Such a process is thought to bring on premature aging, sickness, even death.

Antioxidants are naturally occurring or created molecules that can give up an extra electron to quench the destructive needs of free radicals. The body will produce these if given the proper nutrients in useable forms that are absorbed from foods or from special supplements. The food we eat is generally depleted of many essential vitamins and minerals that used to be found in more natural food sources. Since we often do not eat enough natural foods, supplementation may be the best preventative device we can take to counter our stressful environment and internal attacks by free radicals. Known antioxidants are vitamin A (and beta-carotene), vitamin C (ester C may be most effective), vitamin E (natural forms work best), folacin (folic acid), glutathione, leucoanthocyanin, minerals such as zinc, manganese, and selenium, and lysine (an amino acid). Undoubtedly, more vitamins and minerals which assist or produce antioxidants will be discovered and added to the recommended list as research continues.

The trick may be to not only eat correctly but to find good supplementation that is readily absorbed by the body to make these antioxidants available. However, supplements should not be used as an attempt to balance out negative lifestyle choices. A good multi-vitamin cannot reverse the damage that smoking causes, for instance. Remember that vigorous exercise can deplete our bodies of certain nutrients, also. We must supplement in response to this positive stress as well.

In considering diet and nutrition, remember that too much of almost anything can be unhealthy. Moderation is the key. If you are suffering under stress, you should be careful to increase good things in your diet and limit or eliminate inappropriate things. Everybody is different, but some general guidelines are helpful for all.

If You Are Stressed

Eat as simply as possible, increasing raw or less cooked fruits and vegetables (barring major digestive distress from raw foods). Drink more water: at least six ten-ounce glasses per day. Eat three or four meals per day (smaller but regular is best). Take nutritional supplements, especially vitamin C, vitamin B complex, beta-carotene (and small amounts of vitamin A—check with your physician), vitamin E, and trace minerals that are chelated for easy absorption. Check out the Lifepak supplements from IDN (Interior Design Nutritionals). The author of *Mega Health,* Marc Sorenson, who is an expert on diet, has joined many doctors and nutritionists in suggesting that this particular, unique formulation is superior in effectiveness and technology to most other supplementation products on the market. Ask for help if you are not certain about what to take. Dieticians are most knowledgeable; some health-food store people are also well trained. I wish more physicians were properly trained to offer the nutritional counseling and support so necessary for prevention of disease and enhanced wellness. Finally, eat more grains for energy and complex carbohydrates from fruits. For "fast foods" eat more fruits and vegetables in general.

Do not use caffeine (from coffee, teas, cola drinks, chocolate, and so on). Caffeine increases anxiety, panic, and stress in much the same way that adrenaline acts upon the body. Avoid other stimulants. Do not use too much refined sugar or highly processed food. Reduce fat, especially saturated fat, in your diet. Reduce red meats. A diet of less than 20 percent calories from fat is often recommended, so read ingredient labels carefully. Stop tobacco use! Reduce or eliminate alcohol. Do not become dependent on alcohol or drugs to control anxiety, unless under the care of your physician. Try not to eat close to bedtime (allow a couple of hours, at least, if possible). Try not to eat and do other things at the same time.

ANTISTRESS VITAMINS AND MINERALS

Water-soluble vitamins and certain minerals are rapidly depleted by stress; these are the very vitamins and minerals you need most to combat stress. Nutritional needs vary from individual to individual; even minimal deficiencies can cause physical and psychological dysfunction. Caffeine, sugar, alcohol, and over-refined foods rob the body of vitamins and minerals, especially those needed to help your body adapt to stress. The water-soluble vitamins B complex and C are easily lost, since they are not stored in the body and must constantly be replenished.

The primary functions of vitamins are the prevention of disease, regulation of body processes, facilitation of enzyme action, and the absorption and utilization of all the nutrients. Minerals help regulate body functions and are a constituent of hard and soft tissues. *The following vitamins and minerals are the most important for combating the effects of stress: B complex, vitamin C, calcium, potassium, zinc, and magnesium.* There is an interrelationship between all minerals and vitamins, and they should be taken in concert. The following list will give you some idea of the complex interactions among the stress vitamins and the variety of important functions they perform in the body. This information is not comprehensive and I am not a nutritionist. If you intend to supplement your diet, by all means discuss your nutritional needs with your physician or a nutritionist.

B Complex

The B vitamins function best when they are taken together. The B complex is composed of eleven known vitamins: thiamin (B_1), riboflavin (B_2), niacin (B_3), pyridoxine (B_6), pantothenic acid, biotin, folic acid, cobalamin (B_{12}), choline, inositol, para-aminobenzoic acid (PABA).

THIAMIN

Thiamin is necessary for transforming glucose into energy. In the breakdown of sugar, pyruvic and lactic acids are formed; enzymes containing thiamin convert pyruvic acid into carbon dioxide and water, and lactic acid into glycogen. If there is a thiamin deficiency, these acids are not broken down and remain in the tissues, accumulating in the brain, nerves, heart, and blood. They are eventually secreted in the urine. Adverse personality changes occur from a thiamin deficiency because brain cells derive their energy only from sugar; since glucose cannot be converted without thiamin, the brain cells do not get sufficient nutrients. Also, the acids accumulating in the brain are slightly toxic. These acids irritate the heart muscle, eventually resulting in a rapid heartbeat. Nerves are also exclusive sugar burners, and a lack of this nutrient results in poor nerve functioning. The pyruvic and lactic acids accumulating in the nerves eventually leads to nerve cell damage. A large carbohydrate intake requires a large thiamin intake. Deficiencies can be corrected almost immediately; experiments have shown that resumption of a thiamin-rich diet will eradicate symptoms within two to three days.

Body Use: metabolism of sugar, appetite maintenance, hydrochloric acid production, muscle tone maintenance of intestine, stomach, and heart

Sources: blackstrap molasses, whole grains, sunflower and sesame seeds, pork, organ meats, brewer's yeast, wheat germ

Adjunct Nutrients: B complex, riboflavin, folic acid, niacin, vitamins C and E, manganese, sulphur, zinc

Depleting Agents: alcohol, coffee, tobacco, surgery, raw clams, sugar

Symptoms of Deficiency: depression, lack of ability to concentrate, lack of mental alertness, apprehension, irritability, nervousness, forgetfulness, appetite loss, fatigue, pain and noise sensitivity, shortness of breath

Used in Treatment of: alcoholism, anemia, congestive heart failure, constipation, diarrhea, diabetes, indigestion, nausea, pain, rapid heart rate, stress, mental disorders

RIBOFLAVIN

An early sign of riboflavin deficiency is sensitivity to light. Enzymes containing riboflavin combine with oxygen in the air to supply cells in the cornea; a deficiency of this B vitamin causes tiny blood vessels to form, supplying necessary oxygen from the blood rather than the air. Riboflavin is essential for cell oxidation, a process which releases energy. If you are under stress, more energy is needed, and riboflavin helps supply this energy.

Body Use: antibody and red blood cell formation, cell respiration, metabolism of fat, carbohydrate, and protein

Sources: liver, kidney, milk, brewer's yeast, wheat germ, leafy green vegetables, whole grains, blackstrap molasses

Adjunct Nutrients: B complex, an equal amount of pyridoxine, niacin, vitamin C, phosphorous

Depleting Agents: alcohol, coffee, sugar, tobacco

Symptoms of Deficiency: depression, anxiety, eye problems, sores around mouth, poor digestion, retarded growth, sore and red tongue

Used in Treatment of: alcoholism, arthritis, baldness, cataracts, diabetes, diarrhea, indigestion, stress

NIACIN

Niacin is also known as niacinamide, nicotinic acid, and nicotinic acidomide. The amount of niacin needed varies from individual to individual. Taking niacin usually causes the skin to become red, flushed, and prickly; the reaction can even be frightening. Niaci-namide does not cause these effects and should be used instead of niacin. The first signs of deficiency are an unpleasant mouth odor and psychological imbalance. Niacin is used experimentally in the treatment of schizophrenia.

Body Use: circulation, growth, cholesterol level reduction, hydrochloric acid production, sex hormone production, metabolism of fat, protein, and carbohydrate

Sources: liver, lean meats, fish, wheat germ, brewer's yeast, peanuts, soybeans, milk, poultry, rhubarb

Adjunct Nutrients: B complex, thiamin, riboflavin, vitamin C, phosphorus

Depleting Agents: alcohol, coffee, sugar, antibiotics, excessive starches, corn

Symptoms of Deficiency: nervousness, irritability, loss of humor, suspicion, apprehension, loss of appetite, depression, fatigue, headache, indigestion, insomnia, muscular weakness, nausea

Used in Treatment of: diarrhea, high blood pressure, leg cramps, migraine headaches, poor circulation, stress

PYRIDOXINE

Pyridoxine acts as a tranquilizer and is effective in treating insom-nia, nervousness, and migraine headache. It is necessary for healthy functioning of the brain and is essential in maintaining a proper magnesium level. The need for pyridoxine increases during pregnancy and also when taking oral contraceptives and estrogen-replacement therapy. The amount needed also varies with protein, fat, and fatty acid consumption.

Body Use: antibody formation, hydrochloric acid production, maintenance of sodium-potassium balance in the nerves, weight control

Sources: blackstrap molasses, brewer's yeast, green leafy vegetables, organ meats, wheat germ, whole grains

Adjunct Nutrients: B complex thiamin, riboflavin, pantothenic acid, vitamin C, magnesium, potassium, linoleic acid, sodium

Depleting Agents: alcohol, coffee, tobacco, birth control pills

Symptoms of Deficiency: anemia, arthritis, depression, dizziness, irritability, weakness, learning disabilities

Used in Treatment of: atherosclerosis, high cholesterol level, hypoglycemia, migraine headaches, muscular disorders, nervous disorders, stress

PANTOTHENIC ACID

The need for pantothenic acid increases radically under stress, with the requirement increasing with the severity of the stress. Neither sugar nor fat can be used for energy without this vitamin, and a deficiency adversely affects the adrenal glands. The adrenals become enlarged and unable to produce cortisone and approximately thirty other adrenal hormones. Pantothenic acid is essential in proper blood sugar level maintenance.

Body Use: antibody formation, vitamin utilization, growth

Sources: egg yolk, kidney, liver, brewer's yeast, legumes, salmon, wheat germ, whole grains, mushrooms

Adjunct Nutrients: B complex, pyridoxine, cobalamin, biotin, folic acid, vitamin C

Depleting Agents: alcohol, coffee, stress

Symptoms of Deficiency: depression, lowered resistance to stress, diarrhea, duodenal ulcer, hypoglycemia, intestinal disorders, kidney problems, muscle cramps, respiratory infections, restlessness, nerve problems, sore feet, vomiting

Used in Treatment of: allergies, arthritis, digestive disorders, hypoglycemia, stress

BIOTIN

A deficiency of biotin makes the body particularly susceptible to heart abnormalities and lung infections. Since the ingestion of raw egg white prevents biotin from reaching the blood, large quantities should not be consumed, especially under stress. Depression and panic can result from a deficiency. Biotin is necessary for the utilization of pantothenic acid, which is used up quickly under stress; thus biotin is also depleted under stress.

Body Use: cell growth, fatty acid production, metabolism of carbohydrate, fat, and protein, vitamin B utilization

Sources: legumes, whole grains, organ meats, soybeans

Adjunct Nutrients: B complex, cobalamin, folic acid, pantothenic acid, vitamin C, sulphur

Depleting Agents: alcohol, coffee, raw egg white

Symptoms of Deficiency: depression, dry skin, fatigue, insomnia, muscular pain, poor appetite

Used in Treatment of: dermatitis, eczema, leg cramps

FOLIC ACID

Folic acid is essential for the utilization of sugar and amino acids, and the production of antibodies. Deficiencies are common during pregnancy and when taking birth control pills and estrogen. The production of DNA and RNA and the division of all body cells is partially dependent upon an adequate supply of this B vitamin.

Body Use: appetite, body growth and reproduction, hydrochloric acid production, protein metabolism, red blood cell formation

Sources: leafy green vegetables, milk, organ meats, oysters, salmon, whole grains, tuna, dates

Adjunct Nutrients: B complex, cobalamin, biotin, pantothenic acid, vitamin C

Depleting Agents: alcohol, coffee, tobacco, stress

Symptoms of Deficiency: anemia, digestive disturbances, graying hair, growth problems

Used in Treatment of: alcoholism, anemia, atherosclerosis, diarrhea, fatigue, mental illness, stomach ulcers, stress

COBALAMIN

Essential for proper nerve functioning, cobalamin maintains the nerve tissue sheath which enables nerves to transmit messages. It is also involved in the production of DNA and RNA, the blueprint of heredity, and produces nucleic acid, a necessary constituent of the cell.

Body Use: appetite, blood cell formation and longevity, nervous system, metabolism of fat, carbohydrate, and protein

Sources: cheese, fish, milk, organ meats, tuna

Adjunct Nutrients: B complex, pyridoxine, choline, inositol, folic acid, vitamin C, potassium, sodium

Depleting Agents: alcohol, coffee, tobacco, laxatives

Symptoms of Deficiency: weakness, nervousness, pernicious anemia, walking and speaking difficulties

Used in Treatment of: alcoholism, allergies, anemia, arthritis, asthma, bursitis, epilepsy, fatigue, hypoglycemia, insomnia, stress

CHOLINE

Choline, along with inositol, is part of the structure of lecithin, a deficiency of which results in high blood cholesterol levels and high blood pressure. Choline is part of the enzyme which helps to transfer nerve messages, essential for muscle contraction. The amount of choline needed is related to the amount of saturated fats in the diet; the more fat ingested, the more choline needed.

Body Use: lecithin formation, liver and gall bladder function, metabolism of fat and cholesterol, nerve transmission

Sources: brewer's yeast, fish, legumes, liver, organ meats, soybeans, wheat germ, egg yolks, peanuts, lecithin

Adjunct Nutrients: vitamin A, B complex, cobalamin, folic acid, pantothenic acid, inositol, linoleic acid

Depleting Agents: alcohol, coffee, sugar

Symptoms of Deficiency: bleeding ulcers, heart problems, high blood pressure, impaired liver and kidney functioning

Used in Treatment of: alcoholism, atherosclerosis, high cholesterol level, constipation, dizziness, ear noises, hardening of the arteries, headaches, heart problems, high blood pressure, hypoglycemia, insomnia

INOSITOL

Inositol is one of the most prevalent vitamins in the body and is particularly concentrated in the eye and heart muscles. This B vitamin reduces the amount of cholesterol in the blood and increases the contractions of the eliminatory tract. Along with choline, it is part of the structure of lecithin which is concentrated in the brain. Protective nerve coverings are largely composed of lecithin, and lecithin helps the body digest and absorb vitamins A, D, E, and K.

Body Use: artery hardening retardation, cholesterol reduction, hair growth, lecithin formation, metabolism of fat and cholesterol

Sources: blackstrap molasses, citrus fruits, brewer's yeast, meats, milk, nuts, vegetables, whole grains, lecithin

Adjunct Nutrients: B complex, cobalamin, choline, linoleic acid

Depleting Agents: alcohol, coffee

Symptoms of Deficiency: high cholesterol level, constipation, eczema, eye problems, hair loss

Used in Treatment of: atherosclerosis, high cholesterol level, heart disease, constipation

PARA-AMINOBENZOIC ACID (PABA)

This vitamin makes sulfa drugs ineffective, and as a result it is often excluded from B complex supplements. Not much is known about its function, though it is believed to be useful in hair and skin maintenance and may be necessary for the utilization of folic acid.

Body Use: blood cell formation, intestinal bacteria activity, protein metabolism

Sources: brewer's yeast, organ meats, liver, blackstrap molasses, wheat germ

Adjunct Nutrients: B complex, folic acid, pantothenic acid, vitamin C

Depleting Agents: alcohol, coffee, sulfa drugs

Symptoms of Deficiency: constipation, fatigue, depression, digestive disorders, headaches, irritability

Used in Treatment of: overactive thyroid, rheumatic fever, stress, infertility, dry skin

Vitamin C

The requirements and uses of vitamin C are still being tested; research has shown that some people can utilize over 4,000 milligrams before the excess is excreted. Individual needs vary greatly, and megadoses may be indicated for some diseases. Vitamin C has been promoted as a preventive medication for the common cold by Dr. Linus Pauling and others; researchers are also studying its role in relationship to many other diseases. This vitamin also acts as a detoxifying agent against lead, bromide, arsenic, benzene, and allergens. Absorption of iron is increased as much as 10 percent when taken in conjunction with vitamin C. The B vitamins folic acid and cobalamin (B_{12}) require vitamin C for efficient metabolism, and vitamin C is needed for the manufacturing of adrenal hormones. It appears to be important in all immunological functioning.

Body Use: bone and tooth formation, collagen production, digestion, healing, red blood cell formation, shock and infection resistance, hormone manufacture, protection of circulation from fat deposits, emotional and environmental stress fighter

Sources: citrus fruits, cantaloupe, green pepper, papaya

Adjunct Nutrients: all vitamins and minerals, bioflavonoids, calcium and magnesium are essential for proper functioning

Depleting Agents: antibiotics, aspirin, cortisone, tobacco, stress

Symptoms of Deficiency: anemia, bleeding gums, low infection resistance, nosebleeds, poor digestion, bruises

Used in Treatment of: alcoholism, allergies, atherosclerosis, arthritis, high cholesterol level, colds, hypoglycemia, heart disease, stress

Calcium

Calcium deficiencies are more widespread than most people would think. Though milk and milk products are rich in calcium, a great deal of calcium is lost in the cheese-making process. Roquefort and Swiss cheeses are very rich in calcium, while camembert and cream cheese have the lowest concentration. Muscle cramps and spasms often result from a calcium deficiency; leg and foot cramps are the most common, though cramping can occur anywhere, such as in the spastic colon. Calcium supplementation is often used to prevent menstrual cramps, and along with pyridoxine (B_6) may reduce the severity of migraine headaches. Calcium and magnesium must be taken in conjunction; twice as much calcium is needed as magnesium.

Body Use: bone and tooth formation, blood clotting, steady heart rhythm, nerve tranquilization and transmission, muscle growth and contraction

Sources: milk, cheese, blackstrap molasses, liver, yogurt, bone meal, mustard and turnip greens, soybeans

Adjunct Nutrients: vitamins A, C, and D, and phosphorous, iron, magnesium, and manganese are all essential for proper functioning

Depleting Agents: lack of exercise, stress

Symptoms of Deficiency: heart palpitations, insomnia, muscle cramps, nervousness, grogginess

Used in Treatment of: arthritis, foot and leg cramps, insomnia, nervousness, rheumatism, migraine headaches .

Potassium

Potassium is needed to metabolize sugar and to form glycogen. Excess sugar intake can result in a potassium deficiency; a deficiency of potassium results in low blood sugar because the glycogen cannot be synthesized. Potassium balance depends upon an adequate supply of magnesium. Excessive sodium consumption results in a loss of potassium from the body, and a potassium deficiency can result in water retention and muscle damage. Individual needs for potassium vary, and greatly depend upon salt consumption. Fruits and vegetables are the richest sources of this mineral, though excessively boiling vegetables radically depletes the amount of potassium.

Body Use: steady heart rate, growth, muscle contraction, nerve tranquilization

Sources: dates, figs, peaches, tomato juice, blackstrap molasses, peanuts, raisins, seafood, apricots, sunflower seeds

Adjunct Nutrients: pyridoxine, magnesium; sodium in amounts equal to potassium intake is essential for properly functioning

Depleting Agents: alcohol, coffee, cortisone, salt, sugar, laxatives, diuretics, stress, aspirin

Symptoms of Deficiency: thirst, dry skin, constipation, weakness, insomnia, muscle damage, nervousness, irregular heartbeat, weak reflexes

Used in Treatment of: alcoholism, allergies, diabetes, high blood pressure, angina pectoris, congestive heart failure, myocardial infarction

Zinc

A common symptom of zinc deficiency is white spots in the fingernails; this often occurs during adolescence. Zinc is a trace mineral found in the soil; chemical fertilizers do not allow sufficient absorption by soil or plants. Overconsumption of phosphorus, very prevalent in our society, can cause zinc deficiencies. Zinc is concentrated in the eyes and sperm, and a lack of this mineral can result in sterility and impaired production of RNA and DNA. When vegetables containing zinc are boiled, the mineral is easily lost in the cooking water.

Body Use: healing, carbohydrate digestion, reproductive organ growth and development, sex organ growth and maturity, metabolism of thiamin, phosphorous, and protein

Sources: brewer's yeast, liver, seafood, soybeans, spinach, sunflower seeds, mushrooms

Adjunct Nutrients: vitamin A, calcium, copper, phosphorous

Depleting Agents: alcohol, lack of phosphorous, high calcium intake

Symptoms of Deficiency: delayed sexual maturity, fatigue, poor appetite, prolonged wound healing, white spots in fingernails

Used in Treatment of: alcoholism, atherosclerosis, cirrhosis, diabetes, high cholesterol level

Magnesium

Magnesium deficiency is relatively new to the United States. Like zinc, absorption is restricted by the presence of chemical fertilizers; the agricultural soil east of the Mississippi River is the most deficient in magnesium. Magnesium is lost with consumption of alcohol, and when magnesium is deficient calcium is also secreted. Potassium is also dependent upon magnesium for retention in the cells, and pyroxidine (B₆) needs an adequate supply of potassium for proper absorption. If foods are soaked or boiled, magnesium is easily lost in the water. Every cell in the body needs magnesium for proper functioning, and a deficiency can result in physical and severe psychological dysfunction.

Body Use: blood sugar metabolism, metabolism of calcium and vitamin C, acid and alkaline balance, production of enzymes, synthesis of protein, utilization of fat and carbohydrate

Sources: bran, honey, green vegetables, nuts, seafood, spinach, bonemeal, kelp, peanuts, soybeans, chard, kale, beet greens

Adjunct Nutrients: pyridoxine, vitamins C and D, calcium, phosphorus

Depleting Agents: alcohol

Symptoms of Deficiency: confusion, disorientation, easily aroused anger, nervousness, tremors, rapid pulse, depression, restlessness, insomnia

Used in Treatment of: alcoholism, high cholesterol level, depression, heart conditions, kidney stones, nervousness, sensitivity to noise, stomach acidity

Chapter 12
Tools for Change

YOUR STRESS-MANAGEMENT PROGRAM will reach into many areas of your life. By controlling tension, you may be able to learn more quickly and easily, and remember what you learn for a longer time. Relaxation can increase your efficiency; you will not tire as quickly and may find that you need less sleep. For some people, relaxation twenty minutes a day may take the place of two hours of sleep. Your sleep will be deeper and more restful. Stress reduction, practiced on a regular basis, will help you perform your best and give the most that you are capable of giving.

A relaxed, calm person has a better chance of leading a full, rich, disease-free life. Relaxation may make a radical change in your life. In a profound state of deep relaxation, you may discover new depths in yourself, reexperience and reclaim lost feelings. Some people interpret the changes they experience as a result of practicing stress reduction as spiritual growth. I am not claiming that you will hear messages from the Lord, see burning bushes, or be able to command lightning, but your view of the world will become more positive. Stress reduction practice can make you more receptive to some other tools that can help you alleviate even more stress from your life. Goal setting and communication skills can increase your ability to cope with life in a more positive and effective way. I will not cover these topics in depth, but will give you enough information so that you know where to go to seek additional help.

GOAL SETTING

Many of the people with whom I work suffer anxiety over their present situations and feel apprehensive about the future. They seem to be driving on a highway that has only entrances, with no exits in sight. Their sense of helplessness and hopelessness heightens their anxiety and stress levels. I have watched such people go through a catharsis in their life as a result of stress reduction. After relaxation training, they realize that they have been stagnating emotionally and intellectually—just watching from the sidelines as life passed them by, afraid to take a risk. They learn to jump into life and really live it fully, with its challenges and the possibilities of success or failure.

These people learn that failure is not always bad. They begin to view failure as a potential learning experience and see the importance of risking possible failure. One way to break the pattern of viewing failure negatively is to learn how to set goals and then accomplish them. This provides an experience of success if you start out with a reasonable, attainable goal. Goal setting does not mean daydreaming or deciding to do the impossible. Goal setting is a technique for finding direction and then beginning to take the steps necessary for attaining your goal. No great accomplishment ever just happens. First you must have a dream and then find a way to achieve it.

First establish the goals you wish to achieve, prioritize them, and break them down into achievable steps. If you really want to go to Europe, you will have to do many things, such as collect information about where to go, obtain a passport, and save money to get there. You can't just wish or daydream—you have to act! Cut out pictures of the places you plan to visit. Call and find out the procedure for getting a passport. Break the goals down into short-range goals (less than six months) and long-range goals (one year, two years, five years). Getting a passport may take one month and would be a short-range goal; saving the money might take as long as two years and would be a long-range goal. Even long-range goals can be broken up into shorter time periods. You might plan to have a specific amount of money saved after six months, after one year, and so on. The short-term goals should lead to the long-term goals and be fairly easy to accomplish. *You want to build a pattern of success for yourself, not failure.*

Goal-setting techniques can be applied to social, career, or even health goals. Use the following procedure to break down your goal setting into a realistic plan.

Procedure for Goal Setting

1. Identify your life's values/beliefs/goals.

2. Goals must be realistic and believable. Visualize your goal as accurately as possible; devising a concrete image of exactly what you want helps focus your goal. Your actions will be more realistic if your goal is clear and well defined.

3. Put your goals in writing. Keeping lists of daily, weekly, and monthly goals and accomplishments will help you monitor your progress.

4. Establish goals for all areas of your life: business/professional, family, physical health, spiritual, creative/aesthetic, fun/recreational, social, and emotional.

5. Set short-term goals. Break them down into achievable steps.

6. Set long-term goals. Break them down into achievable steps (daily, weekly, monthly, yearly, etc.).

7. Prioritize your daily list so that your day is not taken up with unimportant activities. Check off your accomplishments and give yourself time to celebrate the momentum of your success.

8. Vividly imagine the accomplishment of your goals. See and feel, if possible, the successful completion in the present.

9. Be passionate and positive. Your goals must be ardently desired for heartfelt reasons.

10. Do not let your list fill you with consuming guilt or anxiety. Be reasonable in budgeting your time and energy. Nothing is so important that your health and well-being should suffer.

After these steps…JUST DO IT!

Further information about goal setting is available in Carl and Stephanie Simonton's book *Getting Well Again.*

COMMUNICATION

Stress is often aggravated by faulty communication or the lack of communication between people. First you must be clear in communicating with yourself and then with the people around you. Getting to know and understand your feelings is a difficult process, but a very important step in becoming aware of your own needs. We often confuse our feelings and emotions with thoughts and end up repressing our real feelings. Feelings are sensations that you experience, and thoughts are the way you try to describe or express the sensations. "My boss is hard on me" is a thought. "I feel angry toward my boss and I am afraid of her" is a feeling. Practicing stress reduction brings your emotions to the surface—they are no longer hidden away deep inside you. Expressing these "new" emotions, whether they are anger or love, may not be easy at first.

Anger is an especially difficult feeling to express. From an early age we learn that other people do not handle anger well, and do not like to see it expressed. We sometimes need to learn anger-release techniques. If you are very angry, allow yourself to discharge the anger. It will be easier for you to gain some perspective on the situation that produced the anger after the feeling has been expressed. Go for a run, take a long swim, yell in the shower, beat your bed or pillow. Using a tape recorder can be very effective release technique. Turn on the recorder and talk until you are completely emptied of thoughts, emotions, and energy. Do not censure your expression. Express your feelings even if they sound childish or irrational—just let them out. You can listen to the tape later to learn about your emotions. But when you are angry, the most important thing is the release.

When you are clear about your own feelings, communicating your needs to other people becomes much easier. Many communication problems develop because people are not aware of their own needs or are unable to express their desires to other people. By clearly communicating your needs you can reduce stress in communication. You must work to send and receive messages more clearly. Visualize the message you want to communicate; this makes you stop just a moment before speaking and gives you time to be really clear on your message. If you are listening, your job is to listen carefully.

Stress can block your ability to hear and receive—your own tension gets in the way. Listening is often difficult if you don't want to hear a certain message, and so block out the other person's words and feelings. Thinking too far ahead about your own reply, before hearing the full message, inhibits communication. You may miss an important point, and your response may be inappropriate. It is important not to send a double message, saying one thing when you actually mean or wish another. You cannot expect another person to read your mind to determine your true intention. Feedback from the listener is important; sometimes you need to ask for feedback to be certain that your message is clear.

Communication involves at least two people, and their relationship to each other definitely affects the quality of the communication. I find a few simple principles derived from Transactional Analysis (T.A.) especially useful. Transactional Analysis sets a simple role model by which most communication can be explained. The three roles that people assume in their interactions with other people are child, parent, and adult. You may slip into any of these roles at various times in conversation or communication. If you assume the child role, you may unconsciously ask your partner to assume the parent role. Talking up or down to another person always sets up the potential for miscommunication. Two people communicating as equals (adults) can get a great deal more accomplished than they can in an unequally defined communication.

If you have a feeling about another person, avoid blaming the other person for your feeling. It is your feeling, your own perception; take the responsibility for it. If you do not like someone because of something he or she did to annoy you, and you want to communicate your feelings, you might say, "I feel uncomfortable." Or "This experience has made me feel uncomfortable." Avoid blaming the other person whenever possible. "I feel our interaction could have been less irritating for me if I had . . ." makes someone more willing to try and work out the problem. Perceive your feelings, and then consider how future communication might be improved.

Communication goes beyond words. Almost 80 percent of all communication is nonverbal, and perceptive people can learn a wealth of information by picking up on all the messages. Body language, intonation, mannerism, gesture, touch, and body movement may often communicate more than words. Relaxation and a calm state of mind increase your awareness of yourself and others and make you more conscious of the different levels of communication.

I feel that relaxation practiced with another person can be a meaningful, consciousness-expanding experience. I have not discussed massage in this book because I wanted to concentrate on techniques people can use alone. If you wish to experience tactile communication and a blissful state of deep relaxation, then learn how to massage and be massaged. Some people have resistance to the thought of being massaged, but massage can be a pleasant, relaxing, healing experience. Touching is both supportive and therapeutic, and a way of breaking through the limits of verbal communication.

I have found in my practice that many people who strive constantly for sexual gratification really want and need more physical contact. In Italian and Greek societies men and women touch and kiss each other as a means of communicating their emotions and thoughts. Such physical contact, especially between men, is considered abnormal in America, a society based on the prudery and self-containment of the Pilgrims. By restricting physical communication, our society increases our stress level. Touching each other, through massage, has become more socially acceptable in our country since the 1970s and can be explored as a technique for reducing stress while increasing communication between two people.

When you receive a massage, you will feel the tightness in your muscles as it yields to the massaging hands. The first time you are massaged, you may be apprehensive about turning your body over to another person. You will learn how to trust the other person's ability to locate and stroke away your tension. When you massage another person, pinpointing where tension is held in his or her body will help you identify your own tension. Once you have shared physical communication with another person, even if only a hug, other levels of communication may improve. Breaking the barrier around your body will make you more sensitive to other people's nonverbal and verbal messages.

ASKING FOR HELP

Stress reduction will significantly reduce your stress level. It may not solve all the problems in your life, and since you have started doing positive things for yourself, you may want to reach out for further help. Psychotherapists, psychiatrists, psychologists, counselors, social workers, and many other types of trained professionals and paraprofessionals are available to you through mental health facilities in your community. You do not have to be "crazy" to avail yourself of these services. Our society has programmed people into isolated, withdrawn, "I can take care of myself" attitudes. Examine your lifestyle and determine whether you are taking time and energy for yourself. If you need assistance, are you capable of asking for support or help?

If you have a specific problem, it can be helpful to work within a group situation. In my stress-reduction classes, I have often seen people with similar problems help each other, even when they couldn't help themselves. They feel less isolated, and once they realize that others have the same problem, it is easier for them to change. Besides stress-reduction classes, and depending upon your specific need, you may be able to find groups in parenting, sexuality, Transactional Analysis, yoga, meditation, assertiveness training, consciousness raising, pain management, gestalt therapy, and many more.

Take care of yourself, and feel good about yourself. I can remember painful times in my own life during which I was confused, hurt, and unable to make any decisions. I had not yet discovered stress reduction and was blindly searching for something to stabilize my life. I would not want to relive these periods in my life—but I would not want to give them up either—because I learned and experienced so much from this chaos and turmoil. I believe most people learn and grow—not when everything is going well in their lives—but when they are experiencing difficulty and pain and have to change. Growth and change are not always easy or fun, but they are a necessary part of being alive. Practicing stress reduction made my life changes easier, and I hope it will do the same for you.

NOW THAT YOU KNOW IT, DO IT

It is important to restate the most vital point. *For you to benefit from having read this book, it will not be enough to just think about these ideas and concepts. It will not be enough to just discuss them with your friends. You will have to give these techniques a chance to work for you by practicing them on a regular basis.* Daily practice for two or three months will really give you the feeling of what is possible. Without this practice, *Guide to Stress Reduction* may become just another book on the shelf and a feeling of failure or waste may be left in the back of your mind.

Remember that by serving yourself by practicing these new skills you will also benefit the people and the projects that surround you.

Chapter 13
Guide to Stress Reduction in Business

I N BUSINESS the costs of stress are too high! Productivity is lowered. Profits are negatively affected. Morale and quality of life are down. Health-care costs are up. Worker's compensation claims are more expensive. Even retention of good employees is severely affected by stress and the company's response to stress and change.

And for executives and senior managers, remember this statement from business consultant and author Jim Clemmer: "The next time you catch yourself pointing fingers at your customers, your frontline employees, managers, supervisors, or support staff, take a look at the end of your arm. There are three times as many fingers pointing back at the real culprit."

In this chapter many of the stress-related business issues will be identified. The answers will require some attention and then the implementation of the solutions will be the next challenge.

Let's begin with managing the stress of change within an organization.

MANAGE CHANGE

The momentum of change continues to build. If you or the organization you work with is not prepared for ongoing change, then you risk being overwhelmed and left for dead by the superhighway of life! This dramatic metaphor is reported constantly by the people who predict business and economic trends. With technology and globalization of trade driving these trends, we must learn to adapt gracefully to these changes or play the very difficult game of catch-up.

Have you noticed any changes to your work or family life in the past several years? Think back to the late 1980s: home computers were just catching on in a big way for productivity at home, not just games. Fax machines were beginning to be used in small and large offices. Pagers were slowly becoming more popular. Cellular phones were still not in widespread use. E-mail was rare outside corporate networking systems and high-tech firms. Cable television only offered twenty choices of programming. The Internet was not widely known or used outside of academic and military organizations. And today?

Some people are actually technophobic about the intimidating rate of change into a technology-driven world. This affects business, education, and even social activities. Technophobia is an anxiety-related disorder that makes people uncomfortable, if not unable to function, in the business world. The competition for dominance in business has driven all the peoples of the world into a race for superiority in high technology. The rate of this change is increasing exponentially.

We are not physically evolving at a rate that can keep up with this economically driven evolutionary trend. We still have a primitive change response mechanism, the fight or flight response, embedded within us. This governs the way we automatically respond to the stress of change. "Overwhelm" is the subjective and often physical response to dealing with the rate of change. What human beings have going for their survival is adaptability. But the rate and need for adaptation have generally outstripped our abilities to keep pace with the rate of change. Younger workers may be more resilient to change and feel pretty good about the exciting new developments, but for the baby boomers in midlife, the resilience and flexibility may give way to the aches and insecurities of reduced adaptation qualities.

Knowing this, we can learn techniques for managing change more gracefully. We can't stop it or control it, but we can learn to respond more appropriately. By being aware of how we respond to change and engaging in preventive actions, we can minimize, if not eliminate, the symptoms of stress and overwhelm. The two keys are awareness and appropriate and effective self-care.

Personal Change Assessment

First, become aware of what transition and change can be like for you as an individual. You must determine how you react in your own personal way to change. Do you ever feel anxious about the changes swirling around you? Do you lose sleep thinking about these events? Have you ever become aware that you lose focus or are distracted more easily when you find yourself in a period of change? Are anger or frustration closer to the surface when you are in the middle of changes? Does your stomach act up or do your shoulders or jaw get tight as a reaction to external changes?

Reread the first chapter of this book on understanding the effects of change and stress. Take the self-guided stress tests. Note the physical and emotional symptoms of stress that you are likely to manifest. This will help you to understand which systems you need to control and minimize the impact of change in your work and lifestyle. Remember these physical and emotional reactions are very primitive and all healthy people have these built-in responses for survival. Awareness of these patterns and your particular way of responding to them can give you some control over your reactions and responses to change.

When you examine the Social Readjustment Rating Scale in chapter 1, note that positive, even enjoyable experiences can be rated as stress producers. A new job, a change in work responsibilities, an addition to your family, or even a change in residence may all be viewed as very positive and yet these may prove stressful as you adapt to these new developments.

Since you cannot avoid the stress of change and don't want to isolate yourself from positive change, you must learn to control the way you respond to these new situations. Adopting new strategies of relaxation, diet, and exercise can minimize the impact of change.

Change and the Organization

After the personal assessment process, you need to become more aware of the actual process of change. Before you can construct a change management system that will enhance productivity through change, you must first develop and understand how you and the people around you will respond to the changes imposed on you. There are four stages of change that have been commonly identified: denial, resistance, exploration-emerging, and commitment.

With the stages of denial, resistance, and exploration-emerging, you or your organization may be subjected to a devastating reduction of productivity. Regardless of whether you are in manufacturing, customer service, or research and development, your productivity, efficiency, creativity, communication, teamwork, and certainly focus can be impaired, if not brought to a resounding halt, as a response to change within your life or your organization's operation. Many organizations are in such denial about these negative effects that they respond by ignoring them and then wonder why key personnel leave to avoid the danger that this denial brings to future developments.

In the first stage, denial, the common response is to pretend that things will just go on and be the same. Assumptions that the changes will just go away or be over soon can foster apathy or numbness. Quick-fix motivational programs usually help for only a brief period (if at all). Managers want the problems to go away, but unless they are addressed in a proactive way, the process can take too long and slow the whole process of change. The best managers will continue to communicate about the change and what will happen. Suggestions of successful actions can be offered and then time allowed for these to sink in. These suggestions can then be followed with a planning session that will put the preparations for change into action.

The second stage is resistance. Symptoms of this stage manifest in many negative forms. Increased anger or disagreements or, perhaps worse, a withdrawal from the team can occur. People can lose sleep. Workers may feel that they are treated unfairly, having given their best and still not being sure that they will survive the coming changes. Self-doubt, anxiety, depression, frustration, and fear often increase. Productivity goes way down as the team flounders. Personnel complain and begin to work on their resumes. Sickness, accidents, and missed work often increase. In a company with poor communication and weak management, resistance may not be addressed in a direct way. People need to come together and communicate to prevent being isolated with their fear and anger. Each person must be made to feel a part of the eventual change and know their role in the successful outcomes of change. Managers should exercise good listening and then acknowledge the expressed feelings. Supportive, encouraging, and empathetic responses by supervisors are a very successful strategy in this phase. Be warned that as a supervisor or manager, it does not serve the organization to slow the change process by trying to talk people out of feelings or by telling them to "change" or "pull together." People need to vent their fear and frustration without judgments made against them. Social activities like picnics, luncheons, and awards can help to enhance communication and community. Even rituals of letting go of the past and the older, familiar ways must be acknowledged and released to make way for the new program. A healthy acknowledgment that you are all in the process of change together and that there are normal fears and discomforts as a response to these developments is beneficial.

Exploration-emerging is the phase that follows resistance. This phase is positive because the energy in an organization can begin to flow again. The difficulty with this released energy is that there is often chaos and uncertainty. People suffer from frustration, confusion, too many new ideas, too much to do, overpreparation, and loss of the ability to focus. For certain people who need structure to function well, there is little or none because the change has removed the foundations of older styles of work. Creative energy is needed to capitalize on the future developments. New teams can begin to form with powerful bonds, forged by common confusion and unclear focus. As a new form begins to emerge, managers must focus on priorities, follow up on projects, provide needed training, set short-term goals, and conduct brainstorming, visionary, and planning sessions.

This will help to lead to the final stage, commitment. This can be seen as the positive developments of teamwork, satisfaction, and clear focus take form. Teams are now ready to refocus on a plan by recreating their mission statement and building their action plans to reach their goals. Adaptation takes place and new ways to work together develop. New roles are established. Successful team members will identify with the new set of goals and become more clear on how to reach these goals. A good manager will now concentrate on team building and validate and reward those who are responding to the changes in positive ways.

Expediting Change Management within an Organization

To expedite the change process gracefully, the skillful manager must be meticulous about good communication. When people are uncertain about the changes they are experiencing, poor communication allows fears to grow and sends the wrong message. Support and full, honest disclosure are important and can speed the change process. If you are managing or supervising a team of people, develop your talents and skills of communication.

Good communication begins with receiving and not transmitting. Most problems with communication, be they work-related or personal relationships, come from the inability of one or more of the people involved to engage in the process of listening. A distracting thought or agenda can keep people from focusing on what is being said in the interaction. If you are thinking of your answer or response, then you are distracted from the present communication. Good listening is difficult, especially when tough emotional issues like survival are included in the communication. To be an effective listener, you need to do more than hear the words. You need to be aware of all the nonverbal messages that are included. Body language, such as facial expressions, shoulders and arms, voice tones and volume, eye contact, and even rate of respiration can tell you a great deal in a communication.

People need to be acknowledged and appreciated. You must listen and then respond to what has been communicated with an empathetic response that indicates your sincere caring for the received message. This is not easy. Communication can be tangled and the process of change slowed or even stopped by poor listening, especially when there is a lack of appropriate acknowledgment for the information that was transmitted. This breakdown in rapport between members of the communication causes retreats into resistance.

The best communication is often done face-to-face in an honest and open manner. Communicating the truth and describing how you truly feel can create trust and empathy for the group involved in the change process. Care should be taken not to fall into the trap of negative gossip or dwelling on the negative any more than necessary. After releasing frustrations, look for the positive rather the negative aspects.

Clear communication is always necessary. In the change management process a supervisor will need to talk to the team or an individual in a face-to-face meeting. Complete and clear communication includes discussion of the situation or change to occur, your feelings about this change, what effect the change will have (on you, the group or team, and on the project), and finally, what you want as an outcome. Then you confirm with your partner(s) that your thoughts and feelings were transmitted in a beneficial way.

TIPS FOR GOOD LISTENING:

1. Reduce environmental distractions and interruptions.

2. Pay attention with your whole body.

3. Make eye contact.

4. Show interest.

5. Ask open-ended questions that encourage discussion of feelings.

6. Listen to the feelings behind the message.

7. Confirm and clarify what you have heard. (Restate the main point if you are unclear.)

Dealing with Resistance

Even when communication has been clear, emotions such as anger and fear may still create resistance to change. This is the hardest part in supervising a group going through change. Awareness is the first step. Resistance can come from insecurity, threats to feelings of competence, comfort with old systems, and fear of learning new systems. Individuals may manifest resistance through complaining, errors, withdrawal by apathy or absence, rigidity, or overt anger. A larger organization may see signs of resistance in increased accidents, worker's compensation claims, absenteeism, sabotage, health-care claims, and reduced productivity.

Managers must realize that even though resistance is difficult, it is a sign that people and the organization are going through the change process and not stuck in denial. Certain individuals may need more support than others, with more frequent communication and mechanisms for releasing resentments and guilt. The organization may benefit from appropriate rituals to release the old systems or beliefs as part of the process of moving on to the new systems. Honoring the outgoing systems by communicating the good-byes and associated feelings of loss will demonstrate support from the organization and help build a foundation to move on to exploration and commitment to the new changes.

After releasing the old systems, the process of embracing the new can begin. For an individual or team, the key to success will be a clear acknowledgment of the purpose of the change and the need to get new goals in place and planning started. This may involve honoring the motivation that drives individuals and the teams within which they work. Developing a positive connection between the motivation and new direction will enhance the rate of success. The process of developing the "buy-in" by participants can be ignored but is a potentially important ingredient. If people do not see their place in the future change or understand why they should participate, resistance and sabotage can slow the change process.

RETENTION AND RECRUITING TIPS

Stress caused by the business environment leads to problems with retaining key personnel or recruiting the "right" person for a key position. The tight labor market has created a stressful situation for many companies. They are competing for skilled people to fill important positions within their ranks. Turnover has increased as the loyalty shown by personnel to their employer has decreased, compared with the workforce of a generation ago. Money and stock options are used to attract people who often do not seem to deserve top dollar based on their experience, performance, or skill set.

Yet some companies have more resumes and applications than they know what to do with. Is it their benefits or rate of pay? Is it their location? Or is it that their senior management has a passion for making their personnel fall in love with their company? There are listings of the best places to work and certain companies understand the strategy that being on this list ensures them of the "cream of the crop" in the employment market. This does not "just happen." There is a plan and it starts with the deep understanding of the value of the labor force. It rewards creative, dedicated, productive people and continuously invests in the ongoing development of this valuable business commodity. The rewards are happy, satisfied workers who perform at a consistently high, profitable level.

GETTING EMPLOYEES TO "FALL IN LOVE" WITH YOUR COMPANY (AND LOVE IT ENOUGH TO STAY):

1. *Capture the Heart:* Offer a compelling vision; emphasize balance and celebration/fun.

2. *Open Communication:* Make listening a priority; maintain multiple lines of communication.

3. *Create Partnerships:* Squash status barriers; open the books; pay for performance (not titles); share the "bad" times and the "good" times.

4. *Drive Learning:* Guarantee employability by encouraging lifelong learning.

5. *Emancipate Action:* Allow freedom to fail; reduce bureaucracy; challenge the status quo.

What are the factors that drive high retention (and the protection of the investment in recruiting and training the workforce)?

Retention surveys show that the rate of pay/salary is usually the fourth or fifth most important factor. Ahead of compensation are factors such as respect, inclusion, compatible values, communication (listening), confidence in the future, sharing the vision, trust (promises and commitments by management are kept), and continuous lifelong learning supported by the company.

RETAINING KEY TALENT:

1. Identify critical staff (pay attention to key people and know their motivations).

2. Find out what they want both in the short term and long term.

3. Create individual plans to tie their goals to business goals.

4. Share critical business information.

5. Encourage managers to build loyalty, commitment, and trust.

Another key to retaining workers is providing attractive benefits, which help by proving the commitment to employees' well-being. A list of these potential benefits includes:

1. *Work Life Benefits:* Preventive medical, EAPs (employee assistance programs), flexible work schedules, family/employee-friendly time off

2. *Family Issues:* Sick kids PTO (parent time off), subsidy for child care, time off for volunteering in classrooms, dependent care spending account, pets at work, vacation/sick time, PTO donations to other employees

3. *Time-off Benefits:* Flextime, telecommuting, PTO versus vacation/sick leave, community volunteering, "well days," part-time positions, job sharing, sabbaticals

4. *Financial Issues:* Loans for computer purchases, financial planning seminars, 401(k)/retirement planning seminars, career placement (in-placement), training and education (inclusive)

5. *Exercise and Health:* Health club discounts, parcourse (a series of exercise stations set up as a fitness circuit) on grounds, longer lunch breaks for exercise, showers, EAPs, health-care spending accounts, classes on site (such as stress management [#1 requested], nutrition, smoking cessation, ergonomics)

It is important to remember that developing a retention program is much better than reacting after the damage is done by the loss of key personnel. Recruiting, training, and waiting for new employees to come up to speed are very expensive compared to keeping your trained workforce happy and in place. (New managers, especially project managers with technical expertise but no management training or experience, need to be coached and mentored in effective management techniques. Without this concern for their training, the company will find mistakes made that will drive good employees from the organization.)

Final note on retention: Senior management must be committed to caring for employees as much as they care for their best clients/customers. Consistent and time-intensive actions will change a low-morale, untrusting workforce into a dedicated, loyal workforce. Once your company is known to be employee-friendly, you will be able to compete for new, highly qualified personnel. They will seek you out with a burning desire to be part of your long-range plans. Attracting and keeping the best people will make a huge difference in your success and profitability.

Assessments: New Strategies for Recruiting and Hiring Winners

- Have you ever made a costly hiring mistake?
- Would you like to know whether an applicant matches up well against the "benchmark" of your top performers?
- Would you like to know how to motivate and then retain your best producers?

Of course you do! Hiring is not magic or intuition; it is greatly aided by tested benchmarking techniques. You can take the guesswork out of hiring and retaining by fully understanding your own top producers and then matching the best skilled applicants up against these internal standards for success.

After recruiting applicants, checking resumes, checking references, and interviewing the very best applicants, hiring decisions should be made with the added information of assessments. These assessments can show your hiring managers whether the applicant has the values that fit with your company's unique culture when "benchmarked" against the assessment results of your top producers. This is especially necessary in sales and customer service positions where customer contact means that the best representation translates into retaining key customers. Technical experts and managers can also be assessed and then compared to the top performers within your organization. Hiring the "right" personnel will save your company lots of money and time. A hiring mistake can cost you three times the annual salary of a manager or technical expert. This can run into the hundreds of thousands of dollars. (Costs include severance buyout for wrong hires, recruiting, hiring, training, and lost productivity.)

Assessments can also show managers how to communicate with or motivate their employees. This key information for your managers can include information regarding the values and interests that motivate a particular employee and information regarding their styles and behaviors. You can also match your applicants with the best work environments for the greatest productivity. Every effective project team needs the "right" balance of talent and skills with respect for the diversity of each team member's style and values. This means matching careful analytical members with decision makers and verbal influencers who may be involved in sales or marketing. They may have different personal styles but, as a team, they may be very effective working together to develop, produce, and then sell your products or services. Communication and team effectiveness are challenges for an organization. When emphasized and effectively addressed, these factors can save your organization time and money and go a long way to solving internal issues that lead to problems with retention of your most important personnel.

There are a wide variety of assessments you can use, including:

1. *360 Degree Feedback:* Assesses an individual's performance based on the combined reports of the individual, the boss, peers, and/or clients (or staff that reports to this individual). This complete report offers assistance and feedback that can greatly improve performance.

2. *Style Analysis—Advanced DISC (Success Discovery Process):* Offers a concise report regarding the behavior of an individual and often his or her value to an organization. It discusses the individual's strengths and challenges and even addresses how to motivate the person. Great for devising retention

strategies for key personnel. This assessment is also one component you can use to "benchmark" your organization's most successful employees. This information can then be used to evaluate developing personnel or potential new hires and match their behavior with that of your key personnel.

3. *Personal Interest, Attitudes, and Values:* Determines the dominant values and attitudes of the individual, which can be benchmarked against those of the organization. This assessment can show how teams can work easily together and where communication challenges might exist.

4. *Work Environment:* Pinpoints ideal work situations for you or for a candidate for a particular position. A good fit makes for a happier, more productive worker.

5. *DNA of Performance (Job Competency):* Helps to determine the specific interpersonal skills and qualities that would match the most successful people with certain job descriptions. Creates ideal questions for an interview to determine an applicant's abilities to meet the needs of the job. Reduces hiring mistakes.

6. *Sales Strategy Index:* Helps determine who has the best skills to be successful in a sales position. Can be benchmarked with your most successful personnel.

I recommend the assessments from Target Training International (TTI). Contact www.dstress.com for more information.

Implementing a successful retention program and/or developing the skills to hire more effectively may require some coaching or consulting. A professional from outside your organization may be able to see clearly your strengths and your challenges. Consider the return on investment for money spent on this expertise to improve the profits for your company.

THE NEW WORLD OF PERSONAL PROFESSIONAL COACHING

An executive vice president of a large international bank came to me for assistance. One of his key project managers was a gifted theoretical expert who was in charge of a large and important project. On paper, he had the knowledge to handle any situation, but like many technology-competent managers, his leadership and managerial skills were deficient and the project was badly lagging. I was asked to coach this new manager in interpersonal skills so that his development team would communicate better and get back on schedule. It was obvious during the early interviews that the team was floundering and even divisive due to poor project management at the personal level. After some initial intensive assessment and team problem solving, I coached the expert in communication, leadership, team building, and review process skills. Our weekly contact reflected the growth of sensitivity and managerial skills this technological expert was developing. He was getting more work done personally and the team began to thrive. Productivity and quality of work life improved so much that the development team was held up as a model for others in the organization. Everyone concerned learned new skills that were readily applied to different projects and different groups of people. The investment of time and money was worth the effort for this department and these key managers.

Coaching

World-class athletes would not attempt top-level competition without the support and teaching skills of an experienced coach. This concept is now becoming more common in business and several other important areas of life.

Executives, business owners, managers, professionals, and even parents are getting the assistance they need to develop the necessary skills and focus and, most importantly, stay on the right track as they move toward accomplishing their goals. These coaches are friends, mentors, and professionals who have the specific information, experience, and skills that are required for success. Their range of skills varies from specific technical information to acting as business managers for technically skilled professionals, experts in interpersonal skill development, and consultants and therapists who make relationships with children or partners more positive.

Coaching can be effective in small business assistance for entrepreneurs, communication, goal development and accomplishment, and parenting.

WHAT SPORTS COACHES DO:

- Teach and review basic fundamentals, determine inappropriate technique

- Strengthen and condition athletes for endurance

- Teach tactics

- Prepare the mind and emotions for success, and to keep focused on steps toward goals

WHAT LIFE AND BUSINESS COACHES DO:

- Teach and review basic fundamentals, determine inappropriate technique

- Strengthen and condition their clients for endurance

- Teach tactics

- Prepare the mind and emotions for success, and to keep focused on steps toward goals

The difference between consultants and coaches is that coaching is an ongoing, committed relationship that works the process through to completion. Coaching is established through regularly scheduled interactions, either in person, by phone, or by fax or e-mail. Criteria are established in a fact-finding interview and then the goals are established. Each interaction is designed to acknowledge progress toward the goal or to refine the goal-attaining process. Specific relevant tools and techniques needed to achieve the goal can be taught by the coach.

Some coaches are experts at business technology, such as writing business plans, grant applications, financial plans, or contract agreements. Other coaches will assist technically oriented business owners or managers in basic business and management skills. Still other coaches, such as myself, offer coaching in future planning, organization development, and interpersonal skill development for business owners and executive managers. All of these coaching relationships are designed to develop the skill levels of key personnel and enhance the efficient attainment of established goals. This is identical to the way athletic coaches work with their athletes to achieve specific athletic achievements. The coaches offer support and, more importantly, hold their clients accountable for the steps toward progress in accomplishing the agreed-upon goals.

For some people, the process of working with an accountability coach is a one-goal process. For others, the coaching relationship may continue to other projects or goals. The process can be a huge benefit to the company or professional manager. The professional support can enhance the motivation and focus of gifted managers and business owners, which can lead to greater than expected success.

Finding the Right Coach

When you are searching for the best person for this mentoring process, certain guidelines may be helpful. All of these listed ingredients are important, though the order of importance varies based on specific projects and personal requirements.

1. Find the coach or mentor who possesses the skills you require. These may be technical business skills or interpersonal management skills.

2. Find someone with whom you are compatible. If their style makes you uncomfortable, this may not be the person you wish to work with over time. However, do not find someone who is so compatible that they will not firmly stand up to you when you have lost your focus or need an appropriate shove in the right direction.

3. Find a coach you can afford. Some are free, but do not offer a long-term committed relationship or the highest level of trained professional support. Coaching can run from $30 to $250 per session. The sessions can range from brief check-ins to one-hour appointments by phone or in person, sometimes combined with daily progress reports by fax.

4. You can find a mentor among your friends, peers, or the people within your circle of influence. Make sure that they have the time and skills to assist you. If you are not paying for this service in some way, establish a reciprocal exchange of time or energy. Many businesspeople and some companies understand the special enhancements that coaching can provide and support this directly or indirectly to improve performance. There are times when this can bring new ideas and energy into an established organization by tapping an external professional coach.

5. If you feel unsure, unsupported, unfocused, or skill-set challenged, you need to be very serious about considering a professional coaching arrangement.

Remember, you do not have to do it all on your own. You can have professional support that can make your life easier and more productive.

Coaching can be found on the Internet (as a World Wide Web search) if you do not have a personal referral. Make sure that you feel comfortable with your selected coach and the program that they recommend. Obviously, if you are risking your time and money, check their credentials and references.

OPTIMUM PERFORMANCE TRAINING

The bottom line for you and the company for which you work can be affected in a positive way by performing at the peak of your abilities. Professional athletes know that their career and value depend on their individual or team performance. Business is just starting to learn that training the workforce in specific skills is not enough to provide the advantage the company needs. Companies must provide the necessary training that allows key personnel or work teams to move ahead more effectively toward the desired company goals and thereby increase productivity.

Optimum Performance Training (copyright © 1992 by L. John Mason, Ph.D.) is an attempt to bring the most effective training methods established for world-class athletic competition into the world of business and individual executive training. This system requires a complete understanding of the desired goals, motivation, and the history of the blockage to these desired results. The initial analysis of the situation can be of great value as stand-alone consulting, but devising a training system and implementing it effectively are the challenges that can make a company, work team, or individual move successfully toward the desired results. As a final step, mechanisms for accountability as a cost benefit analysis are often installed.

The principles of Optimum Performance Training assist individuals in managing the stress that distracts them from their concentration on tasks and their larger focus on important long-range priorities. Individual training in personal stress responses, stress and change management, desensitization principles to overcome fears or blocks, focused long term goal setting, and specific skill development are all included in this comprehensive program. For teams, departments, or organizations, this program can be developed to meet the specific needs of the group, with implementation and necessary revisions installed over the length of the consulting contract.

Many individual training techniques go back thousands of years, based on yogic practices of meditation and visualization techniques for developing patterns of mindfulness and good health. The spiritual teachings from these early disciplines are enjoying a rebirth as business improvement techniques for the twenty-first century. Modern-day athletes, artists, psychologists, physicians, and now businesspeople are learning and practicing these techniques to enhance their performance by ridding themselves of their own self-disrupting response to high-level competition.

The basic premise for individuals who wish to operate at peak performance is to look at the task, make sure it is realistic, uncover the blocks to success, and then create a tailored program. For individuals, this is often done in a coaching format. Each individual has their own way of getting in the way to sabotage the desired results. Often this is a relatively simple problem of internal distractions based on poor stress identification and management. We find the physical and emotional systems that block effectiveness and learn to turn these into a more positive outcome through behavioral techniques of biofeedback, guided relaxation and meditation, and specifically formulated visualizations.

The next step is to look for positive role models with the appropriate skill sets, then move to acquiring the successful patterns. If no role model exists and the tasks are not impossible or unrealistic, a plan must be made to move the individual into the environment for success. Problem solving with the coach is useful at this stage. When a program is established, then the coaching takes on the form more associated with an athletic coaching relationship. This includes regular, usually weekly, contact; regular assignments that bring you closer to achieving the specified goal; and any special skill enhancement that is necessary.

The individual moving toward peak performance will be guided to use specific personal development techniques to ensure balance. The process includes many of the exercises that are taught in this book. The range may include autogenic training or progressive relaxations for basic stress management, desensitization or goal accomplishment visualizations, and processes to integrate the mind with the body and the spirit. The overall process can improve health and quality of life, as well as success in the chosen goals.

Executives who began using these programs as if they were toys to improve their golf or tennis games also found them to enhance focus, concentration, communication, energy levels, and productivity. One executive vice president with a large financial company found that the techniques helped control his high blood pressure, and with the same energies and time, he was able to get eight hours' worth of work done in a very focused six and a half hours. This gave him extra time to work on projects that really motivated him. He found himself moving away from a pattern of burnout and into the benefits of increased productivity.

An important point to remember is that these techniques will not be 100 percent successful for people who are not committed to self-care and life balance. If you practice these exercises just to make a few extra dollars, then you may be wasting your time. Honest, healthy motivation is not self-consuming intensity. A true balance of mind, body, and spirit, when aligned, can give you more focused energy to accomplish your goals and find greater success and happiness in your life.

BALANCE

Is your work or career so demanding that your family feels cheated? Are you so conflicted about how to spend the few hours of your day that you spend all your time worrying and do not accomplish what you know you could? Do you have so many interests and demands that you have difficulty keeping up with all of them or do they come crashing down around you? Does your life need better balance?

If you feel that your life is out of control, then you need to reassess your situation and find our way back into balance. To do this, you must simplify your life. You must strip away the external expectations that are placed on you or that you put on yourself. With the unnecessary clutter placed comfortably to one side, you can look at what is truly necessary, important, and nonnegotiable for quality of life and personal balance.

The basics are clear. We need to eat, to breathe, to sleep and rest, and to have relationships with family and friends. Our first priority is to survive, then to help maintain the survival of those we love and care about. Survival is very different than it was a million years ago when the genetic code was forming to create human life as we know it. We are more stressed and have higher expectations of productivity than we did even two thousand years ago. We no longer go to sleep when it gets dark or stay inside during the coldest winter months, and neither can we depend on our fellow villagers to help us survive common threats. We are more isolated than ever. We get caught up in comparisons of "success," physical beauty, technological knowledge taken as wisdom, and a great many other interesting but not truly important things.

Because we are so far from the basics and cannot provide the simplest things for ourselves and our families, we must submit to the dictates of our society. This often leads us down certain paths that take us away from our most basic needs and can knock us off balance. How many people do you know who structure their activities around paying for overpriced shelter, or worse, for overpriced transportation? How many people grow their own food or at least prepare their own vegetables, breads, fruits, grains and pastas, or meats? Do you go out for exercise every day as your body requires? Do you ever sit quietly by a fire, stream, lake, or the ocean to soak up the life-sustaining natural rhythms of life? Are you too busy to hold your spouse or your children?

When the basics of life are ignored, your body, mind, and soul begin to rebel. The symptoms that develop are designed to get your attention in a rather rude way. We can prevent this through self-care and meticulous attention to the basic details of life. You can ignore the signs and pay the consequences. You can deny personal responsibility and blame many other institutions for your lack of self-care, but you must know that this quality of life is really up to you. Often, we fight to protect things or values that are not life-sustaining priorities.

For better balance, make an honest list of what you need and really want. From this priority list, chart a course that keeps you moving toward your goals with grace.

Toward Better Balance

Balance begins with the principles of self-care. We need to do this for basic survival in our hectic world. It may sound odd to ask you to take time or to make time to take care of yourself. There does not seem to be enough time in your busy schedule. However, time for self-care will actually pay for itself. You will wind up being able to save time by making fewer mistakes, being able to concentrate better, need less sleep, experience enhanced and efficient communication, and develop better problem-solving capabilities.

Basic self-care involves regular physical exercise and activity, proper nutrition and appropriate rest and relaxation.

EXERCISE:

Work your way up to thirty minutes or more per session and five or more sessions per week. This might be walking, jogging or running, bike riding, rowing, swimming, cross-country skiing, aerobics. Try to go fast enough to stay within your breath, within your body, and within the present moment to "ground out" at least a few minutes of these workouts. If you are always thinking of business or other activities and are not in the moment and in your body, then you are not going quite fast enough.

PROPER NUTRITION:

There are many books written on nutrition and most are in conflict. I recommend eating as close to natural as possible, consuming fresh fruits, vegetables, and grains with as many of your three basic meals as possible. Fast foods and highly processed foods are not recommended for your regular diet. Reduce sucrose (processed sugar) and caffeine to a minimum (no caffeine if you suffer from stress, anxiety, or sleeping problems). Do not rely on alcohol or drugs to relax you.

REST AND RELAXATION:

One twenty-minute relaxation period is minimum. Try the Western relaxation methods or styles of meditation described in this book for your personal relaxation requirements. If you are severely stressed or out of balance these relaxations can be used two to three times a day, even at bedtime, to get you back in control.

After self-care, you probably need to do an assessment of your personal priorities. Make a plan to achieve better balance, and then activate this plan. Your assessment should include looking at your plans for the following ten areas: career, finance, relationships/social, family, aesthetic/creativity, recreation/fun, mental/educational development, physical health, spiritual development, and emotional growth and well-being.

Most people will give a lot of attention to their careers. This will help them plan their education and vocational training. Often in midlife the career path loses some of its appeal and the lack of balance can become very apparent. This loss of luster is thought of as burnout, when the real reason has more to do with the lack of attention to the other life-sustaining areas.

Saving for retirement or major expenditures (houses, money for college, and cars) also is a priority. If the individual is dissatisfied with his quality of life, even family and relationships are not enough to make life feel complete.

Attention to aesthetics/creativity, physical health, emotional development, and especially spiritual development is necessary for a well-rounded, healthy lifestyle.

Spiritual development does not necessarily have to do with religious beliefs or organizations. Religions are often needed to satisfy the need for social institutions and the need to belong. The process of spiritual development is deeply personal and individual, based more around developing self-acceptance and guiding beliefs toward a larger sense of connectedness or oneness with the largest community of living beings. When survivors of near-death experiences are interviewed, they can be the most articulate spokespeople for true spiritual acceptance. (Read Ken Ring's *Life at Death* or Raymond Moody's book *Life after Life* to find out more about the changes these survivors have gone through in their priorities in living.)

Pure spiritual growth and development can also come from personal meditation or from insight work with keeping a journal, individual and group process psychotherapy, or deep involvement in one's quest for aesthetic or creative expression. A new resurrection of an old tradition, called "vision quest," is gaining in popularity. These experiential processes remove the participant from many modern distractions and help them to confront the natural world and the challenges of finding one's personal perspective of placement within the universal dilemma. Tribes of indigenous peoples have used this technique for thousands of years as a ceremony to move into the higher circles of spiritually connected members of the tribe. Since Westerners do not have the tribe for social connection, people are seeking consulting groups that can support and provide the vision quest experience. Even corporations are using these consulting processes to create better visionaries and better team members among their key managers.

You must make the time to honor all the major parts of a healthy lifestyle or in the long run you may fall prey to a poor quality of life foundation. Long-term planning and movement on your life quest requires your regular attention, time, and energy. The outcome is balance. Balance will lead to greater productivity, happiness, satisfaction, health, and the positive development of consciousness.

WELLNESS—THE TIME IS NOW!

A change in health-care philosophy began in the late 1960s and continued in the 1970s, but has only recently begun to reach useful and practical manifestation. "Wholistic" or "holistic" medicine developed to offer an alternative to traditional medical practices which allowed little patient input at increasingly higher prices. People became better informed consumers of health care and wanted to share in some of the decision making and treatment of their bodies. Increased media input is in part responsible for this change. With this trend, however, also comes additional stress from the increase of new responsibility.

The sometimes faddish wholistic movement has given way to some very positive developments in terms of increased awareness of health issues and a much greater concern for prevention. More people are getting involved in self-care and are attempting various fitness programs not only to look better, but to help establish more personal power.

Also following a parallel to athletic fitness has been greater interest in and awareness of diet. More people are conscious about the needs for balanced, nutritious foods. In some cases, people are going to extremes to eat more "naturally," and this is not a passing fad. Concern for the foods we consume seems justified in light of all the emerging data on the potentially toxic substances finding their way into our food chain. Consumers are more conscious and careful these days than they have been in the past. This adds more responsibility to the consumer and so more stress in a certain sense on his or her lifestyle. Not everyone is participating in this new health movement, but enough of us are getting involved to radically change the health-care movement and change the course of health-care history.

Corporations have not been in the forefront of preventive health care until very recently when costs of health care, replacement of key employees, lost revenue due to accidents, alcohol and drug abuse, and productivity losses due to sickness have forced the corporate giants into assuming responsibility and providing "wellness programs."

Wellness programs vary greatly because they have not been around long enough to provide data about their effectiveness. They often include physical fitness facilities or time provided as an incentive, nutritional evaluation and counseling, and, very naturally, stress management evaluation and instruction. Some programs also may include alcohol/drug rehabilitation, family or personal counseling, weight control, and, very importantly, smoking control programs. Companies are saving significant amounts of money by contributing to health care through wellness programs (some called HMO—health maintenance organizations).

The necessary ingredients of a wellness program are threefold: stress management, nutritional information, and regular physical activity. Incentives for health—not sickness—need to be established.

Prevention/wellness will work for motivated people. These individuals are people who wish to take responsibility for their good health and who wish to have greater control over their bodies and their lives. Through awareness and vigilance we can contribute greatly to the quality of our lives, adding years for productivity and enjoyment. Research indicates that twenty minutes of deep relaxation/stress management can add two hours to your day by reducing the need for sleep. The sleep you do get becomes deeper and more restful. The relaxation also reduces the stresses and irritations that distract you from your activities. This in turn reduces mistakes and accidents, making your energies more efficient and ultimately more productive.

In consultation for a large electronics firm, I met Tom and Mark. They are electrical engineers, and though their jobs are relatively flexible and creative, true limits create pressures that are felt on and off the job. Their approach to health maintenance widely differed from one another when we met. Mark was an avid athlete. He enjoyed active sports or activities on his weekends. It was not unusual for Mark to lift weights, play racquetball, or jog after work, sometimes even three or four times per week. Tom, on the other hand, preferred less activity, and for recreation he would go out for dinner or to a movie, or might listen to music to "unwind."

The lecture I gave encouraged the wellness approach with a balance of proper diet, exercise, and stress management. Both Mark and Tom came up after the talk, realizing that their lifestyles were not handling the pressures and tensions in an ideal way. My recommendations included that they practice regular stress management, watch their diets for unhealthy foods such as caffeine, sugar, etc., and get a balance of regular aerobic exercise, not necessarily a competitive sport.

Mark was amazed at the difference in his abilities, both mentally and physically. He had not realized the negative effects of caffeine or the great benefits that twenty minutes of complete relaxation would have. Tom slowly began the exercise regimen that we had discussed, and it really surprised him that he would enjoy it as much as he did. It took a while for him to make the time to exercise regularly, but he eventually made it a priority.

After several months on this program, I contacted them to check on their progress. Both Mark and Tom had better endurance and performance on and off the job. They were both surprised that they felt more energetic and that the things that used to "get on their nerves" before seemed much more tolerable now. Mark even suggested that this minor problem with "burnout" was eliminated by this self-care routine.

The wellness model can be adapted to every lifestyle and can be flexible as ability and interests evolve. The benefits to individuals and reduction of health-care costs are not fully documented as yet, but I do not know of anyone who has entered a wellness program of their own motivation and who, after remaining on the program a reasonable length of time (generally six to eight weeks), has not felt great benefits and—barring severe lifestyle changes—has not kept the program going on their own initiative.

TIME MANAGEMENT AND STRESS

A major stress producer is the lack of time. Since we cannot add more hours to the day, we need to learn to use the existing amount of time in a better way. This is true for time at work and time in our personal lives. Few of us actually spend enough time planning our lives, let alone our days, with effective techniques to keep us on track toward our most important goals. We get stressed because we do not feel that we are accomplishing our goals and we find time "slipping away."

Our time is consumed by doing many very urgent activities that do not move us any closer to our important, identified goals. We are unclear about the priority of things we need to accomplish at work. Our performance reviews reflect that we could or should be getting more work done and yet we are consistently pulled away from important assignments to deal with urgent calls, faxes, meetings, interruptions, and requests from the "boss(es)."

There are many time management systems and I could write a whole book just on this topic. The relationship to stress management requires that I mention some basic fundamentals to get you started.

At Work

You have to learn the difference between what is a top priority and what is "urgent." Sometimes there are urgent, high-priority things that have to get done right now. There are also many urgent requests that are *not* high priorities for the long-term plan of the organization. We are bombarded with faxes, e-mails, telephone calls, and memos that are urgent but not necessarily important! Pick the high priorities to focus on.

Sometimes you need help setting priorities. Decide with your boss and co-workers (project team members) what the most important priorities are. Spell them out so everyone has a clear understanding. Clarify the assignment of these top-priority items (e.g., who is responsible and what are the time limits). Find out who will assist you if you are running up against deadlines. If you have more than one boss, find out who and what has the highest priority when multiple activities are coming due. Clear communication is the key! You need to know when you can pass on optional meetings or lower-priority activities. Learn to say "NO!"

Know your most productive parts of the day for getting work done. Are you a fast-starting morning person or do you get rolling in the late morning or afternoon? Plan your serious business during your most productive periods and train the people around you to leave you undisturbed during these times. Try to use your voicemail, hang up a sign, or go find a better place to work, if you have to, so you will be able to concentrate and be more productive during these times. It may not always work out, but you will be more productive if you can plan to do high-priority work in a more controlled environment.

Make sure the top-priority actions are on your schedule and on your desk so you can focus on them. Plan your day either first thing in the morning or last thing before you go home (or before you stop work, if you work at home). Work on the high-priority, urgent things first! Do not leave until you have completed them (if you can) or gotten to a satisfactory stopping place.

Away from Work

Set top priorities in every important part of your life! Determine what your long-term goals are for:

1. Work/career/professional fulfillment

2. Financial needs

3. Educational growth and training (continuous lifelong learning)

4. Emotional awareness and growth

5. Spiritual awareness and growth

6. Aesthetic/creative needs

7. Family

8. Relationships/social needs

9. Recreational/fun needs

10. Health/physical needs

Do not let any of your personal goals be ignored or underrated. You must have balance and a well-rounded plan for long-term health and happiness.

INTUITION IN BUSINESS

Do you hire or put work teams together? Are you developing relationships with clients, advisors, supervisors, or your staff? Do you have to make career choice decisions? Do you make decisions about new products and what quantities to produce, distribute, or acquire? Do you have to stay ahead or at least up on the trends? If you answered yes to any of these questions, then you may want to explore how you can tap your deepest and strongest levels of wisdom.

An executive buyer for a national retail chain of full-service department stores played a "hunch" and created huge profits and national recognition for her stores. Over several years she had learned her job well and understood her customers, but when it came to predicting a fashion trend, she used her intuition instead of depending solely on statistical analysis. On one occasion, her intuition told her that an overlooked style would be a "hit" and she proceeded to order the dress in certain fabrics and in large quantities. The manufacturer, being an honorable business associate, tried to dissuade her, knowing that every other major buyer had overlooked or discounted this particular style. Being very strong willed, the buyer held on to this "gut feeling" and maintained her large order. A large promotional campaign was launched and to everyone's (except the buyer's) surprise, the dress sold out rapidly, causing every other major store chain to demand this product. Thousands of this dress style were sold and the buyer's reputation was elevated by this business decision. Though it seemed to go against logic and current reasoning, this bold act sent the retail market spinning in a new and profitable direction. The buyer developed many projects by intuition in her successful career and she still considers her intuition responsible for much of the recognition that brought her to the very top of her profession.

The story about the buyer has been repeated in every industry. Successful "gut feeling" decisions seem to be increasing with the advent of new technologies and the uncharted arenas that must be negotiated. Many business decisions now must be made quickly and without historical support. In the past decade, many executives with good instincts, especially those in high-tech businesses, have become instant millionaires.

Customer service also can rely on special qualities. When salespeople, managers, or executives can connect in a special way with their customers and create a relationship of trust and rapport, they can develop special loyalty and long-term success. People who are good with people as managers or in providing customer service produce good returns on the company's bottom line.

In training, teaching, or business activities, many executives use metaphors from sports. They play aggressively. They "have their head in the game." They are "in the groove," "hitting on all cylinders," and sometimes totally in the "zone." Athletes describe a state of "being in the zone," where their perceptions are so sharp that time seems to slow down. Their decisions are so clear and precise that they can surgically pick apart the other team's defense and score in almost impossible ways. Examples of this abound. A quarterback, point guard, or sales executive intuitively knows what his teammate or client will do, and in a split second delivers the ball to the perfect position for it to be received, "in stride," to complete the drive for a score! This state of being is a rare pleasure to experience under any circumstance. When you feel this on the playing field or in business, it adds to the satisfaction of the experience. In its way, it has addictive qualities that bring you back time and time again. This feeling of being at the very top can motivate an executive.

Too often we wait for these situations to manifest themselves. We are not proactive in creating the proper emotional, mental, and physical environment to perform at this level and with this satisfaction. Some experienced veterans can pull these qualities out in key situations and use them with great aplomb. Some younger, creative executives seem to have these abilities and can hit a home run early on. But this experience is a subjective emotional skill that cannot consistently happen upon command, without proper training and nurturing of this special sense or skill.

Competitive leaders want every advantage they can develop, and consultants and trainers offer them the latest business techniques. Most business management techniques can be taught through normal teaching methods in classes or through verbal instructions. The "gut feeling" of a clear intentional decision is derived from an entirely different source. It comes through a special connection or feeling that cannot be taught through normal methods. The experience must be provided, guided, enhanced, supported, and nurtured for its full development in a consistent trustworthy "feel set," or skill set with feeling.

Major disruptions to intuition and focus occur in the presence of stress and fear. Controlling fears, insecurities, and your stress response is the first step to preparing for the connection to your intuitive insights. You must control the background noise and distraction that you most often feel when you are not in the present moment and not in your body in a healthy way. More is being written about stress management for business and the optimum performance which can be achieved by athletes or businesspeople through the use of focused relaxation, and then the special visualizations of success and peak performance programming.

After the skill of focused relaxation, the next steps involve immersion through ritual and exercises that reconnect you with certain quiet parts of yourself. Physical and emotional blocks need to be circumvented through awareness, acceptance, and then rechanneling of consciousness. A sensitivity to these feelings must be established and then honed to gain the clarity that will make this more consistent, trustworthy, and predictable. This phase is not the easiest. It requires diligence and practice. The skill of being able to let go physically and emotionally takes some time. You must master your fear in order to trust that the unconscious forces can give special protection and then guidance. The levels of self-awareness and acceptance lead to self-confidence in the special way that successful, creative producers have achieved for consistent success.

The phase of balance and grace is a rewarding and beneficial achievement. No matter what activity you participate in, these levels of focus and of being centered create the proper internal environment for success. These attributes are not just for business, but for all life activities and pursuits. Most people never take the time to achieve these states and never find the deeper satisfaction with their lives. Relationships, families, health, and business can suffer from the lack of balance and grace. At a universal level, the world would have more peace, less crime, and fewer environmentally stupid occurrences if balance and grace were honored and cultivated.

Seven Steps to Intuitive Power

1. *Awareness:* Be exposed to and learn the process of the Intuitive Warrior. Know of historical, cultural, inherited responses.

2. *Self-Control (self-care):* Learn and install lifestyle adjustments for health, wellness, and clarity development. Demonstrate the benefits of centering and connecting.

3. *Self-Confidence (not false confidence):* Learn and know yourself to the core. Develop the control to center yourself: mind, body, and spirit.

4. *Self-Esteem:* Elevate your feeling and knowing of your self. Develop the sense of self-connection and self-love.

5. *Trust in the Universe:* Develop the awareness and the skills to trust the highest levels of connection and consciousness. Prepare for "Letting Go."

6. *Letting Go:* Be able to "let go" physically, mentally, and emotionally to be open for intuition and insight.

7. *Acceptance/Intuitive Insight and Power (also called enlightenment):* Release the fear of failure, death, and conscious level of control. Find your power and deeply connected safety nets of empowerment.

For details and involvement in this evolving process, contact L. John Mason, Ph.D., at the Stress Education Center at (707) 795-2228.

THE ERGONOMICS OF COMPUTER STRESS

Recently, I was asked to consult for a team at a high-tech electronics firm. The main concern was the productivity of the design team: highly trained engineers were working on a project that was of great importance in helping the company remain competitive in its fast-changing field. Market share of the company's products was being threatened by smaller, "lightning-fast" companies. The pressure to perform in this ongoing climate of stress and rapid information development was overwhelming to key members of this development team. When I interviewed the individuals a key theme was apparent: it seems that technology had provided too much information through the Internet and other electronic communication technologies. These engineers were overwhelmed just keeping up-to-date on all the information available. The solution was to work with personal stress and change management strategies and, perhaps more importantly, prioritize the use of time and information handling. This type of analysis and coaching is becoming the necessary alternative to high-tech stress and information overload.

High-Tech Challenges versus Low-Tech Responses

ERGONOMICS. The study of the problems people have adjusting to their environment; esp. the science that seeks to adapt work or working conditions to suit the worker.

By its very nature, high-tech means constant transitions and change, and this means consistently high levels of stress from adapting to these changes. Our primitive mechanisms for adjusting to change are often overwhelmed by the high-tech world of change that we live and work within. Virtually everyone agrees that negative transitions, such as job insecurity due to downsizing, stock market swings, health challenges (sickness, chronic illness, emotional symptoms of stress), relationship insecurities (divorce, dating, family role changes, two-income families), and international or regional political upheavals, are viewed as stressful with potential downsides to your health and well-being.

"Good" Change—Same Results

Transitions and change are not always bad. However, even positive change can create responses within our primitive response mechanisms that can lead to negative symptoms of physical and emotional stress. High-tech advances have increased expectations of productivity and often time commitments to responding to the pressures from work. The pressures of response and keeping up with the changes of technologies are still there, even if you bury your head in the sands of denial.

Recent developments in technology and information systems have created a new dilemma, referred to as "information overload." You can never get enough new information to help you stay ahead of the competition. Hardware and software engineers (and the rest of us who try to keep up with the changes) are often overwhelmed by the glut of information. Wise decisions and prudent choices must be made about which information to read and which e-mail to spend valuable time and energy responding to. The choices are not easy. This can lead to the need for coaching on priorities and long-term goal setting. This is useful at both the personal and professional levels.

Since 1985, more people have developed symptoms of this technology. Eye strain, back strain, wrist and hand strain, neck problems, even weight gain and substance abuse can be loosely linked to long hours in the world of computers and technology. There are even new industries cropping up to take advantage of the health and safety needs of daily computer users and high-tech workers. For the pure physical side of the ergonomics issue, in the consulting work I perform for high-tech companies, I recommend bringing in a physical therapist with preventive ergonomic training to offer seminars to computer workers to protect their backs, necks, wrists, and hands. There is a lot of money to be saved in health-care costs, workers' compensation claims, lost productivity, and reduced morale.

Awareness is half the battle. Know how you respond to stress and what in your life is causing this transitional stress. Then, develop daily habits that combat the negative physical and emotional responses to stress. You can prevent, or at least minimize, symptoms of stress such as headaches, backaches, neck aches, high blood pressure, panic, anxiety, many stomach problems, and sexual dysfunctions. Emotional symptoms such as loss of concentration, withdrawal (depression), anxiety, being accident prone, memory loss, poor motivation, poor communication, poor performance, and some learning disabilities can be linked to stress and reduced, if not eliminated, by awareness and lifestyle changes. Key employees can be given executive/personal coaching and this can prevent them from being liabilities due to inefficiency and poor productivity.

The remedies are as wide as the variables that have created the problems. However, most people perform their functions better when they involve themselves in regular daily self-care that includes relaxation (stress management tapes, exercises, individual counseling), physical exercise (five times a week for thirty minutes or more), good worksite ergonomics, and proper nutrition (including mineral supplements and antioxidants).

Check the guided relaxations in this book or go to the Stress Education Center's website at http://www.dstress.com. The tape and book pages of this website are excellent resources for managing stress and reducing stress-related symptoms.

NEW SYMPTOM OF STRESS: WORKPLACE RAGE

We have recently added several new terms to our vocabulary relating to rage. These expressions were coined to describe violent episodes on roadways ("road rage"), on airplanes ("air rage"), and in the workplace ("going postal," a term that stems from a series of incidents that occurred when employees of the postal service became enraged at work and injured or killed fellow employees). Incidents involving rage are appearing more and more often in the news reports that we read in newspapers and view on television.

Where does this rage come from? It's at least in part a poor response to stress. Overwhelmed by everyday pressures, people interact with other stressed-out people at work, during their commute, in the air—and if they have a poor response to stress, it can manifest itself in tragic ways. More men respond this way than women. Men seem more prone to express their stress and frustration through violence. (This may be related to the role of males as violent protectors or hunters over the course of millions of years of evolution.) Most people can control their reactions to stress, using the coping skills that demonstrate the higher thinking and communication abilities that we have developed and have deemed more appropriate. But some people may respond in an inappropriate way in public or at work when pushed by stress and poor response patterns.

We still have our primitive survival responses within the more basic parts of our brains. In life-threatening situations (such as in war or when confronted by danger on the streets), it is good to survive by running away or fighting, but in today's modern world we have fewer appropriate places to run away to and even fewer times when violence is required to protect us. The world is too small and too crowded to respond with rage. People need to use preventive self-care techniques to maintain more balance and control over their response mechanisms.

The world our children are going to inherit will test them even more than today's stress-filled world tests us. It is thus alarming that the number of children unable to control their impulses seems to be increasing. There are theories about what can cause the lack of impulse control. Too often, children are presented with examples of violence used as a problem-solving technique on television, in the movies, and through the news media. We run the risk that violence, when repeated as often as it is, becomes a "socially acceptable" response for those who are less sophisticated and more impressionable. Another theory suggests that child abuse can cause damage to a developing child's prefrontal lobe, the part of the brain where impulse control is centered. This stress on the child caused by abuse, which may be responsible for the future (possibly violent) actions of the child, in reality stems from an overstressed, poorly coping parent. Lacking societal support, parents sometimes feel frustrations that may be acted out in violence, leading to the development of destructive habit patterns for children growing up in these homes. Stress seems to play a role in this poor impulse control no matter what theory is actually proven true. Providing a good role model of self-care is not common enough.

The feeling of being overwhelmed that many of us experience at work or in relationships can be made more acute by the lifestyle choices we make, such as using caffeine or medicating ourselves with control-altering substances like alcohol and drugs. We may overstimulate ourselves because of an addiction to excitement. We choose dangerous activities to create a focus on the "present moment" and avoid the quiet times of reflective introspection that may cause us to realize the unhappiness with lifestyle choices, overwork, lower self-esteem, and the lack of control that most of us are afraid of at a deeper level. We are surrounded and overwhelmed by change, and unconsciously we fear change. The "unknown" is very scary and most people are forced to change more quickly than they find comfortable. Eventually, this feeling of being overwhelmed can take its toll and cause explosive, inappropriate reactions.

Fatigue can also contribute to responses of rage. Fatigue and stress reduce the ability to be rational and problem solve. Emotions like anger and rage are closer to the surface and less controlled. Today, more and more people are sleep deprived. They are on the road driving. They are operating heavy equipment. They are working on assembly lines, on construction sites, and in hospitals. Sleep deprivation causes accidents and costs all of us a huge amount of money in health insurance, reduced productivity, and workers' compensation claims. Long work and commute hours contribute to this problem. Have you noticed the huge increase in the number of coffee and espresso shops since the late 1980s? Caffeine fights drowsiness and helps people awaken after not sleeping enough, but this may be one of the major causes of this problem rather than a part of the solution. This is a difficult problem to solve. But awareness of the negative effects of poor sleep and action to move (slowly, if necessary) to more positive alternatives will be the job of business and education in the coming generations.

The business world faces many challenges relating to stress that require time, attention, vigilance, and money to address. We cannot stick our heads in the sand and expect productivity and quality of life to increase. Organizations that have begun paying attention and implementing positive alternatives are finding the expense is worth it. Profits are up. People are happy and more productive. Recruitment is easier (though not always easy).

If you believe that you might need some assistance in identifying the issues or finding and implementing solutions, or you just want professional support along the way, please contact us at the Stress Education Center at (707) 795-2228 or through our website at http://www.dstress.com. We will be happy to discuss your challenges and create a proposal, if appropriate.

Please remember to take good care of yourself.

Chapter 14
Teaching Stress Reduction

A Guided Tour

A five-session online stress management course (with tapes and temperature training) is available through the Stress Education Center at www.dstress.com.

THIS IS A PROTOTYPE for a five-week course designed to transmit the basic information about stress, stress reduction, and relaxation techniques. It is based on the program that I have developed and teach regularly. The professional wishing to use or adapt this outline is welcome to do so. I have taught this class fifteen times over the past year and have found that it was satisfying for all the participants.

Class is held one night or one day per week for five successive weeks. Each session runs approximately two and one-half hours and is designed for a minimum of eight people and a maximum of sixteen. The course helps the students isolate their own unique stress responses and find relaxation techniques appropriate for their own lifestyles.

During the introductory session, mention that just passively attending the class will not be adequate for relieving all stress. Home practice and individual participation in class will result in the greatest gains. As in anything else, the more effort the students put in, the more they will benefit. The class will probably be self-selective, because only motivated individuals will enroll and be willing to pay the class fee. Commitment on the part of both instructor and student is absolutely crucial. You are not only teaching stress reduction, you are providing an experience of closeness and intimacy generally shunned by our society. Sharing your own experiences and feelings with the group may facilitate the students' participation.

I describe the first session in depth and explain the process that will be followed in each succeeding meeting. The information for each lecture is found in earlier chapters in this book, as are all the exercises. Be certain to point out the contraindications for any exercise, checking to make sure that none of the students practices any exercise potentially dangerous to his or her health. The questions at the end of each exercise can be incorporated into your class, or you may find others that are more appropriate for your students. I have found it very helpful to make copies of some of the exercises for the students to take home; they can use them to refresh their memories and not feel under pressure to memorize the exercises during class. If you have any questions about a particular exercise, or the course structure in general, feel free to contact me at the Stress Education Center (see contact information at the back of the book).

FIRST SESSION

Seat everyone, yourself included, in a circle. Go around the circle asking people to introduce themselves and describe why they are there and what they expect to gain from the class. Keep notes so you can work individually with each student. Simply asking students to address the group may elicit a stress response from some of the shyer members. This experience will be put to use later in the session when each person describes his or her typical stress response. Be supportive of the participants; reassure them that their stress responses are normal. Ask what form of stress reduction, if any, they practiced prior to the class. Make sure that everyone gets a chance to talk. Encourage an atmosphere of celebration and uninhibited sharing; this takes time, but it makes the experience more valuable.

Now, have everyone join hands, creating a "centering circle." (Use this circle exercise at the outset of all subsequent classes.) Lead a shortened version of Passive Progressive Relaxation emphasizing the calm, relaxed breath and the students' awareness of any held tension. As you lead the relaxation exercise, suggest that the participants mentally review the day's experiences and concerns, allowing the thoughts to flow through and out of their consciousness. Letting go of the day's worries will make them more receptive to new information and experiences. After a few minutes, ask them to turn their attention to the hands they are holding. (Are they hot or cool? Wet or dry?) Tell the students to take a deep breath, stretch, drop hands, and then separate. You may wish to ask for responses to the centering circle and the exercise.

Lecture on the information discussed in the first chapter. Discuss what stress is and how it works; the stress response (fight or flight) and how it affects the body; and the Holmes and Rahe Readjustment Scale. (Duplicate the scale and have the students complete at home.) Allow some time for discussion and a question and answer period. Ask the students to indicate by a show of hands if they have experienced the fight or flight response, particularly its common manifestations, such as tight muscles, cold extremities, and upset stomach.

If you are not a doctor, you cannot legally prescribe or treat, but you can suggest that through stress-reduction techniques students may be able to improve their own health, especially if they practice regularly at home. Briefly discuss stress reduction, and how it can reverse the stress response as explained in the Introduction and the chapter on understanding stress and relaxation. This might be a good time to take a ten-minute break.

Demonstrate, and have the students actively participate in, diaphragmatic breathing. Have them place their hands on their abdomens in the sitting or lying autogenic position, and follow the procedure in the second paragraph of the chapter on breathing. Emphasize the slow, natural breath ending with the full and complete exhalation. Explain how they can associate deep breathing with daily events by discussing the information in the chapter on breathing. Advise them to breathe deeply forty times each day; they should take a deep breath every time they feel tension building. This will help them become aware of how they can breathe tension away. Practice deep breathing as a group. (You will include a new breathing exercise in each session.)

If you have biofeedback instruments, describe their uses. I use galvanic skin response (GSR) and a temperature trainer, and hook some of my students to each device so that they have a chance to use them during the autogenics exercise that follows. Have the participating students discuss what they learned from this experience.

Describe and teach the autogenic phrases to the class. I teach autogenics early on in the course because I find this technique effective, easy to learn, and a good beginning exercise. Give the students a copy of the exercise to take home so they can practice it daily. (Remember to give warnings about adjusting medication levels and contraindications.) Use the Basic Autogenic Training exercise. Repeat each phrase three times exactly how you want the class to learn it. After the forehead phrases, lead a brief visualization of relaxing outdoors on a calm and peaceful day. Discuss the visualization only briefly with the class, as you will go into greater detail on the fourth week of the program. Allow time for class reactions.

Instruct the students to practice deep, diaphragmatic breathing and autogenics for at least twenty minutes a day. If they wish to keep journals of their progress, suggest that they write down reactions each time they practice the exercises. You will allow time for them to share these responses each week after the opening centering circle. I often encourage students to call me if they have any problems.

SECOND SESSION

Begin with a centering circle. You may use Passive Progressive Relaxation, as in the first week, or a modification of that exercise. The important thing is for the students to experience relaxation as a group. Find out how their week went. Did everybody practice daily? Did they have any special problems with autogenics or breathing? If anyone kept a journal, have him or her discuss its effectiveness. Their feelings may change by the next session since they will begin to see changes in their entries. Encourage them to continue with the diary.

Be firm. Remind the class that the techniques will not work if they don't practice on a regular basis. Reemphasize the benefits of twenty minutes of daily relaxation. People may come up with excuses for why they couldn't make the time to relax; don't accept any of them. Discuss resistance to letting go and secondary gains covered in the chapters on understanding stress and specific ailments. Be warm, and help people discuss their problems openly.

Introduce the 1-to-8 Count breathing exercise. Ask the questions at the end of the exercise; go around the room and ask if anyone encountered any distractions. Discuss the different experiences. People who do not easily visualize the numbers should be reassured that this will get easier with practice.

Teach the gentle exercises in the chapter on physical exercise. Begin with Shoulder Rolls, followed by Neck Rotation, Arm and Leg Shakes, Scalp Tapping, and Scalp Massage. These exercises will help people identify where they hold the most tension. Discuss which exercises were the most effective for each participant. Ask the students if they feel increased heaviness, warmth, or blood flow in any of the exercised body parts. Take a ten-minute break.

Teach biofeedback without machines; use the EMG Exercise discussed in the chapter on biofeedback. This is important because it gets people to begin to touch each other and to become sensitive to each other's stress responses. Discuss the questions following the exercises, concentrating especially on how the EMG's perception corresponded to or contraindicated the subject's own perception. Often students can be invaluable in describing one another's style of holding tension. This exercise will also lead into a discussion of tension associated with social interaction.

Discuss the history and theory of progressive relaxation. I usually concentrate on passive progressive because I feel that the active form causes people to tense their muscles too much. You may disagree with this; but I like to use this exercise at the beginning of the course. Lead the 10-to-1 Passive Progressive Relaxation exercise. Allow time for class reactions.

For homework, have them do deep breathing and either autogenics or passive progressive relaxation. Discuss the biofeedback they can do at home as detailed in the chapter on biofeedback. Encourage people who have not tried keeping journals to do so now.

THIRD SESSION

Form a centering circle. You may notice that people are becoming more comfortable with holding each other's hands. Use whatever exercise you wish with the centering circle. Have the students check in for progress or problems. At this point some students may be noticing a sudden improvement in their ability to relax. This is also the point where some students begin to get discouraged. Give these students extra attention at this session.

Have the students do the 1-to-8 Count breathing exercise. Then teach them the 1-to-4 Count; they are probably becoming more comfortable with deep breathing by now. Find out if people are using breathing cues, and if so, discuss the different ways they have found to key their breathing. Take a ten-minute break.

Teach Active Progressive Relaxation. People who have back problems should be cautioned about tensing too much, as this could cause pain. Discuss the musculature of the body, and explain the difference between smooth and skeletal muscles. Ask the questions about the different body parts, ending with a discussion of facial muscles. Have the class look around, and notice how different members use their faces to express emotion. Let them touch each other's faces and feel for any tension. This leads naturally into Eye Stretches or Eye Stretches with Visualization, and then into a head and face massage.

Practice sessions for the next week should include one of the two breathing exercises, and autogenics or a form of progressive relaxation.

FOURTH SESSION

By this week people should be totally comfortable with the centering circle. After the circle discuss how much more comfortable they feel now than at the first session. Point out to them that they can become more comfortable with all the social situations that now make them anxious. Check in for progress and problems, and ask people which techniques they like the best.

Introduce Three-Part Breathing. Explain that the lungs are not actually divided into three parts, but that this is a visualization. Repeat the exercise four times. Observe the students' breathing to see that they are breathing diaphragmatically.

Discuss visualization based on the information in the chapter on visualization. Lead the Visualization for Relaxation. Ask students how their visualizations differed from your suggestions, and have them compare their visual imagery. Were most of them able to easily imagine an idealized outdoor place? Did childhood memories crop up? Did any of them have images that are always associated with relaxation? If anyone is keeping a journal, suggest that visualizations be recorded. Take a ten-minute break.

Discuss diet and nutrition focusing on sugar, caffeine, food additives, and food allergies as explained in the chapter on nutrition. Have each student describe what he or she ate that day. Ask the heavy coffee and sugar consumers to describe their reactions after drinking or eating. This may be a difficult lecture because diet is often closely con nected to body image, and people are sensitive about his subject.

Encourage active exercise discussion based on the material in the chapter on physical exercise. Allow the students who participate in competitive sports to discuss their stress responses in relation to their sports. Suggest the possibility of performing a Zen-like meditation in conjunction with individual active exercise.

Heavy coffee drinkers and sugar addicts should keep a record for the next week of their total consumption of these foods. Everyone should be aware of how he or she feels before or after eating. Have everyone continue with deep breathing and relaxation exercises.

FIFTH SESSION

Form the centering circle and do a passive progressive exercise. Discuss the progress each student has made since the first session. Emphasize that different degrees of success at this point are normal; each person progresses at his or her own natural pace. Find out if the journal-keeping students have benefited from this process. You might have them read an entry from the beginning and compare it to a recent one.

Show the class how to do Alternate-Nostril Breathing, and then have them try it on their own. Talk about Alternate-Nostril Breathing Variation; find out if any of your students has this capability. Review all the breathing techniques, and stress the importance of continued practice.

Lecture on the historical background and physiological benefits of meditation as presented in the chapter on meditation. Explain that meditation may be used purely as a form of relaxation; it is not necessary to embrace a set of spiritual beliefs. On the other hand, for some people, relaxation itself is an altered state of consciousness and may lead to self-awareness. Talk about the different forms of meditation, and then lead Zen Breath-Counting. The visualization of a balloon inflating within the abdomen may be more effective for some people than tripartite division of the lungs in the Three-Part Breathing exercise. Take a ten-minute break.

Seat everyone in a circle again, and lead the Relaxation and Self-Healing Visualization in the chapter on visualization. Substitute the moon for the sun, and cool, healing, blue light for the golden-white light. After the visualization discuss the self-healing properties of this technique, including the information from the chapter on specific ailments. Explain the colors to use for each ailment and any contraindications.

Since this is the last session, reserve some extra time for everyone to socialize. The class has an underlying intention besides stress reduction: to bring the participants together into a unified, caring group as they proceed through these weeks together. Our society continually separates individuals, and this class can successfully bridge the gaps between separated, isolated people and create a more caring support group.

As people gradually reach out for each other and begin to be intimate, the group pulls closer together. The more people try, the more they will get out of this experience. The more intensely people share, the more intensely they will benefit from the group process.

The concern and understanding of the instructor is essential for the growth of supportive group energy. Care should be taken to allow participants to share and be heard, but at the same time students should not be pushed too far. The balance is delicate.

BASIC COURSE OUTLINE

First Session

1. Getting acquainted

2. Centering circle with shortened version of Passive Progressive Relaxation

3. Introduction to stress lecture

4. Diaphragmatic breathing

5. Biofeedback discussion and use of equipment

6. Basic Autogenic Training

7. Brief visualization

Second Session

1. Centering circle

2. 1-to-8 Count breathing exercise

3. Shoulders, neck, arm, leg, and scalp gentle movement exercises

4. EMG Exercise without a machine

5. 10-to-1 Passive Progressive Relaxation

Third Session

1. Centering circle

2. 1-to-8 Count and 1-to-4 Count breathing exercises

3. Active Progressive Relaxation

4. Head and face massage

Fourth Session

1. Centering circle

2. Three-Part Breathing

3. Visualization discussion and Visualization for Relaxation exercise

4. Diet and nutrition discussion

5. Active exercise discussion

Fifth Session

1. Centering circle

2. Alternate-Nostril Breathing

3. Meditation discussion and Zen Breath-Counting

4. Relaxation and Self-Healing Visualization

5. Final class discussion

Glossary

ADRENAL. A gland above the kidney that is responsible for synthesizing and storing certain hormones. There are two adrenals in the body.

ADRENALINE. A hormone produced by the adrenals that stimulates the heart, relaxes the bronchial tract, and constricts the blood vessels. It is often used to relieve asthma attacks.

ALLERGEN. Any substance which causes an allergic reaction. Allergens may be foods, drugs, infectious agents, physical agents, inhalants, and contactants.

ALPHA TRAINING. Biodfeedback training using the electroencephalograph to teach brain wave control by producing an alpha pattern (8–12 Hz) on the cortex of the brain.

AMINO ACID. The building blocks of protein. There are twenty-two amino acids, eight of which are classified as essential amino acids. All the amino acids are necessary for growth or metabolism.

ANEMIA. A condition in which there is a reduction in the number of circulating red blood cells or in hemoglobin. Anemia results in weakness, headaches, gastrointestinal disturbances, palpitation, and general poor health.

ANGINA PECTORIS. A disease characterized by the sensation of choking or suffocation caused by insufficient supply of oxygen to the heart. There is severe steady pain and a feeling of pressure around the heart; the pain often radiates from the heart to the shoulder and down the left arm. There is often great anxiety and fear of approaching death. The attacks may last only a few seconds or as long as a few minutes.

ANTIBODIES. Substances developed by the body, usually in response to the presence of bacteria or toxins.

ARTHRITIS. Inflammation of a joint, usually accompanied by pain and often by structural changes. It may result from or accompany a number of dysfunctions, and there are many forms.

ATHEROSCLEROSIS. A thickening, hardening, and loss of elasticity of the walls of the blood vessels, especially arteries, due to the accumulation of lipids (fats).

AUTOIMMUNE DISEASE. A disease in which the body can no longer distinguish between its own healthy tissue and a foreign substance. The body's immunological mechanism turns against itself, destroying healthy tissue. Rheumatoid arthritis, myasthenia gravis, and scleroderma are considered autoimmune diseases.

AUTONOMIC NERVOUS SYSTEM. The part of the nervous system involved with the control of involuntary functions. It controls the functioning of the glands, smooth muscle tissue, and the heart.

BLOOD PRESSURE. Pressure exerted by the blood upon the walls of the blood vessels, especially the arteries. Blood pressure varies with age, sex, muscular development, and according to different states of emotional upset, worry, and fatigue.

BRUXISM. Grinding the teeth, especially during sleep.

BURSITIS. An inflammation of the connective tissue of the joints. Usually located in the elbow, knee, shoulder, or foot.

CARDIOVASCULAR SYSTEM. The combined organs of the heart and circulatory system (arteries, capillaries, and veins). The system pumps and carries blood, oxygen, and nutrients to the body's cells and carries waste products away from the cells.

CHEMOTHERAPY. The use of chemical agents to treat a disease. Often used in the treatment of cancer.

CIRRHOSIS. A chronic disease of the liver caused by one of the following: nutritional deficiency, poisons, or previous inflammation.

COLITIS. Inflammation of the large intestine (colon). This disease can be psychosomatic in origin and may be the indirect result of excess stress.

COLLAGEN. A protein found in the connective tissue, including skin, bone, ligaments, and cartilage. Collagen represents about 30 percent of the total body protein. Collagen diseases affect the skin, joints, blood vessels, and heart.

CONNECTIVE TISSUE. One of the four main tissues of the body. The primary function is support of body structures and the binding of parts together. Also involved in food storage, blood formation, and defense mechanisms.

CORTEX. The outer surface layer of an organ. The cerebral cortex is the outer layer of the brain.

DIABETES. A disorder of carbohydrate metabolism resulting from inadequate production or utilization of insulin. The pancreas does not secrete an adequate amount of insulin. Principal symptoms are elevated blood sugar, sugar in urine, excessive urine production, excessive thirst, and increase in food intake.

DIAPHRAGM. A thin membrane wall separating the abdomen from the chest cavity. It contracts with each inhalation, flattening downward, permitting the lungs to fill with air. With each exhalation it relaxes, returning to its normal position as the air leaves the lungs. The diaphragm is the breathing muscle.

DIURETIC. An agent that increases the secretion of the urine. Acts on the kidney cells and on the circulation to the kidneys.

DIVERTICULITIS. Inflammation of the intestinal tract, especially the colon, causing stagnation of the feces in little distended sacs.

ECZEMA. Chronic dermatitis caused by a number of external and internal factors, acting either alone or together.

ENDOCRINE GLAND. A hormone-producing gland. Hormones are circulated to all parts of the body. Dysfunction may result from too little production of a specific hormone or excessive production and secretion. The adrenals, the thyroid, the gonads, and the parathyroid are all endocrine glands.

ENZYMES. Complex proteins which are capable of producing chemical changes in other substances without being changed themselves in the process. They are found particularly in digestive juices acting upon foods, causing them to break down into simpler compounds.

EPILEPSY. Recurrent attacks of disturbed brain function. Characterized by altered or complete loss of consciousness, motor, sensory, or psychic malfunction; with or without convulsions.

GASTRITIS. Inflammation of the stomach characterized by pain or tenderness, nausea, and vomiting.

GASTROINTESTINAL. Pertaining to the stomach and intestine.

GENERAL ADAPTATION SYNDROME (GAS). Term coined by Hans Selye for the response to prolonged stress. The body adapts as each system becomes weakened until final breakdown may occur.

GLUCOSE. The most important carbohydrate in body metabolism. It is formed during digestion and absorbed from the intestine into the blood. When it passes through the liver, excess glucose is converted into glycogen and stored for future use.

GLYCOGEN. The form in which carbohydrate is stored in the body for future conversion into sugar. It is converted into glucose when needed by the tissues. It is necessary for performing muscular work or for using body heat.

HYPERTENSION. Abnormally high blood pressure. Results partly from heredity, fear and other emotions, and hormonal activity. The resulting condition may be symptomless or accompanied by nervousness, headache, dizziness, etc.

HYPERVENTILATION. Increased inhalation and exhalation as a result of either the increase in the breath rate or the death of inhalation. It results in a depletion of carbon dioxide and can cause nausea, fainting, and dizziness.

HYPOGLYCEMIA. A condition in which the glucose in the blood is abnormally low. The result is acute fatigue, restlessness, marked irritability, weakness, and mental disturbances.

HYPOTHALAMUS. The part of the brain that activates, controls, and integrates autonomic mechanisms, endocrine activity, and the regulation of water balance, body temperature, sleep, and food intake.

IMMUNOLOGICAL SYSTEM. Protective system of disease fighting within the body, dependent upon the correct functioning of antibodies.

METASTASIZE. Change in location of a disease from one organ or part to another not directly connected.

NERVOUS SYSTEM. A system of nerve cells which regulate and coordinate body activities. It brings about the responses by which the body adjusts to environmental changes, either internal or external. Controls every cell, organ, and structure in the body, including the brain.

NEUROMUSCULAR. Concerning both the nerves and the muscles.

NUCLEIC ACID. A group of substances found in the cell, especially in the nucleus. Nucleic acid forms the genetic material of the cell (DNA and RNA) and directs protein synthesis within the cell.

PANCREAS. A gland whose secretions play a primary role in the regulation of carbohydrate metabolism. Insulin is secreted in the pancreas and is important in maintaining the proper blood sugar level.

PASSIVE CONCENTRATION. Autogenic technique in which the awareness is focused on a particular part of the body and an appropriate phrase is repeated mentally. Passive concentration also includes observing the sensations and emotions that come to mind as a result of relaxation.

PITUITARY GLAND. The pituitary is attached to the base of the brain and is an endocrine gland. The hormones it secretes regulate growth, reproduction, and various metabolic activities. It is the master gland of the body.

PSORIASIS. A common form of dermatitis consisting of pink or dull-red sores and silvery scaling. It is usually chronic and there is no known cure.

RHEUMATOID ARTHRITIS. The most common form of arthritis. An autoimmune disease resulting in inflammation of the joints, stiffness, swelling, and pain. The specific cause is unknown and there is no specific cure.

RHEUMATOID FACTOR. It is a protein found in the blood capable of acting as an antibody. Not all people with this factor in their blood have rheumatoid arthritis, but it is helpful in diagnosing the disease.

SOLAR PLEXUS. An interlacing network of nerves in the abdomen behind the stomach and in front of the diaphragm.

STRESS. Reactions of the body to negative influences, including infections and abnormal states that disturb the body's balance. External stress may be positive or negative (pleasure, challenge, divorce, work responsibilities). Subtle, long-term stress can lead to illness.

TACHYCARDIA. Abnormally rapid heart action.

THYROID. An endocrine gland in the neck which secretes hormones necessary for growth and metabolism. The amount of thyroid hormone secreted is controlled by the pituitary gland.

TOXIN. A poisonous substance of animal or plant origin.

TRAUMA. An injury or wound. A trauma can be a physical wound or a painful, emotional experience.

ULCER. An open sore or lesion, sometimes accompanied by formation of pus.

ULCER, DUODENAL. Broken mucus membrane, sometimes accompanied by a bleeding sore. This type of ulcer is slow to heal because the duodenum, the first part of the small intestine, is constantly irritated by the passage of fluids and foods.

VASCULAR SYSTEM. The heart, blood vessels, and lymph vessels. Responsible for the flow of blood and lymph throughout the body.

Bibliography

Benson, Herbert. *The Relaxation Response.* New York: Avon Books, 1976.

Berkeley Holistic Health Center. *The Holistic Health Handbook.* Berkeley, CA: And/Or Press, 1976.

Berkow, Robert, ed. *The Merck Manual of Diagnosis and Therapy.* 13th ed. Rahway, NJ: Merck Sharp & Dohme Research Labs., 1977.

Berne, Eric. *Beyond Games and Scripts.* New York: Grove Press, 1978.

———. *Games People Play.* New York: Ballantine, 1978.

———. *What Do You Say After You Say Hello?* New York: Grove Press, 1978.

Bernstein, Douglas A., and Thomas D. Borkovec. *Progressive Relaxation Training: A Manual for the Helping Professions.* Champaign, IL: Research Press, 1978.

Brainard, John B. *Control of Migraine.* New York: W. W. Norton & Co., 1979.

Brown, Barbara. *New Mind, New Body.* New York: Bantam Books, 1975.

———. *Stress and the Art of Biofeedback.* New York: Harper & Row, 1977.

Cannon, Walter B. *Bodily Changes in Pain, Hunger, Fear and Rage.* New York: Appleton, 1929.

Christensen, Alice, and David Rankin. *The Light of Yoga Society Beginner's Manual.* New York: Simon and Schuster, 1972.

Colimore, Benjamin, and Sarah Stewart. *Nutrition and Your Body.* Los Angeles: Light Wave Press, 1974.

Dass, Ram. *Grist for the Mill.* Santa Cruz, CA: Unity Press, 1977.

———. *The Only Dance There Is.* New York: Aronson, 1976.

Downing, George. *The Massage Book.* New York: Random House, Bookworks, 1972.

———. *Theme and Variations: A Behavior Therapy Casebook.* Maxwell House, NY: Pergamon, 1976.

Eliade, Mircea. *Yoga: Immortality and Freedom.* Translated by Willard R. Trask. Princeton, NJ: Princeton University Press, 1958.

Fast, Howard. *The Art of Zen Meditation.* Culver City, CA: Peace Press, 1977.

Feldenkrais, Moshe. *Awareness through Movement.* New York: Harper & Row, 1972.

Fink, David Harold. *Release from Nervous Tension.* New York: Pocket Books, 1973.

Fleck, Henrietta. *Introduction to Nutrition.* New York: Macmillan Publishing Co., 1976.

Geba, Bruno Hans. *Breathe Away Your Tension.* New York: Random House, Bookworks, 1973.

Goldsmith, Joel S. *The Art of Meditation.* New York: Harper & Row, 1957.

Green, Elmer, and Alyce Green. *Beyond Biofeedback.* New York: Delacorte, 1977.

Henning, Joel. *Holistic Running.* New York: New American Library, 1978.

Hittleman, Richard. *30 Day Yoga Meditation Plan.* New York: Bantam Books, 1978.

———. *Be Young with Yoga.* New York: Warner Books, 1962.

———. *Yoga: 28 Day Exercise Plan.* New York: Workman Publishing Co., 1969.

Jacobson, Edmund. *Anxiety and Tension Control.* New York: Lippincott, 1964.

———. *Biology of Emotions: New Understanding Derived from Biological Multidisciplinary Investigation, First Electrophysical Measurements.* Springfield, IL: C. C. Thomas, 1967.

———. *Progressive Relaxation.* Chicago: University of Chicago Press, 1974.

Kamiya, Joseph et al., eds. *Biofeedback and Self-Control.* Chicago: Aldine, 1977.

Karlins, Marvin, and Lewis M. Andrews. *Biofeedback.* New York: Warner Books, 1976.

Kent, Fraser. *Nothing to Fear: Coping with Phobias.* New York: Barnes & Noble, 1978.

Kraus, Hans. *Backache, Stress and Tension: Cause, Prevention and Treatment.* New York: Simon & Schuster, Fireside Books, 1965.

Leonard, George. *The Ultimate Athlete.* New York: Avon Books, 1975.

LeShan, Lawrence. *How to Meditate: A Guide to Self-Discovery.* New York: Bantam Books, 1975.

———. *You Must Relax.* New York: McGraw-Hill, 1976.

Lindemann, Hannes. *Relieve Tension the Autogenics Way.* New York: Peter Wyden, 1973.

Luthe, Wolfgang, and Johannes Schultz. *Autogenic Training.* New York: Grune and Straton, 1965.

Martin, Ethel Austin. *Nutrition in Action.* 3rd ed. New York: Holt, Rinehart and Winston, 1971.

McQuade, Walter, and Ann Aikman. *Stress.* New York: Bantam Books, 1975.

Michaels, Andrew. *Why Do You Think They Call It a Deadline?* Berkeley, CA: Self-published, 1979.

Mishra, Rammurti S. *Fundamentals of Yoga.* Garden City, NJ: Doubleday, Anchor, 1974.

Muramoto, Naboru. *Healing Ourselves.* New York: Avon Books/Swan House, 1973.

Ott, John. *Health & Light.* Princeton, NJ: Petrocelli, 1976.

Oyle, Irving. *The Healing Mind.* Princeton, NJ: Petrocelli, 1976.

Passwater, Richard A. *Super-Nutrition.* New York: Pocket Books, 1977.

Pelletier, Kenneth R. *Mind as Healer, Mind as Slayer: A Holistic Approach to Preventing Stress Disorders.* New York: Dell Publishing Co., Delta Books, 1977.

Rohe, Fred. *The Zen of Running.* New York: Random House, Bodyworks, 1974.

Rose, Karl. *You and A. T.: Autogenic Training.* New York: E. P. Dutton & Co., 1976.

Samuels, Mike, and Nancy Samuels. *Seeing with the Mind's Eye.* New York: Random House, 1975.

———. *The Well Body Book.* New York: Random House, Bookworks, 1976.

Selye, Hans. *The Stress of Life.* 2d rev. ed. New York: McGraw-Hill Book Co., 1978.

———. *Stress without Distress.* New York: Signet Books, 1974.

Shealy, C. Norman. *90 Days to Self-Health.* New York: Bantam Books, 1978.

Simonton, Carl, and Stephanie Matthews. *Getting Well Again.* Los Angeles: Tarcher, 1978.

Thomas, Clayton L., ed. *Taber's Cyclopedic Medical Dictionary.* 12th ed. Philadelphia: F. A. Davis Co., 1973.

Wolpe, Joseph. *The Practice of Behavior Therapy.* Maxwell House, NY: Pergamon, 1974.

———. *Psychotherapy by Reciprocal Inhibition.* Stanford, CA: Stanford University Press, 1958.

Index